ELEANOR
OF
AQUITAINE

by Regine Pernoud

TRANSLATED BY
PETER WILES

D1500294

Coward-McCann, Inc.
New York

First published in France under the title
Aliénor d'Aquitaine

COPYRIGHT © 1967 BY WM. COLLINS SONS AND CO. LTD.

FIRST AMERICAN EDITION 1968

Library of Congress Catalog
Card Number: 68-14734

Printed in the United States of America

Second Impression

FOR ANDRE CHAMSON,

who can still speak the same language as Eleanor,
this evocation of the Queen of the Troubadours

ILLUSTRATIONS

Following page 32

Eleanor of Aquitaine
[*Photo Jean Feuillie*]

Her seal
[*Archives de France*]

Eleanor with Isabella of Angoulême
[*Cliché Doloire*]

The tombs of Eleanor and Henry II
[*Photo Jean Feuillie*]

The seal of Louis VII
[*Society of Antiquaries of London* and *Photo Giraudon*]

The vase which Eleanor gave to Louis
[*Cliché du Service de Documentation Photographique des Musées Nationaux*]

Ampulla given to the abbey of Saint-Denis
[*Cliché du Service de Documentation Photographique des Musées Nationaux*]

Abbot Suger
[*Photo Larousse*]

Choir of the abbey of Saint-Denis
[*Photo Jean Feuillie*]

The Emperor Manuel Comnenus
[*Vatican Library*]

The Crusader's Return
[*Photo Jean Feuillie*]

The cathedral of Le Mans
[*Photo Giraudon*]

The seal of Henry II
[*Society of Antiquaries of London*]

The keep of Dover Castle
[*National Monuments Record*]

Scenes from the Life of Becket
[*Mansell Collection*]

ILLUSTRATIONS

Following page 128

Eleanor's palace at Poitiers
[*Photo Roger-Viollet* and *Bildarchiv Foto Marburg*]

Notre Dame la Grande, Poitiers
[*Photo Giraudon*]

The city ramparts, Poitiers
[*Archives Photographiques des Monuments Artistiques*]

The abbey church of Fontevrault
[*Photo Jean Feuillie*]

The kitchen and refectory at Fontevrault
[*Photo Giraudon*]

A knight does homage to his lady
[*Bibliothèque Nationale*]

Bernard de Ventadour
[*Bibliothèque Nationale*]

The murder of Becket
[*Mansell Collection*]

The ruins of Glastonbury Abbey
[*National Monuments Record*]

Tintagel Castle
[*Mansell Collection*]

The seal of Richard I
[*Society of Antiquaries of London*]

The Kings of France and England leave for the Third Crusade
[*Bibliothèque Nationale*]

The ruins of Château-Gaillard
[*French Government Tourist Office*]

The castle of Niort
[*Photo Roger-Viollet*]

The castle of Gisors
[*Photo Giraudon*]

King John
[*British Travel Association*]

Matilda of Saxony
[*Bildarchiv Foto Marburg*]

Richard Coeur-de-Lion
[*Photo Bulloz*]

TRANSLATOR'S NOTE

To induce a degree of consistency unattempted by the Mediaeval sources, I have given proper names in their English forms wherever possible, despite the fact that historical figures of the twelfth century can seldom be ranged arbitrarily on one or other side of the Channel, which—to quote Miss Pernoud—'was thought of as being literally a channel, a means of transport, and not a barrier'. Nor is there any uniformity among historical writers. Reference to the *Dictionary of National Biography*, and to the works of individual historians, has not helped me to decide whether Henry II was the son of Empress Maud or of Matilda Empress; whether his daughter's name was Joan or Joanna; whether Peter of Blois should be styled Peter de Blois or Pierre de Blois.

Yet to write 'Christian of Troyes' would be no less absurd than to write 'Guillaume le Conquérant'. Clearly, there are exceptions to my rule. So I have kept the names of the troubadours in the language to which their works have added lustre, and Bernard de Ventadour, Peire Vidal and their fellows appear in their more widely known French forms. Nor did I think it wise to tamper with the names Hubert de Burgh and Richard de Luci, which have received the sanction of standard English usage.

Similarly, I have evolved no uniform terms to denote the value of money in the twelfth century. Instead, I quote the figures given as a basic measure in the second volume of *English Historical Documents*. The average agricultural wage at that time was a penny a day, while 'at the other end of the social scale the chancellor, the highest paid official in the king's household, received shortly after the death of Henry I [1135] a salary (in addition to perquisites) of five shillings a day.'

Peter Wiles

PREFACE

Eleanor of Aquitaine has been likened now to Messalina, now to Muséline. The comparison with Messalina is not worth dwelling on. And yet it is scarcely less forbidding to speak of Muséline, who according to folktale was half fairy, half human; her husband became so alarmed at her mysterious disappearances that one night he followed her and met with a painful surprise—she had turned into a snake.

A sorry reputation then, and I have to admit that I accepted it without demur in one of my own previous books. But when I had occasion to take a somewhat closer look at the lady, there occurred what often occurs when we forget hearsay and turn to the prime sources (especially in matters pertaining to the history of the Middle Ages, on which so much spadework still needs to be done): I found myself confronted by an Eleanor utterly different from my preconceived notion of her. A woman beyond compare, towering above the age in which she lived. And what an age! It saw the Gothic style emerge, but not until the Romanesque had achieved the height of magnificence. It saw the city burghers cast off the feudal yoke, at the very time when chivalry was in full flower. In literature it was the great age of the lyric of courtly love—in the south, the troubadours; in the north, the early romances, Tristan and Iseult and the inventiveness of Chrétien de Troyes.

Now, in the light of contemporary evidence Eleanor emerges as fully worthy of this background. Indeed this background is partly her own creation, for Eleanor played a dominant role in politics and literature alike, and upon social and economic matters her influence was strong. That posterity should be mindful only of a youthful indiscretion on the part of a woman twice queen and the mother of two kings, a woman who defied an emperor, threatened a pope and ruled her twofold realm with the utmost lucidity and control—this ought surely to give us pause.

11

The reader will arrive at his own conclusions. Rather than weigh the story down with notes and references, I have given my sources at the end. However, I should like to emphasize that the conversations and utterances reported in the text do not contain one word of invention: they are all drawn from the writings of the day. It was never my intention to write a novel; my book, though it endeavours to keep pace with a life as romantic as any, is but a straightforward historical study.

Régine Pernoud

I

Maïstre, gran benanansa
Podetz aver si sofretz . . .
Gran be vos venra de Fransa
Si atendre lo voletz.

Master, great good luck may chance
Your way, if you'll but patient be . . .
A boon shall come to you from France,
Well worth your while to wait and see.

CERCAMON

ON SUNDAY, July 25th 1137, a great wedding took place in
Bordeaux. The bells of the ancient cathedral rang out as Eleanor of
Aquitaine was given in marriage to the youth who was heir to the
royal crown of France. From the chancel, where two thrones had
been set on a velvet-covered dais, it was easy to hear the clamour of
the festive throng which had gathered about the great building.
Eleanor was seated on one of the thrones, very upright in her scarlet
robe; she wore the gold diadem which had been set on her head by
Louis, her bridegroom. Louis had the rather frail look of a boy
whose health has been taxed by immoderately rapid growth. He
was sixteen. Indeed the combined age of the bride and groom was
only about thirty, for the chronicles give Eleanor's date of birth as
either 1120 or 1122. Yet it was apparent from her bearing that here
was a young princess full of self-assurance, alert to the powers of
her magical spring-like beauty and not at all overawed that she
should be the focal point of everyone's attention—stared at by the
barons and prelates, as well as by the common people. No one
could have acknowledged the cheers of the crowd with an easier
grace when, at the end of the ceremony, she emerged through the
main doorway on the arm of Louis of France and took her place at
the head of the procession which was to conduct them to the
Ombrière Palace. And all along the route, with its festoons and

13

streamers and its carpet of leaves withered from the stifling heat, her subjects roared out their acclamation; they were a people of warm and rapid impulses, and it enchanted them to see so gracious and winning a young duchess. As for her bridegroom, they looked at him with kindly eyes and murmured, as onlookers were to murmur all his life long: 'He might almost be a monk.'

———————◆———————

It was a turning-point, this marriage between the ruling families of France and Aquitaine. Exactly a hundred and fifty years had passed since Hugh Capet, 'duke of the Franks', had taken the throne after securing recognition as king from the barons who had gathered at Senlis when the last descendant of Charlemagne died. In those early days there had been little to suggest what a long and remarkable history was in store for the Capetians. The initial struggle had been hard. For over a century Hugh's successors, like Hugh himself, had been filled with but one ambition—to endure, to pass on the crown from father to son. Lacking the imperial prestige of their Carolingian predecessors, they had been regarded in the Western world as determined upstarts who, staking all on survival (and in those days survival counted for more than anything else), had continued to hold sway because, as feudal lords dealing with other feudal lords, they had known how to derive maximum benefit from the feudal oath. The oath—that personal bond between one man and another—united barons great and small throughout the length and breadth of the country in a web of reciprocal rights and duties, a vast interwoven complex which is hard for us to unravel since it differs so greatly, in total effect, from the centralized State we know today. By ensuring that their sons were crowned within their own lifetime, and that their vassals rendered homage to those sons, Hugh Capet and his successors had shaped a dynasty; they had persuaded people to forget that in the first instance Hugh had been elected by his peers—his equals.

Yet how much power did they really exercise, as rulers of a country which had already (more or less) taken on its present dimensions, save for that eastern portion—approximately to the left of the Rhône and Saône and to the right of the Meuse and

14

Scheldt—which was subject to the control of the Empire. They had the moral authority invested in them by their anointment; they had the right to settle internecine disputes among their vassals; they had a duty to take police action at times when there was looting or abuse of authority. All this, however, was in no way comparable to the absolute sovereignty of a Holy Roman Emperor or of a monarch such as Louis XIV. A good many lords—the dukes of Normandy, for instance, or the counts of Champagne—acknowledged themselves vassals of the king of France, yet were the masters of domains bigger and wealthier than his. The king did not 'rule', as we understand the word today, except within his own feudal area, where he owned fiefs, administering them directly and garnering their resources. At the time of the Aquitaine marriage, this feudal area was confined to a strip of land extending from the course of the Oise (level with Soissons) to the vicinity of Bourges; it was made up of Ile-de-France, Orléanais and part of Berry. When the reigning king, Louis VI, managed to secure direct control of the fortress of Montlhéry, between Paris and Orleans, he rejoiced (according to Suger, his historian and confidant), as if someone had 'plucked a mote from his eye or battered down the doors of a prison in which he was incarcerated'. This shows how limited were the ambitions which he could realistically entertain.

Set against the scale of this paltry domain, Eleanor's own position was a formidable one. The dukes of Aquitaine were also counts of Poitou and dukes of Gascony. They held sway over nineteen of the departments of modern France, from Indre to the Basses-Pyrénées. Among their vassals were barons powerful in their own right: in Poitou, the viscounts of Thouars and the lords of Lusignan and Châtellerault were men of great substance—a Lusignan was one day to be crowned king of Jerusalem. Next came the lesser barons of Mauléon and Parthenay; of Châteauroux and Issoudun, in Berry; of Turenne and Ventadour, in Limousin . . . Then there were those Gascon lords with the high-sounding names—Astarac, Armagnac, Pardiac, Fézensac and many others, all the way to the Pyrenees; to say nothing of the viscounty of Béarn and the various counties of the March: Auvergne, Limoges, Angoulême, Périgord —every one a rich and extensive fief. This large team of vassals provided any duke of Aquitaine with a full-size court of his own;

15

they rendered homage to him and were under an obligation to supply aid and counsel. In short: marriage to Eleanor would give the king of France direct control over regions where hitherto his authority had been purely nominal.

This increase in political power was backed, to express it in modern terms, by an appreciable step forward in the economic sphere. In these days of tidy budgeting, strict accountancy and regular financial rewards, it is hard to estimate the resources of a feudal king. For instance, the king of France owned thirty farms at Marly, a glass furnace in Compiègne, several barns at Poissy, some mills in Chérisy (near Dreux); he levied a tax on Argenteuil market and on the fishing waters around Orleans; most oddly of all, the people of Senlis had no further obligations towards him once they had provided his kitchen staff with the saucepans, porringers, garlic and salt needed during his periods of residence in the town! Thus his resources were made up of a plethora of rights which often appear small beyond consideration. The least we may conclude is that, in an age when most revenues were furnished in kind and when the fruits of the earth were the principal source of wealth, the increase in the royal resources was going to be directly proportionate to the extent of the bride's domain.

Eleanor's domain was not only bigger than Ile-de-France but richer as well. 'Opulent Aquitaine,' writes Heriger of Lobbes, a monk living at about that time, 'sweet as nectar thanks to its vineyards, dotted about with forests, overflowing with fruit of every kind and endowed with a superabundance of pasture-land.' It had a long seaboard and its harbour towns were thriving. Bordeaux had been exporting wine and salt since earliest antiquity, and in recent years it had been joined in this trade by La Rochelle—which did not exist as a port until the Middle Ages; Bayonne had made a speciality of whale-fishing. The dukes of Aquitaine (some had dubbed themselves 'Dukes of the Entire Monarchy of the Aquitainians') commanded wealth in so many different forms that they had long enjoyed the reputation of living on a grander scale than the kings of France.

So the significance of the occasion did not need explaining to the men and women gathered at table for the huge banquet which took place after the religious ceremony in the cathedral—nearly a thousand guests, to say nothing of the countless humbler folk who were joining in the good living all over the castle estate; for whenever there was a wedding between two great noble families, casks of wine and huge hunks of meat were distributed to all and sundry.

The Ombrière Palace—a name whose undertones of coolness were soothing in these torrid days of summer—stood at the southeast corner of the great quadrilateral formed by the ramparts of the old Roman city, whose outlines are still discernible today; the whole of twelfth-century Bordeaux lay within the oblong area contained between the Place de la Bourse, the Rue de la Vieille-Tour, the Place Rohan and the Place du Palais, which in fact owes its name to the Ombrière Palace. The Ombrière was a powerful fortress and its keep rose high above the banks of the Garonne—a stout rectangular tower known as the 'Arbalesteyre', sixty feet by forty-five, with thick well-buttressed walls. The present-day Rue de la Palais-de-l'Ombrière runs clean through the middle of what was once the palace courtyard; this courtyard was still there in the eighteenth century, and so was the main hall; both were surrounded by a curtain-wall about three hundred feet long, supplemented by a pair of towers, one semi-circular, the other hexagonal.

We have to picture this hall and courtyard bustling with activity as the squires and pages circulated among the tables, diligently carving and pouring. Everyone of any rank in Aquitaine had come to Bordeaux for this wedding, not only the great vassals—as for instance Geoffrey of Rancon, lord and master of Taillebourg—but also those petty nobles whose titles had been conferred more or less at random and whose names are to be found dotted about the countryside: there was a William of Arsac and an Arnold of Blanquefort, as well as the minor governors of distant fortresses in Labourd or Lomagne. And for his own part the king of France had been determined that his son should have an impressive escort: some five hundred knights, and knights to reckon with, for among them were such powerful feudatories as Theobald, count of Champagne and Blois; William of Nevers, count of Auxerre and Tonnerre; Rotrou, count of Le Perche; and Count Raoul of Vermandois, seneschal of the realm. With them had travelled the foremost prelates of Ile-de-France—including Geoffrey of Lèves, bishop of Chartres, who according to one chronicler was bidden welcome to Bordeaux by 'the clergy of all Aquitaine'. Most significantly of all, the official deputation which had followed the young prince up hill and down dale in the July sunshine was headed by Suger, abbot of Saint-Denis, the king's lifelong confidant—and there can be no greater proof of the importance which Louis VI attached to this wedding between his son and the heiress of Aquitaine.

The betrothal had been rather hurried, unlike most betrothals of the period, which were often entered into when the parties principally concerned were still in the cradle. Three months earlier, in fact—towards the end of April 1137—some messengers had ridden up to the royal castle at Béthisy, where the king of France was then in residence. Their mission was to inform the king of the death of their overlord, William, duke of Aquitaine. An unexpected death, if ever there was one. William was only thirty-eight and had looked uncommonly well when, a short while previously, he had set out on an Easter pilgrimage to the shrine of St James, at Compostela. But he never reached his destination. On Good Friday, April 9th, an unspecified illness laid him low—this giant of a man whose sheer physical strength was as legendary as his insatiable appetite (for it was said that at a single meal he could devour as much as eight ordinary mortals).

When he realized he was going to die, his chief concern was for his elder daughter, Eleanor. Aigret, his only son, had died seven years earlier, leaving Eleanor as sole heir to the vast and onerous domain of Aquitaine, with its redoubtable neighbours and turbulent vassals. Among the former, the counts of Anjou could hardly wait for an opportunity to improve their common frontier with the duchy. Among the latter, the Gascon lordlings had always been recalcitrant and were hungering for independence.

It was in compliance with the duke's last will and testament that a few of his fellow-pilgrims had turned back and journeyed to Ile-de-France. In the meantime the duke's death was kept secret, for it was essential to forestall any attempts at rebellion or self-enfranchisement. They were bowing to feudal tradition by bearing the news straightway to the king of France; for one thing, it was the sovereign's duty to offer a vassal lady his protection and to contract a suitable marriage for her if she were a widow or an unbetrothed girl. But there was more to it than this. The messengers had been instructed to communicate the dying wishes of the duke of Aquitaine: he wanted his daughter to marry the heir to the throne of France.

King Louis VI had spent his whole life quelling unrest within his own borders and safeguarding the possession of uninspiring acres. Who better than he to gauge the importance of an offer which would extend the influence of the Crown beyond his wildest dreams and bring one of the finest domains in the kingdom under the direct control of the House of France? He was a sick man at the time, gravely afflicted with what was known as 'flux of the belly'—an attack of dysentery. This tireless campaigner had been laid low by the same disease two years before. He had recovered from the first attack, but this time his condition was obviously critical, so critical indeed that he had already summoned the trusty Abbot Suger to his side. On receipt of the message from the Aquitanian nobles, Suger had immediately followed traditional procedure and called the royal councillors together. They were unanimous in their view that the Crown must accept the duke's offer, reply without delay and make every effort to indulge the pride of the people of Aquitaine and do honour to their young duchess.

Suger lost no time in organizing the expedition. He had a mind for everything, this resourceful little monk who had risen from serfdom to become principal adviser to the king of France. His energy and efficiency were amazing. Some five hundred knights— the largest royal deputation ever, and the first to be sent to Aquitaine since the accession of the Capetian line—called for a good deal of planning and timing; vehicles and pack-horses had to be assembled, and so had the tents, the portable kitchens and all the other paraphernalia for making camp. Unfortunately, not many details have been handed down regarding this journey to Bordeaux. It would be fascinating to know what presents were taken for the young bride and her entourage. One contemporary history, the Chronicle of Morigny, boasts tantalizingly that it would take 'the lips of Cicero and the memory of Seneca to unfold the richness and variety of these presents and the pomp paraded for these nuptials'. Suger himself, in his account of the life of Louis VI, is content to speak of 'abundant riches'... He is considerably more forthcoming as to the gifts which the king conferred on the abbey of Saint-Denis under the terms of his will, drawn up at about the same time: a magnificent Bible with a bejewelled gilt binding; a forty-ounce gold censer; some gold candelabra weighing a hundred and sixty ounces; a gold chalice encrusted with precious stones; ten silk copes; a superb hyacinth which Louis had inherited from his grandmother, Anne, daughter of the duke of Kiev, and which he wanted set in the crown of thorns upon the great crucifix at Saint-Denis.

At all events, preparations for the journey were completed at speed and on the eve of departure, June 17th, Suger sent for Hervé, his prior, who was to be in charge of the abbey while he was away. He took him down to the crypt below the basilica and showed him the spot, just to the right of the altar, where the king was to be laid to rest if the worst should happen during his absence.

That same day, Louis VI bade farewell to his son. He had taken a turn for the worse. All the vigour had gone from his great frame; he was tired and gasping for breath; his brow was bathed in sweat. To this heir whom he might never see again, and who was the repository of the kingdom's hopes, he addressed these final words of counsel: 'Protect the clerks, the poor and the fatherless, safeguarding the rights of each and every one.' And young Louis, deeply moved, went down on his knees as the king delivered his valediction: 'May Almighty God, through Whose Grace kings rule, watch over you, my dear child... for if by ill chance you should be taken from me, yourself and the companions I have given you, there would be nothing left to reconcile me to kingship or to life.'

The young man was unlikely to forget such words as these. At sixteen, Louis the Young displayed all the earnestness and sobriety that could be demanded of a future king; indeed, there were times when his father would have preferred him to show a little more fight and a little less meditation. As a child, never dreaming that he would one day be called upon to rule, he had studied hard at the abbey of Saint-Denis, where his piety had been an inspiration to the monks themselves; work was all he cared for, and he lived only for the time when he might permanently mingle his voice with theirs. And then one morning he was abruptly torn away from this life of studiousness and prayer. Suger sent for him and explained that the king required his presence urgently: Philip, his elder brother, was dead. A senseless accident had occurred while the boy and a few companions were riding back to the Cité Palace; they had just forded a bend in the Seine when a stray pig from a near-by farm blundered into his path; his horse took fright and reared, and the young man, excellent horseman though he was, pitched forward over its neck. When his companions went to his aid, he was already dying. The tragedy was over in a few moments. Three days later Philip was buried beneath the vaults of Saint-Denis and Louis's dreams of a secluded life were at an end. On October 25th, 1131, his father took him to Rheims so that the principal vassals of the kingdom might swear homage and fealty to this nine-year-old boy.

Afterwards he had quietly returned to the royal abbey and gone on with his studies. And then once again, no less suddenly, he was wrenched away and informed that he was to marry the heiress to the duchy of Aquitaine. By now he was resigned to doing whatever was asked of him, whether or not it suited his own wishes; so he had spent day after day riding towards Bordeaux and the Ombrière Palace, with Abbot Suger on his right hand and a deliberately imposing escort strung out behind him.

As he sat beside this dazzling girl who was now his wife, Louis in common with the knights around him felt a trifle disconcerted by his surroundings. He and his party had difficulty in keeping up with the ceaseless flow of *langue d'oc*, and they were taken aback by the boisterousness of these people, so much more lightly clad and forthcoming than the men from Ile-de-France or Champagne. Only gradually, amid the general jubilation as the banquet proceeded, was the gulf between northerners and southerners overcome. The wines of Guyenne, poured unstintingly by the squires and pages of the baronial households, were largely responsible for the change—and so were the songs of the troubadours which rang out all the time, punctuated by the guests' applause and the rhythm of the tambourine. All the gaiety of the south was given

21

free rein before the young duchess of Aquitaine, to whom the role of hostess came quite naturally; she had fulfilled it often enough at her father's court. She was beautiful and she knew it—she had already been told so many times, in verse and prose. It came as no surprise to her that destiny, within a few weeks of making her duchess, should today be promising her the royal crown of France. She had known all along that she would never give her hand to anyone but a high lord, and the dukes of Aquitaine were ever ready to rank themselves equal with their sovereign. This particular sovereign turned out to be a somewhat frail and retiring but essentially likeable young man. Eleanor was as alert as she was self-possessed, and from the glances which the young prince kept directing at her she was amused to realize that he was madly in love.

The wedding festivities went on for several days, as was usual at the time. There were continual comings and goings between Bordeaux and the Lormont hills, where the tents pitched for the royal party were visible from afar, bright specks amid the green. The little ferry-boats plied back and forth between the banks of the Garonne —for as yet there was no bridge at Bordeaux, much to the amazement of the northern barons. In the heady atmosphere, only Suger continued to wear a look of concern. His brow furrowed as he thought of the old king slowly dying on the island in the Seine. He held long conversations with the archbishop of Bordeaux, Geoffrey of Loroux. Between them, they cut the celebrations as short as possible without causing undue disappointment either to the local populace or to the barons who had ridden all the way from their distant estates in Gascony and Poitou solely to do honour to their sovereign lady.

Events continued at a giddy pace until the moment of departure. Feast succeeded feast and there was no end to the presents that were showered on the bride. The flutes and tambourines were still resounding as Eleanor made her farewells to her young sister, the members of her household and to the Ombrière Palace itself, where she had spent the best part of her girlhood. Cheerful and resolute though she was, after crossing the Garonne she must have turned and bestowed a long last look upon the city silhouetted against the setting sun. Bordeaux's shadowy ramparts stood out against the golden sky, and so did the bell-towers of its cathedral and nine churches, and the pillars of the ancient Tutelle Palace which was built quite close to the town. Farther off stood the old abbeys of Saint-Seurin, Sainte-Eulalie and Sainte-Croix, down by the shore. The whole of this venerable land could be taken in at a glance from the margin of the gently winding river. It was the region which had given birth to the tales that had enriched her early childhood—St Etienne appearing to a poor townswoman, Charlemagne himself laying Roland's horn upon the altar of Saint-Seurin. And she must have recalled the old religious song:

> *A beautiful maid was Eulalie,*
> *Fair of body and fairer of soul . . .*

The long line of horsemen stretched out along the road towards Saintes. Not until they reached Taillebourg castle, on the far side of the Charente, did Louis and Eleanor find themselves alone in the bridal chamber that had been made ready for them.

II

Sant Jacme, membre us del baro
Que denant vos jai pelegris.

St James, be mindful of that knight
Who prays on pilgrimage to thee.

CERCAMON

THE JOYFUL ACCLAMATIONS in Bordeaux found their echo in Poitiers. No doubt the populace was not quite so vociferous and demonstrative, but plainly it was all in favour of this marriage between the lily and the olive-tree. The ceremony in the Cathedral of Saint-Pierre—not the present-day building, but an earlier edifice which was rebuilt in the course of the twelfth and thirteenth centuries—was every bit as important, from the feudal point of view, as the one in Bordeaux. For it was here in Poitiers that the young couple were to receive the ducal crown of Aquitaine. For hundreds of years the old Merovingian city had been the dukes' favourite residence and principal fief; it was here that they were crowned and here their vassals came to render homage to them. Bordeaux may provide the earliest personal traces of Eleanor (for it is generally believed that she was born in the near-by castle of Belin, and at least part of her childhood was unquestionably spent in the Ombrière Palace), but Poitiers is the obvious place for piecing together the history of her dynasty. It was history already rich in contrasting episodes by the time Louis and Eleanor were crowned, and dominated by the personality of her grandfather, William the Troubadour.

He was one of those wholly exceptional human beings whose excesses shock and offend even the most tolerant of observers, yet who redeem their wild acts by their physical splendour, their great-heartedness, their capacity for repentance and the fact that they are as unmindful of themselves as they are of other people. As Louis and Eleanor sat side by side in the cathedral, receiving oaths

24

of fealty from their vassals and undertaking to provide them with protection, more than one member of the congregation must have had personal recollections of the dramatic scene enacted some twenty years earlier on this same spot, when William the Troubadour had been excommunicated by the bishop, Peter. Suddenly, quite overcome with fury, he had flung himself upon the prelate, brandishing his sword and shouting: 'I will kill you if you do not absolve me!' The bishop had pretended to comply, so as to get free, and then calmly finished reading out the excommunication. After which, he thrust out his neck and said to his antagonist: 'Now strike! Go on—strike!' William was dumbfounded. He stood hesitating for a moment, then sheathed his sword and retrieved the situation with one of those timely rejoinders for which he had a special gift: 'Oh, no! You needn't think I'm going to send you to Paradise!'

Then there was the occasion when another bishop, Girard of Angoulême, pleaded with him to submit to the Church's authority. William's answer might be rendered in modern speech as: 'All right—you win! Keep your hair on!' The worthy bishop was completely bald.

These were only two of the many quarrels which William IX of Aquitaine had with senior churchmen in his feudal area. They occurred time and again throughout his life, and affairs with women were nearly always at the root of them. Perhaps the most notable liaison of all, and it was paraded quite shamelessly, was with a certain viscountess of Châtellerault who bore the fateful name of Dangerosa. In Poitiers she was nicknamed La Maubergeonne, for William had not hesitated to install her—rather than his lawful wife, Philippa of Toulouse—in the beautiful new keep, known as the Maubergeon Tower, which he had just added to the ducal palace. His own son had fallen out with him over Dangerosa.

Yet for all his ribaldry this powerful noble was also a poet of genius. He was the earliest French troubadour, and by one of those unexpected twists in which his life abounded no less richly than his verse, he was the first to give voice to the courtly ideal which was to nourish the best and highest in mediaeval French poetry. Moreover, William IX *did* mend his ways in the end. His last poem reveals that the apparently incorrigible sensualist had repented with all his heart. Whereas, unlike most nobles in those days, he had never given much thought to endowing religious foundations, he finally donated one of his estates, L'Orbestier (close to the vast acres of the Talmond woods, which were the favourite hunting-grounds of the dukes of Aquitaine), so that a priory of the Order of Fontevrault might be established there; his wife Philippa had entered this order, and so had their daughter Audéarde.

Some of the local barons, familiar with the past history of the Aquitaines, must have directed a questioning glance at Eleanor and wondered whether she was likely to take after her terrible grandfather. She had the same physical beauty, which was a family characteristic, the same feeling for poetry, the same cheerful disposition, and perhaps a measure of the same wilfully irreverent high spirits. As for her husband, it was clear at a glance that he did not belong to the breed of men who get themselves excommunicated over affairs with women.

Still, whatever the past may have held, it did not seem to weigh on the young couple. Youthfulness and joy radiated from them, and as soon as the ceremony was completed they found themselves presiding over yet another enormous banquet—this time in the great hall of the ducal palace. Interlude succeeded interlude: performances by minstrels and the songs of troubadours rose above the hum of talk and the bustling of the pages as they recharged goblets and set further roasts upon the carving tables. The general gaiety was at its height when a member of the royal household went up to Abbot Suger, who was seated at a table close to the young couple's. He mumbled a few words into the prelate's ear, and when he heard them Suger turned pale. He looked at the prince sitting at Eleanor's side, smiling and unconstrained: Louis was certainly growing into his part; the wedding and the ducal crown appeared to be making a new man of him, even though he had been wearing the royal signet for several years. Suger hesitated for a moment, then he stepped forward and solemnly bent his knee to him who was henceforth king of France.

A messenger had ridden over Montierneuf bridge an hour ago, bearing news of the king's death. On August 1st the sickness tormenting Louis VI had suddenly grown worse. He had expressed a wish to be conveyed to the abbey of Saint-Denis, but it was already too late for that. He was being attended by Gilduin, abbot of Saint-Victor, and Stephen, bishop of Paris, and each of them gently opposed his request. The king was quite clear-headed. He realized that his corpulence, the seriousness of his condition and the unbearably hot weather were strong arguments against his being taken to the place where he would have preferred to die. And so he resigned himself. He requested that a carpet be laid on the floor and sprinkled with ashes in the shape of a cross. He had them lower him on to the cross, and there he died an edifying death. His body now lay in Saint-Denis, wrapped in a silk sheet, close to the altar of the Holy Trinity, in the spot decreed by Suger.

Once again the festivities were cut short and the procession moved on towards its final destination. And all the way from Poitiers to Paris, crowds of people turned out to acclaim the king and queen of France.

It is easy enough to imagine the feelings that stirred in Eleanor as she journeyed towards Paris, turning over in her fifteen-year-old mind the events which had led to her becoming first duchess of Aquitaine and then queen of France. What can Paris have meant to a southern girl in August 1137? Certainly not what it would mean to one today. Paris was a royal city, but not more so than Orleans—where indeed Louis VII's forebears had preferred to reside. The prestige bestowed by its antiquity was no greater than that of Bordeaux and decidedly less than that of Marseille or Toulouse, for example. And from the religious point of view (religion was an important factor in those days) Paris was of less consequence than a good many other cities of the realm: it was only an auxiliary diocese of Sens and did not exercise the influence of metropolitan sees such as Rheims or Lyons. True, the diocese abounded in abbeys—those of Saint-Médard, Saint-Victor and Saint-Vincent-et-Sainte-Croix, for instance, as well as the old Merovingian foundation which was known even then as Saint-Germain-des-Prés after a Parisian bishop; but their renown was far exceeded by Cluny, whose vast edifice had been completed some thirty years earlier and was to remain the vastest in all Christendom until St Peter's, Rome, was rebuilt in the sixteenth century. Nor at that time could Paris boast monuments as perfectly wrought as Durham Cathedral or as magnificent as the Palace of Aix-la-

27

Chapelle; nor, of course, anything able to stand comparison with the almost fabulous reputation of cities like Rome or Venice or Constantinople. And the royal house of France could hardly lay claim—as rulers liked to do in Eleanor's day—to imperial roots, let alone an heroic past. In the hundred and fifty years since the last descendant of Charlemagne had been plucked from the throne by the sturdy grip of one of his own barons and Hugh Capet had won the recognition of his fellow-nobles at Senlis, not one of his descendants had added lustre to the Capetian dynasty by an exploit of any note. When Pope Urban II had called upon western Christendom to go to the aid of the Holy Places, the king of France—Philip I, a fat, selfish, sensual man, wholly engrossed in his illicit love-affair with the beautiful Bertrada of Montfort—had not lifted a finger. And indeed the *chansons de geste*, first conceived at approximately the same period, had concerned themselves with the deeds of mere barons, real or imaginary (Godfrey of Bouillon, Roland), nostalgically evoking as king the spirit of Charlemagne, who had not been afraid to draw sword and cross the mountains against the Saracens.

Yet something was already astir in Paris in the early twelfth century; and Eleanor, with her open mind, would be quick to respond to it. As the daughter of an exceptionally literate family, she must have appreciated her husband's feeling for the arts, even though his cultural upbringing had been quite different from her own. His, almost monastic, had unquestionably been made up of what used to be known as the seven liberal arts, in other words what was then regarded as the complete cycle of knowledge: the four physical sciences (arithmetic, geometry, music, astronomy) and the three sciences of the intellect (grammar, rhetoric, logic), all heavily steeped in theology. Eleanor, on the other hand, had probably received a far more secular education; though this has to be interpreted in the light of the standards then applying; in other words, her Latin studies may have led her to Ovid, but only after she had mastered the language through the Bible and the writings of the Church fathers. Above all, she had spent her childhood listening to the songs of the troubadours. Of those residing at her father's court, we know at least one by name—a Celt called Bledhri, who was probably Irish or Welsh; while in the beautiful *planh* which

28

he composed on the occasion of the duke's death, Cercamon extols
the generosity which William X had always displayed towards
poets.

Although Paris did not yet enjoy the immense international
reputation which its university was to win for it, the place re-
echoed with those impassioned arguments which are a sure sign
of intellectual activity. Already within the shade of the great
abbeys—Saint-Victor, Saint-Médard, Saint-Marcel, Sainte-Geneviève—masters and pupils were hotly debating the major philosophical issues and striving towards syntheses with an ardour which
augured well for the future: Paris looked like eclipsing the great
schools that had hitherto enjoyed most fame—monastery schools
like those at Bec and Fleury-sur-Loire, episcopal schools such as
those at Rheims and Laon and even Chartres. Eleanor cannot have
failed to hear all about Abelard, that beguiling and insufferable
figure who as a young student had not been afraid to challenge
the teachings of even the best-established masters, yet whose fame
—amid all the pyrotechnics of a triumphant intellectual career—
stemmed chiefly from his love for Heloïse. It was barely twenty
years since the scandal had erupted and since Heloïse's uncle, in
his fury at seeing his niece dishonoured, had set ruffians on to
Abelard with orders to castrate him. And Eleanor would not need
telling of the extraordinary career of Heloïse herself—of how,
renowned for her learning even as a girl of seventeen, she was now
abbess of the convent of the Paraclete, separated for ever from the
lover to whom her heart remained hopelessly loyal. With her taste
for the romantic, the young queen must have been spellbound by
a tale which retains its magic even after eight hundred years and
which in those days derived especial potency from the fact that
both protagonists were still alive.

As she approached Paris, she no doubt delighted in the coolness
of its surrounding woods and loved her first glimpse of the old city
beneath the soft blue sky of Ile-de-France. From the slopes of
Mont Sainte-Geneviève, where the Seine bends, she could discern
the largest of the green islands dotted on the river: the Ile de la
Cité. There were its ramparts, erected some two hundred years
earlier for fear of a recurrence of the Norman invasions; and there
were the two bridges, lined with houses and flanked by fortresses—

on the left bank, the Petit Châtelet; on the right, that same Grand Châtelet which lent its name to one of the squares of modern Paris.

All this while she had been journeying, though in the reverse direction, along the pilgrims' route to St James of Compostela; at the other end lay the shrine for which her father had been making when he had died the previous Good Friday. Almost certainly, as she approached Paris itself, her attention was directed to the tomb of Isoré the Giant, a menhir standing at the termination of the Roman road whose course can still be traced on the map, cutting clean into the hills on the left bank, via the Rue Saint-Jacques, and sloping down to what was then a great marshy plain dominated by the high hill of Montmartre and the more distant hill of Chaillot (later the Templars lost no time in draining the plain and turning it into market-gardens). Her heart must have warmed to this landscape patched with vineyards, enlivened on the right bank by the fleet of watermen and, on the left bank, by the ceaseless tide that flowed from the lodging-houses and taverns frequented by the students. It was with firm tread that she ascended the steps of the old Cité Palace, having stepped down on to the stump of moss-grown olive-wood which traditionally served as a dismounting-block, lovingly assisted by her attentive young husband, the king of France.

III

Quant ieu la vey, be m'es parven
Als huelhs, al vis, a la color
(Quar aissi tremble de paor
Cum fa la fuelha contra'l ven);
Non ai de sen per un efan,
Aissi sui d'amor entrepres;
E d'ome qu'es aissi conques
Pot Domn' aver almorna gran.

When I see her, my feelings flow
Into my eyes and face; my hue
Betrays the stress I'm subject to,
I'm like a leaf when tempests blow.
So deep in love am I that tho'
A man, I'm witless as a child;
To one so hopelessly beguiled
His lady should great mercy show.

BERNARD DE VENTADOUR

VITRY
1143

THE FLAMES ascended with a thunderous roar. From time to time
brilliant flashes rose above the pall of black smoke that seemed to
engulf the little town. The army, under King Louis VII in person,
had succeeded in crushing the resistance of Vitry-en-Perthois; by
way of lanes and side-streets, the footsoldiers had penetrated to the
heart of the city, and in their fury—which no one had attempted to
restrain—they had set fire to the buildings. Panic-stricken and
frightened out of their wits, the townspeople had taken refuge in
the church, hoping to find security and asylum in accordance with
the traditions of the time.

This was in 1143. Six years had gone by since Eleanor's marriage
to Louis. The king, who had watched his troops advance on the
little township from his encampment on the La Fourche hills, was
no longer the shy and hesitant youth who had been so warmly

31

Hugh Capet head of the Capetians, a Royal family ('328)
France. Became King in 987. Direct descendants ruled

acclaimed in Bordeaux Cathedral. He was a young man determined
to display resolution and self-assurance. From his vantage-point he
gazed silently down at the roaring blaze in the dusk below the hill.
Suddenly the flashes intensified. A jet of flame shot up above the
rest and a muffled tumult carried to the hillside camp. The shrieks
of the crowd began to mingle with the roar and crackle: the church
was on fire. A few minutes of unbearable suspense, and then the
pandemonium grew worse than ever. The framework of the building was caving in, burying the hundreds of men, women and
children who had fondly thought to find refuge on consecrated
ground.

Louis's companions grew alarmed at his stillness and silence.
When they went up to him, they saw that his face was white and
haggard and his teeth were chattering. They led him away and
made him lie down in his tent. When at last he found his tongue,
he merely asked that they should leave him on his own. For several
days the king continued to hold aloof, refusing to eat or drink or
talk to anyone, lying prostrate and motionless on his couch.
Engaged in dark self-scrutiny, he was reckoning the cost of the
past six years. They had been happy years, the years of a young
husband madly in love with his wife—yet they had culminated in
this horror. How had he ever come to commit such a heinous
crime?

———◆———

In fact this pious and peace-loving prince, whose early life had
been spent within the walls of the abbey of Saint-Denis, and who
may well have dreamed of becoming a monk there, was now in
active revolt against every religious authority; his kingdom had
been laid under an interdict by the pope—no church bells rang,
no church services were ever performed; he had quarrelled with
his mother; Suger, his father's right hand, no longer came to the
Cité Palace; and now, to cap it all, his armies—fighting a war for
which he himself had given the signal—had burned down a
church, a holy place, a place of asylum, killing the entire population of a town, some thirteen hundred human beings . . . In the
mind of even the least biased observer, there could be little room

Eleanor of Aquitaine, from her tomb in the Abbey of Fontevrault

All that remains of her seal,
from a charter in the
Archives de France

Eleanor with a companion, probably Isabella of Angoulême, from an early 13th c. wall painting in the Chapel of St. Radegund, Chinon

The tombs of Eleanor and Henry II of England in Fontevrault

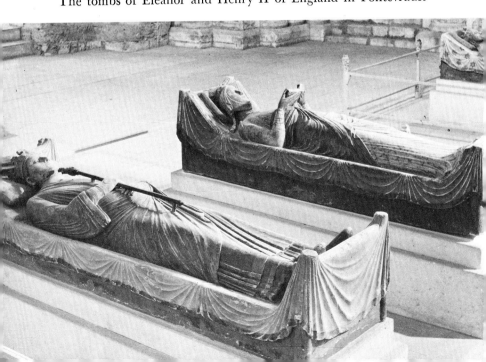

The seal of Louis VII of France, showing (left) his title
as Eleanor's husband: Dux Aquitanorum

A crystal vase, given by Eleanor to Louis VII, who gave it to Abbot
Suger, and an ampulla of 10th c. Saracen workmanship, given to
Suger by Theobald of Champagne—both now in the Louvre

Abbot Suger, from a stained-glass window in the Abbey of Saint-Denis, and an ambulatory in the choir of Saint-Denis which Suger built

Left, Emperor Manuel Comnenus, Eleanor's host in Constantinople, from a 12th c. manuscript in the Vatican Library. Right, 'The Crusader's Return', from the 12th c. tomb of Hugues de Vaudémont, now in the Archæological Museum, Nancy

The south doorway of the Cathedral of Le Mans, capital of Anjou

The seal of Henry II. Barely visible (left) is his title of Dux
Aquitanorum. Below, the keep of Dover Castle, built by Henry II

The crowning of the Young King, and his father, Henry II, serving him at table. Below, Thomas Becket excommunicating his enemies and arguing with Henry II and Louis VII. From a 13th c. French manuscript of the Life of St. Thomas, written in England

for doubt. Lurking behind every one of the decisions that had led to this imbroglio of private rifts and public outrages, of family squabbles and feudal wars, was the figure of Eleanor. In her pretty hands lay both ends of the skein which seemed to have been wantonly tangled for her own girlish amusement.

Louis and Eleanor had barely arrived in Paris, in fact, before they were on bad terms with the queen mother, Adelaide of Savoy. This was hardly surprising; there was bound to be friction between the young wife and an ageing mother-in-law who, having failed to influence her late husband, had no doubt been hoping to make up for it with a son who was conspicuously shy and inexperienced. Let an exasperatingly young and pretty girl intrude upon the scene, and a breach became inevitable. It occurred almost at once; the queen mother withdrew from court and retired to her own estates where, so soon afterwards that it seemed almost an act of revenge, she married a certain lord of Montmorency, only a minor noble but a fine figure of a man.

It is not hard to imagine what a woman like Adelaide would have against her daughter-in-law, this southerner who was bound to take after her godless grandfather and whose bold ways could hardly fail to give offence to those about her. It had happened before, in the previous century: Hugh Capet's son Robert had married a southern girl, Constance of Provence, and her behaviour had utterly scandalized the sobersided barons of the north; they had considered her immodest of dress and brazen of tongue. Adelaide must often have levelled the same charges at her son's wife.

But these petty personal frictions were as nothing beside the storms that were soon to break over the young king's head. Within a year of his accession he was leading an expedition against Poitiers, where the burghers had made so bold as to form themselves into a commune; following the example of the burghers of Orleans, whose rebellion had been put down in the recent past, they had taken a joint oath to repudiate the count's authority. Poitiers! The fief of her forefathers, the town most beloved of William the Troubadour! Eleanor's anger and humiliation in the face of this blow to her ducal authority may be gauged from the ferocity of the measures applied once the uprising was crushed. For Louis VII

33

lost no time in taking the field with a small army, whose paucity of knights was more than compensated by the exceptional number of sappers and siege devices. He captured the city easily enough, without shedding a drop of blood, covering himself with glory in the eyes of his entourage and, an even more precious achievement, in the eyes of his wife.

But his demands as victor were positively barbarous: not only must the commune be disbanded and the oath unsworn, but the sons and daughters of the leading burghers were to be led away as hostages. This seemed excessively harsh even to some of the king's own followers. Suger, who had been keeping in touch with events from Saint-Denis, hurried to the king's side and had a series of long talks with him. Eventually, speaking from a palace window overlooking the old quarter of Chadeuil, the abbot was able to tell the assembled populace that the king had relented: Louis had decided against taking hostages; he was going to let the burghers off. The city went wild with rejoicing—and the king's generosity had been lauded ever since, with an ardour commensurate with the sense of relief which had been felt in Poitiers. But Eleanor was clearly riled at the abbot's decision to intrude in a matter pertaining directly to her own feudal powers. In the months that followed, Louis never once turned to Suger for advice. The abbot understood and did not press his views.

His absence had a grave effect on the administration of the kingdom's affairs. There was no voice of wisdom and experience to temper the young couple's often ill-considered reactions, which were ruled by Eleanor's slightest whim. Louis's every act bore the stamp of her inspiration; his every expedition was directed towards the area under her ducal control. He dealt with William of Lezay, who had refused to render homage at the time of the coronation and who had purloined the white gerfalcons belonging to the dukes of Aquitaine from their hunting preserve at Talmond, of which he was joint holder. He carried out a senseless and totally unsuccessful foray against Toulouse; Eleanor was determined to stake her claim to the county, maintaining that it was rightfully hers through her grandmother Philippa, wife of the Troubadour (the wife whom he had forsaken and who had entered the abbey of Fontevrault). On his return, Eleanor recompensed him for his pains with a magnificent crystal vase which is still preserved in the Musée du Louvre; its chased gold base and neck were inlaid with pearls and precious stones.

Clearly the king of France was not powerful enough to make a mighty vassal like the count of Toulouse relinquish his fief—nor, incidentally, was there any justice in the demand; so Alfonso-Jordan was not unduly perturbed. Louis's own difficulties, on the other hand, were only just beginning. Eleanor had gone to Toulouse with him, and on the way back she collected her young sister, who is referred to in some contemporary sources as Petronilla (or Peronelle, the diminutive form of the same name) and in others as Aelith. The latter was of marriageable age and her eye soon lighted on one of the king's familiars, Raoul of Vermandois, who had served as counsellor to Louis and to his father before him; indeed he had just been appointed seneschal. Raoul was well-preserved, even though he was more than old enough to be the father of this girl, who cannot have been a day over seventeen at the time—i.e. in 1141. His delight in being cast as the greying seducer must have been all-consuming, for he quite forgot that he was already married—and married not just to anyone, but to the niece of the powerful Theobald of Blois, count of Champagne. It was obvious to anyone even moderately well-informed as to the affairs of the realm that here was fuel capable of setting an entire province ablaze. As indeed it did.

Eleanor took up her sister's cause and Louis, who could never deny the queen anything, persuaded three of his bishops (those of Laon, Senlis and Noyon) to rule that Raoul's first wife, Eleanor, was within the prohibited degrees—a point on which canon law was very strict at the time. The bishops were therefore able to declare an annulment and Raoul lost no time in wedding the triumphant young Peronelle, before the contented gaze of the queen.

This was a direct affront to the count of Champagne and more than enough to rekindle the ancient quarrels which had long divided the counts of Champagne and the lords of Vermandois, who had traditionally strengthened their position by alliances in Flanders; anxious to avert these quarrels, which might spread and provoke internecine strife throughout the length and breadth of the kingdom, Louis VI had reconciled the two families a short while before his death. Now suddenly they were at loggerheads again, all because of a feminine whim. Theobald of Champagne was so furious that he complained to the pope; a council assembled at Lagny, within his domain, during the early months of 1142, and the papal legate (Yves of Saint-Laurent) excommunicated the newly married couple and the bishops who had stretched the law of the Church in their favour.

This was not the only matter in which the king of France was defying religious authority. At more or less the same time, Louis VII had become embroiled over the archbishopric of Bourges. He had taken it into his head to appoint his own candidate—in the shape of his chancellor, a man named Cadurc. When the archbishop officially elected and invested by the Holy See, Peter of La Châtre, arrived to take up his duties he was unable to get in: Louis had given orders for the city gates and cathedral doors to be bolted against him. This was a momentous decision, for the papacy believed that, after more than a century of struggle, it had succeeded in safeguarding the liberty of ecclesiastical nominations and quashing lay investiture. That such a decision should be taken by a scion of the Capetian dynasty, which had tended to support the papacy against the emperors, was therefore somewhat startling. But it was less startling on the part of a duchess of Aquitaine. Indeed, Eleanor's grandfather had on several occasions decided to confer bishoprics within his feudal area upon prelates whose first loyalty was to himself, and he had not been afraid to defy the papacy on this score; worse, he had at one time espoused the cause of an antipope, Anacletus, against this same Innocent II who still sat on the throne of St Peter. So members of the royal entourage were quick to blame Louis's indiscretions on his wife—not without justification.

And so France now lay under an interdict, and Louis himself was in danger of being anathematized for lending armed support to his excommunicated sister-in-law. Now that the fighting in Champagne had culminated in this terrible holocaust at Vitry, he sensed sharply that he must take a fresh grip on himself and put matters right. For France's sake as well as his own.

Moreover, at the end of these days of gloomy meditation the

young man received a sharp recall to the path of duty. It came from the highest spiritual authority of the day, a counsellor of popes and kings and a man universally regarded as a saint—Bernard of Clairvaux.

Some thirty years had passed since Bernard had presented himself at the gates of the monastery of Cîteaux, seedbed of the reformist movement which was to be brought to fruition under him: by the time he died, the abbey of Clairvaux comprised seven hundred monks and a hundred and sixty daughter-houses, and the Cistercian order had spread all over Christendom, from England to Portugal, from Italy to Scandinavia. This mystic, who aspired solely to the silence of the cloister and the austereness of the solitary cell where he slept on the bare floor, had been constantly embroiled in the affairs of his time; he was for ever being called upon to settle quarrels, throw light on difficult situations and breathe fire into the practice of the Christian faith. He had already addressed several reproofs to Louis VII, but the young man had turned a deaf ear. This time the tone was really stern: 'When I consider the innumerable acts of violence for which you are responsible, I begin to rue the fact that I have always ascribed your misdeeds to youthful inexperience; from now on I am determined, so far as my feeble strength allows, to tell the whole truth. I shall state loud and clear that . . . you are always killing, burning, destroying churches, that you drive the poor from their homes and that you consort with plunderers and armed robbers . . . Be sure of this: you will not go unpunished for long . . . I am speaking harshly to you, but only because I fear that an even harsher punishment may be in store for you.'

This time, everything suggested that his exhortation would be heeded. Louis returned to the Cité Palace, leaving his brother Robert to terminate the war in Champagne by occupying Rheims and Chalons. And it was not long before he showed by his behaviour that a profound change had been worked within him.

37

[Handwritten annotations:] abbey of Saint Denis = a N. suburb of Paris. Pop: 68,595, Seine Dept. Metal works, chemical plant. Town grew around a Benedictine abbey, founded 626 at tomb of St. Denis, the patron saint of France. Played a prominent part in Fr. history.

[Handwritten left margin:] Foundation (12th & 13th C) acppey influenced evolu-tion of Gothic architecture; revolution. Includes tombs of 6-11 1144 Kings of new abbey France dedicated

[Handwritten:] 6-11-1144

IV

Estat ai com om esperdutz
Per amor un lonc estatge,
Mas era'm sui reconogutz
Qu'eu avia faih folatge.

Long time I lived in wretched wise,
By love distracted and oppressed;
But today I recognize
I have behaved like one possessed.

BERNARD DE VENTADOUR

THE ROAD between Paris and Saint-Denis was even busier than on market days. Clusters of pilgrims hurried along, and again and again the haycarts had to give way to some procession of prelates and barons whose steeds were tired of pawing the ground while a pair of lay brothers—their skin and clothing grey with dust—did their best to manage a flock of sheep. The bustle grew steadily worse towards Saint-Denis; the carts were loaded with sacks of flour, barrels of wine and piles of vegetables, for the market-gardens of Ile-de-France had been picked bare, and in these early days of June other foodstuffs had been ordered from far and wide. The royal marshals, sent to reinforce the abbey's own guardians of the law, had a difficult task ensuring that the shifting mass of animals and men was properly channelled. And along the edge of the fields, as far as the eye could see, the tents were going up which for three eventful days would shelter the squires and clerks and lesser folk who had been unable to find accommodation either in the guest quarters of the abbey—reserved for those of higher station—or in any of the local households.

They were all on their way to attend the dedication of the new abbey of Saint-Denis on Sunday, June 11th, 1144. Bustling and beaming, the tireless Abbot Suger was extending a personal wel-

38

come to all visitors of rank and pointing out the various lodgings which had been assigned to them. This frail little prelate, whose health was so delicate that he was always thought to be at death's door, was unquestionably one of the most extraordinary figures of his time. He had never been dismayed by the amazing turn of fortune which had lifted him from his lowly rustic background and placed him in sole charge of the royal abbey, and was soon to place him in sole charge of the kingdom itself. He had been equally undismayed by his fall from favour during the past few years: he had immediately taken full advantage of the resulting leisure to devote himself to hastening the work of reconstruction on the great abbey. Up before dawn and active far into the night, he had the satisfaction of knowing that never once—not even in the days when he used to journey all over Europe on the king's business— had he neglected to say daily mass, in accordance with the rules of his order. He was a man of great culture and his writings abound in classical quotations, but—and in this he is very much a man of his time—there was nothing of the intellectual about him, nothing of the desk-bound scholar. Suger had a good deal in common with the modern executive-style prelate (there is nothing intrinsi- cally damning about the phrase) who in the United States and the young Christian nations of our own day builds churches, founds schools, launches Catholic newspapers, and so forth. He himself has described, with a complacency which hints at the self-made man, how his abbey was rebuilt stage by stage; and his own zestful labours emerge clearly from his account. One day he was informed that the carpenters had been compelled to stop work owing to lack of materials: it was proving impossible to find beams of the right length in the abbey woods, already plundered for timber. Suger immediately left his cell and went scouring in the Yvelines forest; it was he who led the woodcutters to the dozen entirely suitable oaks which had escaped everyone else's attention.

Moreover, as so often happens in the case of those who are enter- prising and alert, luck seemed to be always at his elbow. If he was faced with the problem of transporting building-stone from the Pontoise quarries, word would arrive that the local peasants were willing to help out. Were the goldsmiths in urgent need of precious stones to set in the great cross which was to hang above the altar?

A messenger came, announcing the count of Champagne's offer of a magnificent collection of topazes and garnets. Only three days before the official opening, when there was great concern as to how they were to feed all the guests (for the local flocks had been hit by an epidemic), a Cistercian brother drew him aside as he was about to say Mass and announced that a flock of sheep was on its way—a gift from his own order, as a way of sharing in the great occasion.

A sudden stir in the crowd, followed by an outbreak of shouting and cheering, indicated the arrival of the king and queen. It was an important day, this June Sunday, for it marked also a major reconciliation.

There was no hint of regal majesty in the attire or bearing of King Louis VII. To the surprise of the crowd, he wore neither silk tunic nor ermine-lined cloak but had donned the grey garb of a penitent and a pair of plain sandals; lost in the crowd, he might well have been mistaken for a humble hermit on pilgrimage to the shrine of St Denis. He could not have provided a sharper contrast to the great nobles who were present—his own vassals—clad in the glowing colours which were then so much in vogue; nor with the bishops, whose embroidered mitres trimmed with gold shone in the sunlight. Eleanor, for her part, wore a brocade dress and a diadem of pearls; she was making the most of the occasion; opportunities to array herself in splendour were becoming few and far between at the court of France. In her first years of married life she had been able to give free rein to her fondness for outward display. Their joint coronation as king and queen of France, celebrated in Bourges during the Christmas of 1137, had been marked by the most splendid pageantry. Louis had already been crowned in Rheims; but coronation rites were repeated several times in those days, whenever the occasion warranted—and what more suitable occasion than a marriage? Ever since, constantly seeking new ways to please her, he had showered gifts on his young wife. She had done her best to bring a little brightness to the austere old palace on the Ile de la Cité. The tapestry workshops—and already there were some in Bourges which had won high renown—had carried out commissions for her; and the merchants who were beginning to import products from the Near East (musk; sandalwood to

40

sweeten the vast and cheerless rooms; light silk veils; rose preserves; ginger to purify the breath) travelled regularly along the roads leading to the various royal residences, in Paris and Etampes and Orleans. Most important of all, Eleanor had lost no time in sending for the troubadours. Life would have seemed drab to her without them. She needed their songs, the strains of viol and tambourine, of flute and cithara, and above all the poetic interplay of words, the repartee, light-hearted and sometimes slightly daring, which had always found favour at the courts of her father and grandfather and which she had been anxious to introduce into France.

But it had not always been to the taste of her husband, whose love was possessive and easily roused to resentment. The troubadour Marcabru learned this to his cost.

Marcabru is a typical figure of his age. He was a foundling, brought up somewhere in Gascony and given the name Panperdut. Initiated to the craft of poetry by Cercamon, a familiar of William X of Aquitaine, he had won respect for his talent and his songs were now in general circulation, from the court of Castile to the banks of the Loire. Eleanor had invited him to Paris, despite certain reservations on the part of her husband. But any troubadour is unfailingly in love with the Highborn Lady who inspires his verses. He told her so in burning stanzas, and one fine day Louis flew into a rage. He dismissed the impudent troubadour without further ado. Marcabru got his own back as best he could, with a set of treasonous verses. He wrote of a tree which was 'big and tall, branchy and leafy . . . and spreading out in all directions, reaching from France to Poitou . . . Its root is Spite, by which Youth is confounded . . .'

Moreover, Louis had changed a good deal of late. That appalling incident at Vitry had obviously upset him deeply. No more celebrating, no more dancing and feasting, no more songs or poetry-recitals: he had grown gloomy and had no mind for anything except doing penance; he fasted several days a week and was to be observed saying his prayers at all hours. To commemorate the dedication of the chancel at Saint-Denis, he had insisted on presenting Suger with the beautifully wrought vase which Eleanor had given him. He was thinking of making the old abbot his chief

41

adviser again, and this—as she was quick to realize—could only mean that Eleanor's influence was on the wane. Already Suger had brought about a peace settlement with Theobald of Champagne, and following the death of Innocent II the king had lost no time in making his submission to the new pope. 'Sometimes I feel I've married a monk,' she confided to her intimates.

At an even deeper level, there was a nagging sense of unease between the young couple: they did not have a child. Hopes had arisen in the first months of marriage, but they had soon been dashed. Those close to the throne were beginning to murmur (and never a whisper went undetected by the queen's sharp ear) that this marriage which had seemed to promise so much might not be such a boon after all. Not only was Eleanor extravagant, not only did she start wars out of sheer capriciousness, but she had yet to bear a child to safeguard the future of the dynasty . . .

Eleanor, however, had a plan in mind. The abbots of every great abbey in the realm would be present at the ceremony in Saint-Denis, a ceremony which Suger was determined to invest with unparalleled magnificence. She had taken advantage of this fact to seek a private audience with Bernard of Clairvaux. Bernard was commonly regarded as a saint, even in his own lifetime, and he was in the habit of addressing her husband as though Louis were a mere pupil. There seems little doubt that Eleanor herself was drawn to the abbot more out of curiosity than veneration. Her father before her had clashed with Bernard of Clairvaux. The scene has become famous in the annals of Aquitaine. One day William X, smarting under the abbot's threats of excommunication, had burst fully armed into Parthenay church where Bernard was saying Mass. But the latter had simply advanced on him, bearing the Host and the ciborium, and the duke—vanquished, subjugated by the ardour emanating from his incandescent adversary—had suddenly prostrated himself, filled with repentance. The powers of this world could no more hold out against St Bernard than could the powers of heaven.

At present, Eleanor had need of his influence with God and with men. She wanted a child in whom she could instil the ambition and taste for regal magnificence which shape great kings; and she was equally anxious that the ban be lifted from her sister and

42

brother-in-law. Who better than Bernard of Clairvaux to help her achieve this twofold ambition?

———————◆———————

Just as Suger had anticipated, the ceremony marked an unforgettable date in the history of the Church and the history of art. Indeed, the new abbey at Saint-Denis evoked a general response in the twelfth century comparable with that evoked by the new churches at Assy and Vence and Ronchamp in the twentieth; it was a major architectural step forward, and everyone was immediately alive to the fact. Never before had the rib vault been employed in a building of any great size. It was an object-lesson to the visiting prelates (some of whom, like the archbishop of Canterbury, had come from far away) and Eleanor must have been especially delighted to see among them Geoffrey of Loroux, archbishop of Bordeaux, who had officiated at her marriage. When the prelates returned to their own dioceses several decided to apply similar principles to the reconstruction of their cathedrals, now too small for populations which were growing at an unbelievable rate. The use of the rib vault made it possible for the supporting walls to be hollowed out boldly, and in consequence light and colour flooded down from the stained-glass windows on to the twenty altars due for consecration that day. In the centre, supported by a gilt pillar above the high altar, rose the magnificent twenty-foot gold cross, glittering with enamel-work and gems and pearls, a masterpiece representing two years' hard work by the goldsmiths of Lorraine, the foremost craftsmen of their time. This vision of beauty was intensified as the congregation joined in the psalms, lay voices alternating with the choir of several hundred clerics amid the age's general atmosphere of religious fervour . . . It all made a deep and lasting impression on everyone present. And however spacious the abbey might seem, there was no room for the thousands of ordinary people milling about in the open air. When the time came for the clergy to process round the church, sprinkling holy water on the outside walls, the king himself energetically assisted his own officers to clear a passage for them. Indeed he had several opportunities during the day of giving practical expression

43

to his fervour; as the bishops turned aside to collect the reliquaries containing the 'holy bodies'—the relics of St Denis and his companions—he left his place, hurried forward and asked permission to shoulder the silver reliquary of St Denis. 'Never,' concludes Suger, 'never was there a more solemn and soul-stirring procession, never were bystanders moved to greater joy.'

At least a few of these bystanders must have glanced uneasily towards Bernard of Clairvaux and wondered what he thought of such display of gold and precious stones and liturgical riches—he who had spoken out so strongly against priestly pomp and had gone so far as to banish colour (a supreme act of self-denial for a man of his time!) from the windows of Cistercian churches. In fact the two men were in complete harmony, however wide the seeming gulf between them. Some twenty years earlier, Suger had remodelled his personal style of living in response to St Bernard's appeals: the Cistercian was insistent that his fellow-priests should return to the poverty of Christ and the early disciples; since then, Suger's cell had been bare except for a crucifix, and his daily fare as frugal as a monk's should be. But he had put all his longing for visual splendour into his abbey. The two men thus embodied the two opposite yet unconflicting poles that the Church habitually steers between: austerity and magnificence.

And Eleanor herself would remain incomprehensible if she were not viewed against this essential background to her personality and to the age—the love of splendour, which was manifested in the lavishly painted churches, with their bejewelled crosses and rings of blazing candles; or in those tales of chivalry in which heroes with shining swords and shields engage in awesome combats and dream luminous dreams. This obsession assumed many guises, from the mystique of light, which was later to achieve its full expression in Gothic architecture and in the solemn philosophical treatises of such men as Robert Grosseteste and St Bonaventure, down to the general hankering after 'gold and glitter' in which—to judge from her life and her tastes—Eleanor shared to the full. She must have revelled in a setting which Suger described in ebullient verse, playing on words as the sunlight played on the precious stones scattered profusely about the building.

As the celebrations drew to a close, she and Bernard of Clairvaux

44

met in a private room and began their tête-à-tête. Saint and madcap queen—they made an extraordinary pair. Eleanor's beauty was youthful, earthly, wholly corporeal. That she *was* beautiful, and radiantly so, her contemporaries testify, though in keeping with the tiresome habit of the times they have not handed down the slightest detail as to the nature of this beauty; they are content to tell us that she was *perpulchra*, in other words that her beauty went beyond the ordinary. We may assume, however, that her appearance tallied with the contemporary ideal of womanhood—that is to say that she was blonde, for fair hair and fair complexion were considered indispensable in the twelfth century.

We are given a far more adequate picture of the extraordinary human being confronting her, for nothing fascinated the men and women of the time so much as saintliness and they strove to preserve every detail relating to the saints' lives on earth. We know that Bernard was handsome and that in youth he had been, as William of Saint-Thierry tells us, 'more dangerous to the world than the world was to him'. He was tall, with very delicate skin and red hair which was fast turning white. But at the time of this discussion with Eleanor (he was fifty-four and had only nine more years before him) his outward appearance had been wholly transfigured by the nature of his inner life. 'His body, wasted from fasting and the deprivations of the desert, gave him—together with his pallor—what one might call a spiritualized appearance,' wrote Wibald of Stavelot. One of his contemporaries said of him: 'He is a Voice.' Ardour of the spirit had literally consumed the flesh and he had become no more than a voice, in the sense in which, say, John the Baptist was. 'The very sight of this man,' we are further assured, 'was enough to persuade his audience even before he opened his lips.'

However, Eleanor remained sufficiently self-possessed to tell him composedly what troubled her. 'During all the seven years that she had lived with the king she had remained barren, apart from one hope in the early days, which had been quickly dashed; she despaired of ever having the longed-for child.' Would Bernard of Clairvaux intercede for her and move heaven to answer her prayer?

His reply was as uncompromising as the fiery gaze which had

45

stemmed her father's onslaught years before: 'Strive for peace within the realm and I promise you that God in his infinite mercy will grant what you request.'

Within a year of this encounter, the kingdom had been purged of strife and a child was born to the royal couple—a daughter whom they christened Marie in honour of the Queen of Heaven.

1145

married
of Eleanor
Louis VII

Solitary success in 2nd Crusade was LISBON
... mixed Co. of Flemings, Lorrainers & English
in 200 vessels started for Holy Land.
... Alfonso — son of Duke Henry of Burgundy
wanted to capture Lisbon from Moors
... Persuaded "crusaders" to help him.
... 17 week siege.
... Took Lisbon   10-24-1147

V

Ver ditz qui m'apella lechai
Ni desiran d'amor de lonh
Car nulhs autres jois tant no'm plai
Cum jauzimens d'amor de lonh.

Who calls me greedy does not lie;
I hunger after love remote.
No joy within my grasp can vie
With that of winning love remote.

JAUFRE RUDEL

1146

LEAGUE AFTER LEAGUE the wagons stretched, strung out in line. The peasants, busy with the hay harvest, dropped their tools and hurried across the fields to gape at the seemingly endless wake of vehicles to rearward of the itinerant army. Heavy four-wheeled wagons they were, pulled by big strong draught-horses and piled high with iron chests and rolled-up tents for sheltering under at the next halting-place, all carefully protected by coverings of leather or canvas.

The length and opulence of the baggage train may have inspired wonder among the populace of the Rhineland, but it prompted entirely different feelings among the king's entourage, whose members were wondering apprehensively how an army so heavily encumbered was ever going to stand up to the enemy and stave off his surprise attacks.

This procession, which had set out from Metz at Whitsun and headed towards the plains of the Danube, was none other than that of Louis VII and the companions who had elected to join him on the road to Jerusalem. For at the end of the year in which their first child was born, Louis and Eleanor had announced to the chief feudatories, who had gathered for the annual Christmas court in Bourges, that they intended to take the Cross. Louis was thereby proposing to fulfil the vow which had been made years before by

47

his elder brother Philip, the boy whose premature death had made him heir to the kingdom of France; and doubtless his remorse at the savage burning of Vitry was not unconnected with his resolve.

In 1144, shortly after the dedication of the abbey of Saint-Denis, the whole of Christendom had been deeply disturbed by the news from the Holy Land: the renowned city of Edessa had fallen to Zengi, governor of Aleppo and Mosul. Edessa had been conquered about fifty years earlier by Baldwin of Boulogne (younger brother of Godfrey of Bouillon, that legendary hero of the First Crusade) with the help of the considerable number of Armenians living in the town—who were now, as a result of the fall, being subjected to renewed persecution by the Turks. Northern Syria, the border-land-fief of the Latin kingdoms, was at present more or less un-defended and wide open to the attacks being launched by Zengi. In his hands lay the three strongholds closest to Antioch, whose capture had cost the early crusaders such a price in blood and endurance. He was a redoubtable warrior, this Turk, and all kinds of legendary tales were told about him. He was rumoured to be sprung from an amazon—Margravine Ida of Austria, a celebrated beauty and intrepid horsewoman who had taken the Cross at the same time as William the Troubadour and vanished in the course of her ill-fated expedition; according to the story, she had been taken prisoner and packed off to a harem, where she had eventu-ally given birth to the Muslim hero.

The fall of Edessa constituted a serious threat to the Latin king-doms, especially at a time when the titular head of Jerusalem itself, Baldwin III, was a mere boy of thirteen still in the care of his mother, Queen Melisande. Yet although there might be anxiety as to the fate of the Holy Places, and sympathy for the Armenian victims of the appalling massacres which the Turks had perpe-trated after their victory, nobody seemed in any great hurry to renew the large-scale expeditions which had been launched half a century earlier. Since the recapture of Jerusalem, the preservation of the Holy Land had been guaranteed solely by such spontaneous acts of assistance as might be afforded from time to time; driven by personal piety or appetite for adventure, a youngest son—or, more rarely, some great lord—would vow to go on crusade, recruit some men, muster some other pilgrims who were animated by the same

48

desire, and then ride forth and offer his services to the Latin kingdom, which had already, despite its precariousness, taken on the
appearance of an established institution.

So the decision of King Louis of France had come as a shock. He
would be the first monarch ever to undertake an armed pilgrimage.
Geoffrey, bishop of Langres, had delivered a sermon in Bourges
exhorting the barons at the Christmas court to follow their
sovereign's example; but only gradually did they make up their
minds to do so. Even the pope—it was the reign of Eugenius III, a
Cistercian—displayed certain reservations before he finally lent
approval to the project. As it happened, His Holiness was unable to
preach the crusade in person; he entrusted the task to Bernard,
abbot of Clairvaux. History has preserved the scene enacted among
the hills of Vézelay at Easter the following year (March 31st, 1146).
St Bernard stood on the tall platform which had been erected for
the king and himself and delivered his ardent exhortations to the
mighty lords and common people crowded together within the
amphitheatre of hills. Pennants and standards fluttered in the
breeze, and soon the air resounded with the cheers of a great host:
so many rushed forward and clamoured for crosses that there
were not enough to go round and the abbot had to snip more from
his own habit. St Bernard's power of utterance was gradually reawakening in western Christendom that same enthusiasm which
had characterized the Council of Clermont and the prodigious
launching of the First Crusade.

Eleanor had taken the Cross at the same time as her husband.
Contrary to what is sometimes believed, there was nothing very
extraordinary about this. Far from it: even on the first expedition,
a good many lords had taken their wives with them. Baldwin of
Boulogne, victor at Edessa, had taken his; so had Raymond of
Saint-Gilles, one of the principal leaders of the expedition. Indeed,
the latter's son—heir to the county of Toulouse—owed his name,
Alfonso-Jordan, to the fact that he had been baptized in the waters
of the river which had once heard the voice of John the Baptist;
for he had actually been born in the course of that epic journey to
Jerusalem. Visions of the scorned wife, excluded from her husband's exploits and living immured in a gloomy castle until such
time as he chose to return, may still be firmly rooted in many

49

minds; but they have almost as little to do with reality as talk of serfs patrolling ponds to keep the frogs quiet, and other non-sensical ideas inherited from those neo-classical days when the barbarism of the Middle Ages was an article of faith.

And indeed it was not for taking his wife with him that Louis VII incurred criticism from some of his contemporaries (incidentally his great-grandson, St Louis, was to do the same a century later); no, what they objected to was the fact that Eleanor and the other women taking part in the expedition—the countess of Blois, Sybilla of Anjou, the countess of Flanders, Faydide of Toulouse, Florine of Burgundy, all doubtless led astray by her example—had insisted on bringing their chambermaids and were determined not to forgo a moderate degree of comfort during this long and arduous journey. Hence the daunting line of wagons lumbering towards Hungary across the plains of central Europe. Far too many wagons, grumbled the men-at-arms; far too many, echoed the churchmen. And while the former were troubled by intimations of the disasters that could easily befall an army with so many useless mouths to feed and so much surplus baggage, the latter railed against the dissolute conduct which was bound to result. The presence of so many maidservants could not fail to lead to a lot of snickering when camp was pitched of an evening, and after dark there would be a good deal of furtive coming and going around the tents. They would scarcely provide moral reinforcement for men engaged upon a mission of piety. In the words of one chronicler who did not shrink from dubious puns: there was nothing chaste about these encampments (*castra non casta*).

That Eleanor had played a really active part in preparing the expedition, there can be no doubt. A study of the old title-deeds of the area shows that a remarkably high proportion of these crusaders came from Poitou. This is very probably due to the fact that she had made a personal tour of her private estates. Her own example must have been highly persuasive. Everywhere she garnered financial support and rallied men to her side. A great many Gascon and Poitevin knights took the Cross—among them Geoffrey of Rancon, owner of Taillebourg castle where Eleanor had spent her wedding night. Among them, too, was a goodly number of knights whose names will reappear more than once in the story of Eleanor's life: Saldebreuil of Sanzay, whom she termed her constable, Hugh of Lusignan, Guy of Thouars; and many others. All over western France, the barons were responding to the voice of St Bernard. Almost certainly among the nobles riding with the count of Toulouse was that delicate poet Jaufré Rudel, prince of Blaye, bard of that 'love remote' which generations of commentators have tried to fathom: even his thirteenth-century biographer was none too clear as to what Jaufré meant by *amor de lonh*. He believed that the poet may have been in love with the princess of Tripoli and taken the Cross on her account. And doubtless we shall never know precisely what the troubadour wished to convey by this phrase 'love remote' which recurs in all his poems; but with its rich undertones of mysteriousness and longing it is admirably expressive of the impulse which was fundamental to his age and which manifested itself in the urge to seek adventure in far-away places, in the quest for a love which exceeded the self, in men's readiness to strive beyond the here and now. *Amor de lonh* . . .

Marcabru, for his part, added his voice to the preachers' and composed some beautiful crusading-songs, though even in these he contrived to exercise his poetic verve at the expense of the king of France. 'Woe unto King Louis, by whose doing sorrow has entered my heart!'—such are the words he puts into the mouth of a girl bewailing her lover's departure on crusade, in his remarkably beautiful poem entitled *A la fontana del vergier*. Marcabru was not a man to bear a grudge lightly.

On several occasions during her tour of Aquitaine, Eleanor is known to have renewed the special privileges enjoyed by abbeys, presumably in consideration of their financial support for the crusade; she is also known (and this is the first time that contemporary documents provide evidence of these particular donations) to have made a gift to the abbey of Fontevrault. All crusaders were in the habit, before setting out, of offering alms to monks and nuns and beseeching their prayers. This gesture of Eleanor's, guaranteeing the monastery a profit of five hundred sous from the fairs held in Poitiers on the eve of her departure, was the first of a series which was to extend throughout the rest of her life; henceforth, whenever anything important happened to her the repercussions would in one way or another be felt at Fontevrault. She may not have given the matter much thought at the time, for the gift was more or less the same as those which she made simultaneously to Montierneuf, the abbey of Saint-Maixent, the church of La Grâce-Dieu and many other religious foundations. But viewed in terms of her life as a whole, it is a striking indication that she had reached a turning-point.

Eleanor must have sensed as much: the vigour with which she participated in the preparations shows how keenly she was looking forward to the crusade. True, it meant deliberately exposing herself to the risk of death and worse. The road to the Holy Land was strewn with the bodies of rich men and poor who had set out along it at the time of those first expeditions which had driven the infidel from the common fief of Christendom. Nor did anyone need telling of the sufferings endured by those who had stayed the course: three years of journeying through deserts and treacherous defiles, with only hunger and thirst: and Turkish arrows for companions. But their sacrifices had won them glory in the sight of God and their fellow men; and now others yearned for this same glory, feeling that it was worth any amount of suffering and hardship.

In addition, the Orient must have called to Eleanor as strongly as it called to most other members of her family. Her grandfather, the blithe and shameless troubadour, had taken the Cross. He had cheerfully and stoically withstood the calamities of an expedition which had proved ill-fated from first to last, and when he got home he had even gone so far as to write some comic songs about his sufferings. His younger son—Eleanor's uncle and one-time playmate (for he was barely eight years older than she)—was in the Holy Land as prince of Antioch. No doubt the prospect of seeing him again contributed to the queen's obvious enthusiasm, a fact which was to strike others even in the planning stages of the expedition.

Most of the planning was done at Etampes, early in 1147. Louis called together all the chief barons who were to ride with him on the crusade. Their meeting lasted three days, February 16th–18th. They had to decide—by process of open debate, as always—what route the expedition was to take. A public reading was given of letters received from the monarchs whose lands it would have to traverse; for messengers had been sent far and wide across central and eastern Europe to broach the subject with them. The main choice confronting the meeting was this: ought the land route to be taken or the sea route?

The former meant relying on the good offices of the emperor of Byzantium, the latter accepting the hospitality of King Roger II of Sicily.

The latter was clearly very keen that the crusaders should put into port in his kingdom; not content with sending letters to this effect, he had dispatched special envoys to the meeting. Were his intentions altogether pure? Roger was a Norman, and the word Norman was never uttered in those days without at once earning the epithet wily. The king of Sicily was at war with the Byzantine empire at the time, and obviously his position would be greatly strengthened if the army of Christendom were to lie at anchor in one of his harbours.

Before they had even set foot outside their own frontiers, the French barons could gauge the extent to which human scheming was to dog their enterprise, and how, once again, tares had sprung up among the wheat.

Perhaps the best wheat grew beside the banks of the Bosphorus? The emperor of Byzantium was almost equally pressing with his offers of help. Remarkably enough, relations between East and West had taken a turn for the better during the past few years. There had been prickliness and even open hostility between Alexius Comnenus and the first crusaders, but in the intervening period they had become almost friendly. The improvement was largely the work of Eleanor's uncle, Raymond of Poitiers. A year after assuming control of the principality of Antioch, he had knelt and rendered homage to Emperor John Comnenus; this had been done with the complete approval of the Latin king of Jerusalem, who in his letter of reply had displayed admirable sense and fair-mindedness: '. . . We all know that Antioch formed part of the Byzantine empire until the Turkish conquest and that the emperor's assertions are strictly truthful when he speaks of our fathers' undertakings with regard to the city; can we oppose truth and justice?' In these words he was plainly acknowledging the validity of Byzantium's claims, although they had always been rejected by earlier princes of Antioch—by Bohemond, the Norman, and his descendants. That very year John Comnenus entered the Syrian capital in triumph and set the seal on his agreement with Raymond. It put the latter on bad terms with the king of Sicily, but he had right on his side and his action was in the truest interests of Christendom. The pope felt it was still possible that full communion might one day be restored between Greece and Rome and he was quick to encourage any step likely to put an end to previous disagreements; at his request, therefore, the prelates attending the meeting at Etampes came out in favour of the emperor's proposal.

It won the day. The envoys of the king of Sicily withdrew in dudgeon, forecasting dire catastrophes and assuring the leaders of the expedition that they would very soon discover to their cost how little the word of a Greek was worth. Eleanor was exultant, however: her uncle's work of reconciliation had tipped the scales against the Sicilian offers.

Three months later she was riding forth at her husband's side, with a multitude of maidservants and that superabundance of four-wheeled wagons for which history would never forgive her. Naturally she needed carpets for underfoot comfort at every halt, several tents as an insurance against loss and bad weather, enough dresses to allow of a frequent change of clothes, furs to keep her warm and light veils to stave off sunburn, spare saddles and harnesses, bowls, ewers, jewellery, all the things that would enable her to look well and eat well and withstand the hardships of the journey—though at the age of twenty-four she had an iron constitution and was superbly endowed for such an enterprise.

The date was May 12th, 1147. The days leading up to it had been charged with excitement and emotion. Louis and Eleanor had been staying at the abbey of Saint-Denis, where the press of people was so great that when they attempted to leave the basilica it was impossible to clear a path for them; they had to make their exit by way of the monks' dormitory. In accordance with a tradition which was from this time forward zealously observed by all kings of France, Louis had venerated the relics of St Denis and then taken the famous oriflamme from the altar—the red-and-gold royal banner which was the 'ensign of France'. Eugenius III had jour-

54

neyed to Saint-Denis especially for the occasion, and it was he who handed the king his pilgrim's scrip and staff. For although we tend nowadays to see the crusades in the light of military expeditions, they were first and foremost an act of pilgrimage. If the pilgrims bore arms, they did so primarily for self-protection and to safeguard the security of the Holy Places. Up to the time of the Arab conquest—even later, indeed, until the arrival of the Turks—it had been possible to reach Jerusalem in perfect peace.

Following the path taken by the first crusaders fifty years earlier, the army set off through central and eastern Europe in the direction of Constantinople. Difficulties arose at the very outset: shortly after crossing the Rhine, near Worms, quarrels and scuffles began to break out between the crusaders and the German villagers and townsfolk. The Germans were accused of every crime under the sun: they were drunkards, they were brawlers, they weren't to be trusted, and so on *ad infinitum*. Later, in Hungary and Bulgaria, food was hard to come by: this again was the fault of the Germans, who had travelled the same route not long before and emptied the markets. For St Bernard had persuaded the emperor, Conrad of Hohenstaufen, to take the Cross too.

Godfrey of Bouillon and the other nobles taking part in the first expedition had been wise enough to plan different itineraries so that provisions would be easier to obtain. No such foresight had been displayed by the king of France and his barons. As the party moved eastwards, the peasants—whose supplies were dwindling and whose greed had been stimulated by previous bouts of haggling—began to demand really extortionate prices of the crusaders, and this gave rise to increasing acrimony. Louis VII had given strict orders against looting, but he was alarmed to discover that costs were everywhere exceeding his expectations; each time they broke their journey he was obliged to dispatch further monetary demands to Suger, who was minding the affairs of the realm during the king's absence.

It was almost five months before they at last reached Constantinople on October 4th, 1147.

Constantinople . . . It seemed like a vision of splendour. All who visited it at the time, from the first crusaders to those who were later—in the thirteenth century—to seize the city in defiance of their undertakings, expressed wondering admiration at the magnificent city, 'the glory of Greece, renowned for its richness and exceeding even what is claimed of it'. No capital had ever enjoyed such a setting: a triangle jutting out into the Bosphorus, with the sea of Marmara on one side and the famous Golden Horn on the other. And its concentration of palaces would have outrivalled any man's dreams. All the way along the high walls, which half a century later were to make such an impression on Villehardouin, rose towers that would have been objects of admiration in their own right, even considered individually. The harbour was the biggest in the world, and no other city could boast such a quantity of marble monuments, triumphal pillars, porticoes and mighty domes. On the tip of the peninsula, down by the old Acropolis, the Great Palace was a prodigious tangle of buildings overlooking the port of Boucoleon. One state-room succeeded another, and each had its own particular use: the palace of the Chalce and the palace of Magnaura, where solemn assemblies were held; the Triclinium, or Tribunal of the Nineteen Beds, scene of banquets and sometimes of coronations; the palace of the Daphne, containing the private apartments of the emperor and his family who were waited on by a veritable army of servants and eunuchs; the Porphyra, where the empresses gave birth to their children; the Chrysotriclinium, or Hall of Gold, the palace of Justinian, reserved for the most solemn of audiences . . . A series of terraces linked this cluster of buildings—part administrative centre, part imperial residence—with the shore where the emperor had his private harbour, while on the north-west side the palace of the Daphne led out into the Hippodrome, the scene of frequent public demonstrations.

Beyond lay the city—more than four thousand dwellings lined the straight, beautiful streets and dominated the hills above; for the most part they were built on sturdy vaulted earthworks which concealed and protected an equal number of cisterns. A positive maze of lanes, small squares, porticoes, churches and fountains was wedged between the three main thoroughfares which formed a Y within the triangle, one arm pointing to the Golden Gate and the other to St George's church and the walls of Theodosius. Admittedly the intervening area contained many dark, filthy, evil-smelling quarters, teeming with riff-raff from the arsenals and the port; but this did not detract from the peerlessness of the scene when considered as a whole.

At the time of Louis's and Eleanor's visit, the economic power of Constantinople was still more or less intact, even though most of its territory had fallen to the Arabs and Turks. Two-thirds of the world's wealth was said to be concentrated within its walls.

But in the past half-century or so its emperors had appreciably simplified the almost legendary magnificence of their predecessors' style of living; they no longer lived in the Great Palace but in the palace of Blachernae, situated at the northern corner, its walls merging with those of the city itself; the air was better here than in the old residence, which stood directly above the port and was hemmed about by a veritable labyrinth of narrow lanes and streets—and it afforded a view of the surrounding countryside as well as of the Golden Horn.

As soon as they arrived within a day's march of Constantinople the royal couple were met by envoys of Emperor Manuel Comnenus, with a great many salutations, tokens of respect and enthusiastic words of welcome. A procession of dignitaries was waiting to escort them to the Blachernae palace. And a great crowd of ordinary people had turned out to meet them, anxious to set eyes on these Franks—these 'Celts', as they were still generally called. All Greeks, whatever their rank, were in the habit of regarding themselves as the exclusive heirs of ancient civilization; they viewed any outsider as a semi-barbarian and it was a convention of Byzantine diplomacy that effusiveness increased in proportion to the suspicion harboured. Louis's and Eleanor's own escort on the road to Blachernae was a small one, consisting of the king's brother, Robert of Le Perche, a few of the great barons and the queen's attendants.

As part of the process of modifying their way of life, the Comnenus family had done away with a goodly number of the ceremonies which had previously turned the emperor, on state occasions, into something very like a god; for Christian prohibi-

57

tions had not entirely stamped out the habit, inherited from ancient times, of offering worship to him. Anyone granted an audience of the emperor had to be flanked by two dignitaries as he stepped forward; they would hold his arms up until the moment came for him to prostrate himself on the ground. Whatever simplifications may have been introduced, the degree of ceremony at court was still extreme—and the Franks had occasionally been scandalized to see ambassadors from certain countries go down on their knees before the emperor. At all events, their own reception in the Blachernae palace made a profound impression on the royal party: this is abundantly clear from the account given of it later by the king's chaplain, Odo of Deuil. They were dazzled by the palace itself, with its huge marble-paved courtyard, its pillars decorated with gold and silver leaves, the brilliant mosaics depicting the emperor's wars and victories, and the golden throne ablaze with precious stones, from which he presided in the great hall.

Throughout the three weeks of their stay, the king and queen of France were treated to an endless series of receptions and banquets and hunting expeditions. To Eleanor these delights, experienced amid settings worthy of an oriental tale, must have come as a revelation. Constantinople eclipsed everything that she had seen until now: here, dreams of splendour became reality. She and her husband were lodged outside the city walls in a residence which the emperors used as part country seat, part hunting lodge —the Philopation, no great distance from Blachernae. Inside the great building, sumptuous carpets yielded to the tread, a host of servants anticipated every need and the air was sweetened by scents burning in silver perfume-pans. Vast woods grew round about, full of wild beasts which the sovereign had imported at great expense.

A banquet was given in the visitors' honour after a religious ceremony in St Sophia, whose mosaics shone resplendently by the light of a multitude of candles and oil-lamps in the great crown-shaped chandeliers. The basilica of Justinian, with its immense dome sparkling in the sunlight between the Acropolis and the Great Palace, could have been taken for the private chapel of the vast imperial residence, a memorial to the days when Byzantium, capital of the known world, eclipsed even Rome.

manuel Comnenus

The reception was held in a hall in the Sacred Palace, with Emperor Manuel Comnenus presiding at one of the tables. He was a strikingly handsome man, quite magnificent in his bearing; he had adopted western customs to an even greater degree than his predecessors, and he took pride in the fact that he had made tourneying a fashionable pursuit in Constantinople. Never had a man been so manifestly born to wear the imperial purple. An impression of might emanated from his entire person. He was tall and powerfully built and his enviable features were darkly bronzed. Marvellously gifted, he excelled at the most violent forms of sport —bear-hunting in the mountains, for example—as well as more elegant games like polo, his favourite pastime. Side by side with this, he was endowed with a keen and cultivated mind which was as responsive to the sciences as to the arts: his passion for theology did not keep him from showing a lively interest in geography and even in astrological studies. Medicine itself was not outside his scope —he had personally tended his brother-in-law, Conrad of Hohenstaufen, when the latter was taken ill in Constantinople. On the battlefield, he was adept not only at leading his troops against the enemy but at bearing lance and shield just like them, if the need arose; his own weapons were rumoured to be so heavy that very few of his men could have wielded them. Yet how relentlessly charming he could be at the rich social functions in which his court abounded; his reputation as a gay seducer was unrivalled.

In 1146 he had married Emperor Conrad's sister-in-law—a German woman, Bertha of Sulzbach. She was fond of remarking that 'no man on earth had ever added so much fame and glory to his name, within a single year, for the sole purpose of pleasing and doing honour to his Lady'—adding that she knew what she was talking about, 'stemming as she did from an unsurpassably warlike breed'. Eleanor could scarcely believe her eyes and ears. Retaining all her self-possession and exercising her remarkable critical faculties amid the bedazzlements of the imperial banquet, she thought what an ill-assorted couple they made: on the one hand, the thoroughbred Byzantine; on the other, this woman whose features were already lumpish despite her youth, whose hair was unsightly and who did not know how to use cosmetics. Even at that time, Frenchwomen had a reputation for elegance. Eleanor herself may have been responsible for the recent introduction of the long, silk-lined sleeve, sometimes trailing to the floor; the material parted to reveal a forearm tightly sheathed in bright satin to accentuate the slenderness of the wrist. Manuel Comnenus behaved with assiduous courtesy towards her; shrewd as ever, she noticed the caressing gaze which he was continually directing at his niece, the beautiful Theodora, with whom shortly afterwards he was to carry on a scandalous affair. Obviously the Frenchwomen made a great impression on the high dignitaries of the court. During their stay one of Eleanor's attendants was sought in marriage by a relative of Manuel's; the king's brother Robert had to help the girl steal out of her lodgings so that she might escape the ardour of his wooing.

The banquet went on for several hours. Course succeeded course and the royal party was introduced to such delicacies as artichokes served in silver dishes, stuffed kid, fried frog, and caviar which was consumed in great quantities at the imperial table. The wines of Greece were served in unbelievably light and colourful glasses, while sauces flavoured with cinnamon and coriander were displayed in beautifully wrought boats; these were as unfamiliar to western eyes as the two-pronged silver forks. The floor was strewn with rose petals, and behind the hangings an orchestra was playing softly; from time to time during the entremets, these hangings would be drawn aside to reveal juggling of the most astonishing virtuosity or miming and dancing in the oriental style.

In the days that followed there were exhilarating hunts in the grounds bordering on the Philopation, with falcons, sparrow-hawks and even tame leopards. And then there were the races in the Hippodrome, which the Byzantines had made a forum for popular opinion as well as the home of their favourite entertainment: demonstrations in the Hippodrome had several times been the making or breaking of emperors, while choosing between the drivers in green tunics and the drivers in blue (green and blue being the traditional colours for chariot races) was merely another way of manifesting a political tendency. Up to thirty thousand spectators could be packed into the giant enclosure of the Hippo-drome (sixteen hundred feet by four hundred) and the works of art decorating it were so many reminders of Byzantine splendour. On top of the stables stood the group of bronze horses which had been brought home in triumph from Alexandria and which fifty years later were to be carried off by the Venetians as an adornment for the main portal of St Mark's. The obelisk standing in the centre came from Heliopolis and had been carved seventeen hundred years before the advent of the Christian era. A bronze pillar in the form of three coiled snakes had been brought from Delphi. Also to be seen here was the famous bronze group of the she-wolf suckling Romulus, a fantastic trophy which did much to sustain national pride. In fact the whole city was like a museum, and even in those days being a guide was a highly lucrative occupation.

Three weeks in such a setting would have been pure enchantment but for the worries which still somehow came to light. The Frankish soldiery were not getting on at all well with the ordinary people of Byzantium. In the crusaders' encampment there were complaints about the exorbitant prices which the Byzantine traders were charging for provisions. Despite the outward show of politeness to which they were treated, the French could all—from humblest to grandest—sense the profound disdain in the hearts and minds of their hosts. Here and there serious incidents occurred. As he was walking along the Mese, the main street and centre of business where the goldsmiths and money-changers had their shops and stalls (money-changing being then the most lucrative trade in Byzantium), a Flemish soldier was so dazzled by all the piles of gold and silver that he suddenly lost his head and with a shout of 'Haro!'—the cry which marked the opening of fairs in the West—hurled himself upon the tables and carried off as much as he could; this caused a good deal of panic and commotion among the money-changers and the noise quickly attracted a large crowd. No doubt the poor devil was merely seeking to compensate himself, and his companions, for the grossly unfair prices that were being charged in the market-place. Louis VII took the culprit out of the count of Flanders's jurisdiction and gave orders for him to be hanged forthwith.

At the same time, the king himself was finding their stay in Constantinople hard to endure. The over-refined protocol at the Byzantine court irritated him a great deal. Every single dignitary

61

was invested with some high-flown title or other; there was the Most Illustrious Protosebaste and the Panhypersebaste; even the lowliest official was, at the very least a nobilissime or protono-bilissime or even a hyperperilampros (of the most dazzling merit). All this was somewhat aggravating to a man who was simple by nature and who further regarded simplicity as a duty. He was tired of these obsequious men who unfailingly addressed him in flowery language, and whose speeches were full of empty phrases; behind the importunate politeness he seemed to detect irony, even treachery. His advisers began to put him on his guard: there were strange rumours to the effect that the emperor was conducting negotiations with certain mysterious emissaries, allegedly Turkish. He therefore accelerated the departure in so far as he was able. When Manuel Comnenus called to take his leave he informed Louis, with a beaming smile, that he had just received news from Emperor Conrad: the forces of the Holy Roman Empire had won a great victory over the Turks in Anatolia; the enemy had lost over fourteen thousand men.

The crusaders had not travelled many miles from Constantinople when, on the outskirts of Nicaea, they ran into the vanguard of the German army: lamentable-looking troops, hungry and exhausted. The truth is that on the very day when he told Louis of Conrad's so-called victory, Manuel Comnenus had received information that the Germans had been put to rout. They had been utterly misled by the Byzantine guides, who had assured Conrad that he need carry only a week's supply of food and water to cross the deserts of Anatolia. Then they had stealthily decamped one night, leaving the army trapped in a seemingly endless series of defiles. It would have taken the Germans more than three weeks to reach northern Syria—three weeks under constant attack from Turkish bowmen, with no supplies except what they had with them. Conrad had decided to turn back and even thought of discontinuing his crusade when he saw how many lives this ill-fated escapade had cost him. Sure enough, Manuel Comnenus was in collusion with the Turks and had been negotiating with them even while he was showering honours on the king and queen of France.

To avoid meeting with a similar fate, Louis VII decided to adopt a longer but safer route. Bypassing those deserts which had invariably proved disastrous to crusaders from the West, he planned to send his men via Pergamos to the gulf of Smyrna, whence they would proceed to Ephesus, Laodicea and the port of Adalia: Ionia and Lydia afforded a less difficult approach than the desert gorges in which the German army had sustained such heavy losses. And with so much baggage weighing him down, the French king must at all costs avoid dispersing his troops over too long a line. Orders were given for the journey to be made in as close order as possible; responsibility for the vanguard was given to the king's uncle, the count of Maurienne, and to Geoffrey of Rancon, the knight from Saintonge who, as we have seen, was one of the queen's vassals.

All went well until they came to the gorges of Pisidia, not far from Mount Cadmos. The king, who was in charge of the rearguard, enjoined all the armed crusaders to be even more wary than usual. Danger might well be in store for them that day (it was the feast of Epiphany, 1148). They were going to have to negotiate some narrow defiles and would be extremely vulnerable to attack... What exactly happened? Can it be that Geoffrey of Rancon disobeyed orders? At all events he rode on into the defiles which were not supposed to be entered until the following day, and thus lost contact with the main body of the expedition. This is exactly what the Turkish squadrons were waiting for as they lurked on the ridges of the surrounding hills. Suddenly the main force, strung out in a slender line in order to give cover to the baggage train, was being attacked on all sides by these lightly armed warriors. The French did not even have time to form up; they were thrown into terrible confusion as the arrows began to fall. The womenfolk screamed and there was general panic. Even so, it was some time before the king and his companions in the rearguard realized what was happening. When at last he hastened to the scene, it took him only a moment to appreciate the size of the calamity which seemed about to befall his army. That day he demonstrated his powers of leadership to the full and showed the courage he had in him. It

63

was he who rallied his men-at-arms and with a hurriedly assembled force drove the enemy from the points of maximum exposure. For a time he found himself completely cut off from his companions, and the manner in which he survived was fully worthy of a *chanson de geste*: he grabbed hold of some branches of a tree trailing down to his height, and used these to swing himself up on to a boulder; there, with his back to the mountainside, he made a lone stand against a howling pack of besiegers. Luckily they did not recognize him: he was clad in a simple coat of mail; at the time of the attack he was armed only with sword and buckler and wore none of the insignia that might have distinguished him from his men. To this he owed his life. His assailants began to weary, and as the daylight faded the Turks fell back to their positions on high ground.

Next morning Geoffrey of Rancon and his companions, uneasy at finding themselves cut off from the rest of the force, made their way down into the valley again and saw the tragic price that had been paid for their negligence. They were lucky not to get their throats cut.

What was Eleanor's part in these nightmarish events which, but for her husband's valour, might have resulted in the annihilation of the crusade? Nobody knows. The chroniclers are silent on this point. We cannot even tell whether the queen, as some have insinuated, was with the vanguard when it acted so irresponsibly or whether she was among the attacked; but the fact that one of her favourite vassals was in command of the advance party was sufficient to earn her a share of the blame. There was much bitterness against her and the Aquitainians in general. It was the fault of these madcap southerners, always so shy of discipline, that the army of Christendom had come within an inch of destruction.

The crusaders spent several days burying the dead, nursing the wounded and repairing the damage as best they could; then they moved on, at a slower pace than before, until at last they came to Adalia. There, realizing that the land route presented almost insurmountable difficulties for so cumbersome a force, the king decided to sail as far as Antioch. He dispatched messengers to Constantinople, asking for vessels. The Byzantines undertook to provide some, but did not send even half the number they had

64

promised. However, they renewed their assurances and Louis decided to put his faith in them. He was exasperated by these continual delays. March was already here: it had taken nearly five months to cross Asia Minor. And so, confident that the rest of the fleet was about to follow, he embarked with most of his knights and put to sea in the direction of Syria.

VI

Per erguelh e par malvestat
Dels Christias ditz, luenh d'amor
E dels mans de Nostre Senhor,
Em del sieu Sant Loc discipat
Ab massa d'autres encombriers;
Don par qu'elh nos es aversiers
Per desadordenat voler
E per outracujat poder.

It is through arrogance that we,
Christians in name but not in love,
Dishonouring Our Lord above,
Are from Jerusalem forced to flee
With such a rain of plagues on us;
In wrath God turns his face from us,
To quench sinful desires in us,
And overweening pride in us.

GUIRAUT RIQUIER

THE LITTLE PORT of St Simeon was abuzz with animation. A host
of small craft milled round the vessels of the royal fleet, while on
shore the bells rang out a full peal as a procession of clergy in white
surplices worked its way through the festive throng. The king and
queen of France disembarked to the singing of the Te Deum
and were greeted by exuberant demonstrations of friendship
by a large group of knights. In the midst of these, clearly distin-
guishable by his height, his handsome face and his elegant
silk tunic, was Eleanor's uncle, Raymond of Poitiers, prince of
Antioch.

After their slow, unsafe and harsh journeyings, she and Louis
were on friendly soil at last, the soil of the Holy Land for which
they were bound as pilgrims. The date was March 19th, 1148. It was

66

ten months since they had set out. To them, as to their companions, Antioch was a welcome haven. The magnificent city, sloping gently down towards the sea with the hills of Djebel Akra in the background, was an oasis of greenness and coolness. A veritable corridor of gorges opened out at the foot of the city, and through these the river Orontes conveyed the mountain air as well as the water from the melting snows. Antioch was capped by a series of terraced gardens, rising to a point high above the water-front. Its ramparts stretched for eight miles, regularly interspersed with three-storey towers: there were said to be three hundred and sixty of them, one every thirty yards or so. Afterwards, the town suffered extensive damage from the great earthquake of 1170. But at the time of Louis's crusade its monuments were intact, having been either restored or newly built by the first crusaders who—at what cost!—had finally won possession of a city generally regarded as impregnable. One of the major items of interest in St Peter's cathedral was the tomb of Bishop Adhémar of Le Puy, who had served as papal legate on the first expedition. And other churches too—SS. Cosmas and Damian, St Mary Latin, St John Chrysostom —raised their spires above the narrow streets, whose bazaars were filled with all the merchandise of the Middle East. The markets offered fruit of every kind, for the surrounding countryside was so broadly irrigated that it was like a great fertile garden and the wind stirred gently in the grey-green foliage of the olive-trees rising in tiers on every hillside.

If Constantinople had dazzled her with its ornate and exotic splendour, Antioch was quite different—and in Eleanor's eyes even better: a paradise of sunstrewn greenness in which she was continually finding something to remind her of her Poitevin estates and her beloved Aquitaine. The patriarch who headed the procession of clergy and gave the royal couple his blessing on their arrival in Syria was one Aimery of Limoges; the chaplain officiating in the palace of Antioch was a Poitevin called William; Charles of Mauzé and Payen of Faye, two knights in the prince's service, had been neighbours and vassals of her father. *Langue d'oc* was spoken in Antioch. Above all, there was the magnificent figure of Raymond himself. She found that she still looked up to him, just as she had in their childhood games together, and they were united by memories of the days when they had both lived in the Ombrière Palace.

This son of the Troubadour and younger brother of William X of Aquitaine had become prince of Antioch as the result of a series of adventures which were as close to the spirit of farce as of knightly romance. In 1136—the year prior to Eleanor's marriage—Raymond was at the English court. Henry I (Henry Beauclerk) had knighted him and taken him into his service. One day a Hospitaller came in search of him, a man named Gerard Jéberron who claimed to bear letters from King Fulke of Jerusalem. And sure enough, as soon as he and the young man were alone he revealed the nature of the mission with which he had been entrusted. The king of Jerusalem was alarmed that the principality of Antioch—northern Syria, in other words the most vulnerable of the Latin kingdoms—should be in the hands of a woman, the dowager Princess Alice. Alice was the widow of Bohemond II, son of the first prince of Antioch—a Norman whose remarkable exploits and no less remarkable guile had been much talked and written about at the time of the First Crusade. Legally, Alice was merely acting as regent for their daughter Constance. But she was an ambitious woman and had not been afraid to entertain relations with the notorious Zengi when, as ruler of Aleppo and Mosul, he first began to threaten the principality of Edessa. Constance must obviously be found a husband who knew how to wield a sword and was capable of standing up to the Turks, not to mention a redoubtable mother-in-law. King Fulke had conferred with his barons and reviewed the list of possible candidates. The man of his choice was Raymond of Poitiers.

The proposition could not have commended itself more strongly to Raymond: it was agreeable, it was hazardous and it contained the touch of comedy which any son of the Troubadour would find hard to resist. For Jéberron warned him that he would have to journey surreptitiously to his future fief, so as to avoid arousing the suspicions of the king of Sicily who was out to get his own hands on Antioch; that he would have a difficult task persuading the widow to let him rule in her stead; and finally that he would have to reckon with the patriarch of Antioch, Raoul of Domfront, a

Norman who was more at home on the battlefield than before the altar.

Shortly afterwards Raymond and a few companions left the English court and set sail with great secrecy, disguised as pedlars. His first move on reaching Antioch was a very shrewd one: by putting forward a great many promises and winning the priest's trust, he succeeded in making the dangerous patriarch a party to his scheme. The two men drew up their plan of campaign. Raoul went to see Alice and gave her to understand that the handsome knight who had just arrived in Antioch was desirous of making her his wife. Alice was highly flattered. She welcomed Raymond with open arms and let him confer with her barons as much as her wished. She was still quietly awaiting her wedding-day when word reached her that the patriarch was in the cathedral, solemnizing Raymond's marriage to her daughter. At this she had no choice but to retire to Latakia and gnash her teeth, leaving Raymond undisputed ruler of Antioch.

alice retired to Latakia

According to contemporary accounts, he was 'taller, better-built and more handsome than any man of his time; he surpassed all others as warrior and horseman.' In sheer physical strength and prowess in the lists, he was the equal of Manuel Comnenus. In addition he loved poetry and the troubadours and courtly life and had, like his father, the gift of turning unhappy memories into amusing anecdotes. A joyous atmosphere prevailed at his court, and it was for him that Richard the Pilgrim composed the *Chanson des Chétifs* which, written at the time of the crusade, gives a detailed and colourful account of the exploits of Peter the Hermit and his companions.

Louis and Eleanor spent only ten days in Antioch, but those ten days had such an effect on the course of history and on their personal destinies that one longs for a day-by-day or even hour-by-hour account of their stay in the city. Yet Odo of Deuil, who so faithfully recounts all that had happened since the start of the expedition, terminates his narrative on the very day of the arrival in Antioch. Why this silence? Are we to assume that it would have troubled his conscience to describe what followed? After all, as the king's confessor he must have had intimate knowledge of the mental tussles afflicting Louis in those crucial days. Could he

69

record them without, to all intents and purposes, betraying the secrecy of the confessional? Or was he reluctant to implicate the queen—of whom he says not one word—by going into the events which led up to the crisis? Whatever the truth of the matter, his reticence is cruelly tantalizing. We may know what occurred, but we can only conjecture at the whys and wherefores.

The first thunderbolt came when, after a few days of rest and enjoyment, the crusader-barons met to draw up their plan of campaign. As might have been expected, Raymond's intentions were very plain. His objective: the reconquest of Edessa, whose fall had first given rise to the crusade. Zengi, the man who had captured the city, had been assassinated two years later by his own troops, in accordance with a custom seldom broken in the annals of the Turkish army. But the son who succeeded him, Nureddin, was showing himself to be no less redoubtable in the struggle against the Franks. The security of Antioch was dependent on this constantly threatened hinterland, where such bulwarks of Turkish might as Aleppo and Hama could probably be won if only full advantage were taken of the terror inspired in the foe by the simultaneous arrival of the emperor of Germany and the king of France. For after so nearly abandoning the crusade, Emperor Conrad had remustered his forces as best he could and was now on his way to the Holy Land.

To everyone's amazement, Louis VII came out strongly against the scheme: he had vowed to make the journey to Jerusalem and he had no intention of doing anything else until he had made it. Conrad would be arriving in Acre any day now, and so would the count of Toulouse. Melisande, the dowager queen of Jerusalem, was anxious that Louis should join forces with them.

Raymond knew all about Queen Melisande. She was the sister of that same Princess Alice whom he had dislodged from the throne of Antioch twelve years earlier. She was a 'passionate creole' whose amorous adventures had once been the talk of all Christendom. Now that she was of mature years, this widow of King Fulke had found a different outlet for her fiery nature: politics. Her son, Baldwin III, was of age; though only sixteen, he had already given proof of his military prowess. Far from leaving the reins of government to him, however, she was engaging in more and more hazardous ventures of a kind which could only imperil the kingdom of Jerusalem. Only the previous year she had sent an expedition to Hauran to fight the sultans of Damascus, who had a longstanding alliance with the Franks and who had even sought their help against fellow-Moslems. This was an obvious blunder and must never be repeated.

The king of France remained adamant, despite the cogent arguments which were put forward. Raymond called a second meeting, and this one was attended by all the knights who had so far reached Antioch. But he was wasting his time: Louis resisted him, point by point, with that dumb obstinacy which is the weak man's way of showing will-power. The king intended to go straight to Jerusalem, and nothing and nobody could deter him. But surely, insisted Raymond, the defence of Jerusalem lay along the Orontes? The kingdom was extraordinarily vulnerable, with a frontier-length totally disproportionate to the small number of troops at its disposal. Did not reason demand that the pressures be eased by destroying the enemy's major strongpoints? Suppose Nureddin or someone like him were to overthrow the weak Damascene dynasty and get his hands on Damascus and Aleppo, the twin gateways to Syria? Besides, who could deny that the prime purpose of the crusade was the recapture of Edessa?

It was all to no avail. The king simply announced his intention of leaving Antioch as soon as possible.

It was at this point that Eleanor spoke up. Raymond sought one last interview; this time the queen attended. She sided passionately with her uncle, and before long husband and wife were raising their voices to each other. Eleanor had quite obviously grasped the strategic merits of Raymond's plan. After all, he was in a better position than anyone to appraise the needs of the situation and assess the comparative strengths of the opposing armies. If he were denied the support of the crusade, then she would remain in Antioch with her own vassals.

An untimely remark: her vassals had already made themselves only too conspicuous . . . And so the quarrel went on, becoming more and more personal and heated until finally Louis threatened to assert his marital rights: he would *force* her to leave Antioch. By these words he laid himself open to a devastating and totally un-

Louis VII and Raymond of Poitiers disagree on strategy.

R. wants to take Edessa. L. wants to go direct to Jerusalem.

Eleanor sides with Raymond.

Eleanor + L. VII related.

expected reply: he would do well to examine his marital rights, for in the eyes of the Church their marriage had no validity—they were related to a degree prohibited by canon law . . .

———————◆———————

This sudden savage turn in their already angry discussion can only be explained in the light of attendant circumstances which have always been the joy of the fiction-mongers. They have embroidered this background zestfully, most of them making Eleanor out to be a woman of easy virtue, a sort of Messalina who flitted from lover to lover, scarce bothering to conceal her misconduct, not only with great barons like Geoffrey of Rancon but with subordinates such as Saldebreuil, constable of Aquitaine (why him, for heaven's sake?); the more restrained have been content to make her fall into the arms of the handsome Raymond of Poitiers.

If we adhere to historical fact, it seems unchallengeable that the queen acquired a bad reputation in Antioch. Did she really have a weakness for her young uncle? One chronicler—William of Tyr, who cannot be dismissed lightly—*does* level the charge; the others are more evasive. What cannot be doubted is that events exacerbated the fundamental disharmony between a man and wife who were clearly not made for each other. Eleanor was no longer the girl of fifteen or sixteen who had waited by the banks of the Garonne for the husband sent to her by God's will, or at any rate the will of the king of France. She was a young woman of twenty-five, with a keen sense of her own maturity and self-possession. Intuition told her that she was no less capable than this rather weak husband of arriving at decisions and carrying them through to a successful conclusion; consequently the last few years had been distinctly irksome to her. The king still displayed the same passionate feelings, but he was no longer willing to be guided by her advice. Suger had regained full dominion over him, and when Eleanor declared that she felt she had married a monk it may well be that she was alluding not only to what she regarded as Louis's over-addiction to prayer and fasting, but also to the fact that the governance of the realm was to all intents and purposes in the hands of the abbot of Saint-Denis.

ELEANOR 25 Fr. ruin by Suger

72

All this had been brought to a head by the intoxicating and liberating experience of Constantinople, where she was shown a world ideally suited to her feelings and aspirations. Its splendours had filled her with admiration, its refinements had been entirely to her taste; she must have revelled in the subtleties of the diplomatic game as played at Manuel's court and sensed with a quiver of delight the disquieting and sometimes amoral things which were concealed behind all the ceremony and glitter. Her response to the temptations, unknown pleasures and intellectual subtleties of the Byzantine way of life must have been diametrically opposed to the reactions inspired in her pious and simple husband. After Constantinople had come the hardships of an unbelievably strenuous expedition in which she had daily been exposed to winds, storms, Turkish arrows, the aridity of the mountain regions and the perils of a direct clash with the enemy. She may not always have been in agreement with the marching orders; on their side, Louis and his entourage felt ever-increasing rancour at the deportment of the queen's hot-headed and undisciplined Poitevin vassals.

Then Antioch. An open-hearted welcome by a well-loved relative, long conversations in *langue d'oc* under the shade of the olive trees, the joy of listening to the troubadours . . . Life was worth living again, life had richness and colour. For Eleanor but not for Louis. Louis was still feeling the effects of their long trek and wondering anxiously what had become of that portion of the army which he had been compelled to leave in the gulf of Adalia; he was still awaiting news of these men. It displeased him that anyone engaged on a mission of faith should even think of listening to troubadours. He had undeniably taken umbrage at the degree of warmth which had immediately marked the exchanges between uncle and niece, and had felt left out during their conversations in *langue d'oc*, a language of which he had no command. Doubtless he had hoped to salvage a situation which was visibly deteriorating, but as on so many other occasions in his life, he had gone the wrong way about it. And now, quite suddenly, an irreparable rift had occurred. It struck at his pride and it hurt him deeply, for he had never ceased to love his wife. Where had she acquired this sudden familiarity with canon law which allowed her to suggest

73

that their marriage was without validity? Afterwards, when he had time to think things over, he probably recalled that, in order to marry Eleanor's sister, Raoul of Vermandois had been allowed to cast off his first wife on the grounds of unlawful consanguinity.

Bringing the argument to an abrupt close, Louis went and consulted one of his familiars, a Templar named Thierry Galeran. Here was another bone of contention between king and queen, for she loathed Thierry and his feelings for her were equally uncordial. He knew that Eleanor derided him behind his back—often in risqué terms, for he was a eunuch. But Louis gladly turned to him for advice; his father, Louis VI, had often done so to advantage. Thierry and the other barons had no hesitation in urging the king to take a strong line with his wife. The Frankish army left Antioch that same night—and Queen Eleanor had to leave too, whether she liked it or not.

VII

Be m'agrada la covinens sazos,
E m'agrada lo cortes temps d'estiu
E m'agradon l'auzel, quan chanton piu,
E m'agradon floretas per boissos,
E m'agrada tot so qu'als adregz platz,
E m'agrada mil tans lo bels solatz.
Don per mon grat jauzirai lai breumen,
On de bon grat paus mon cor e mon sens.

This pleasurable season suits me well,
I like the gentleness of summer days,
I like to hear the warbler's sweet throat swell,
I like to see flowers spring along the ways.
Things that please noble minds can never pall,
Yet courtly discourse is the best of all,
Such as I hope to enjoy again ere long,
Gladly devoting heart and mind and tongue.

PEIRE VIDAL

SUBSEQUENT EVENTS demonstrated all too clearly that Raymond of Poitiers had been right. There had never been any wisdom in launching the crusade against the Damascenes; after all, relations with them had been cordial ever since the formation of the Latin kingdoms. And in the event the campaign was conducted so ineptly that it proved a lamentable failure. The consequences were to be highly detrimental to the kingdom of Jerusalem. The arrival of these Franks and Germans had put fear into the Turks, yet they were departing without a single worthwhile achievement to their credit. Emperor Conrad set sail on September 8th. The king of France, however, protracted his stay until Easter 1149. Unwilling to admit failure, he did his best to realize other plans; rather than rely on the Byzantines, who had deceived him quite

75

odiously (not only had they failed to deliver the ships which they had promised, but they had made the Turks a present of all those crusaders who had been compelled to stay behind in Asia Minor), he endeavoured to form an alliance with Raymond of Poitiers's enemy, Roger of Sicily. Perhaps he was simply trying to delay his return to Europe, where a twofold humiliation awaited him—as a king whose expedition had been disastrous, and as a husband whose marriage seemed in ruins.

Eventually he and Eleanor set off as members of a Sicilian convoy, sailing in two separate ships. Their journey home could hardly have been more dramatic. The king of Sicily was still at war with the emperor of Byzantium, and spring had brought a renewal of fighting at sea. As it drew level with the Peloponnese peninsula, the fleet clashed with some Byzantine vessels off Cape Malea. During the ups and downs of the engagement, the ship bearing Eleanor and her attendants was captured by the Greeks. The pirates were already making for Constantinople with this unexpectedly valuable hostage when she was freed by a sudden counter-attack on the part of the Sicilian Normans. Meanwhile Louis's vessel had landed in a Calabrian harbour on July 29th. The king was without news of his wife for three long weeks; only then did he learn that she was safe and sound in Palermo. Each then travelled to Potenza, where they were received in great style by the Norman king of Sicily—the very man whose offers they had previously spurned. It must have been here that they learned of the death of Raymond of Poitiers: he had been killed on June 29th, giving battle to the forces of Nureddin, and his handsome blond head had been sent by the victor to the caliph of Baghdad.

For a time physical and mental exhaustion (grief too, perhaps) overcame the remarkable stoicism which Eleanor had always displayed until now. She fell ill, and for the sake of her well-being the remainder of the journey was made in short stages, with a fairly long halt at the famous Benedictine monastery of Monte Cassino.

Pope Eugenius III had been kept informed of the mishaps which had befallen the crusading army and of the royal couple's arrival in Italy. So had Suger, who received a regular flow of letters from the king. He had continually advised restraint: let the king come to no decision in present circumstances; let him first return to his kingdom, which was in growing need of him; the disagreements between him and his wife might be simply the result of tiredness and of the dangers to which they had been exposed. And the abbot of Saint-Denis had lost no time in apprising the pope of the bad times through which the couple were passing.

Beneath his stern exterior, Eugenius III was a kindly and sensitive *1145-53* man. He had given them his personal blessing when they had set out on this campaign, with all its perilous, exhausting and disappointing experiences. Deeply moved at the thought of the long series of ordeals which they had suffered during the past two years, he invited Louis and Eleanor to his residence at Tusculum: he was unable to reside in Rome at the time because of the upheavals caused by Arnold of Brescia, into whose hands the city had fallen.

The king and queen of France did not reach Tusculum until mid-October, but the welcome which they then received was memorably warm. The pope had a long private talk with each of them. He explained that he longed with all his heart to bring the young couple together again and help them return to a full partnership on which they had embarked for the good of their two peoples; he wanted to listen to their grievances, smooth out their resentments and effect a full reconciliation. As for the question of consanguinity, they must not give it another thought; the Church was always ready to allow for special circumstances and would be able to grant a dispensation in their case.

Louis's sense of relief was obvious. His exact conscience had undeniably been troubled over the problem. For their consanguinity was real enough: Eleanor's great-grandmother, Audéarde of Burgundy, had in turn been a granddaughter of his forebear Robert the Pious. This made them cousins nine times removed under civil law, but only four or five times removed according to canonical reckoning; which was sufficient to render their marriage invalid. And he was still in love with Eleanor, despite the bitter feelings which may have been awakened in him by the events in Antioch.

By the end of the audience, husband and wife appeared to be on good terms again. The pope conducted them to the bedroom which, at his instructions, had been prepared especially for them.

It was a sumptuously furnished room adorned with silk hangings (he knew Eleanor's tastes), and there was only one bed in it. The couple spent a few days in Tusculum before riding away the richer for the generous gifts and words of Pope Eugenius. 'When they took their leave,' records John of Salisbury, 'this man, for all his sternness, could not restrain his tears. On their departure he blessed them and the kingdom of France.'

———————◆———————

It was round about Martinmas (November 11th) when Louis and Eleanor returned to the banks of the Seine. Living proof of their reconciliation came the following year, when a second child was born to the royal couple. But it was not the male heir for whom both had been longing; it was another daughter, Alix.

For Eleanor the outlook seemed drab. There was no joy in living by the Seine after living by the Orontes. The lemon groves had given place to these banks covered with dead leaves which were beginning to rot in the November drizzle; the tiered palaces on the shores of the Golden Horn had been spirited away in favour of this penny-plain old residence in the middle of the tiny Ile de la Cité. She was surrounded all the time by the looks of reproof which had been levelled at her ever since the disaster at Mount Cadmos and which had intensified after Antioch. Her only consolation lay in having a considerate husband who was as eagerly attentive as ever; but she knew he would never put his trust in her again. Even on the journey home he had made it abundantly clear that he proposed to rule without her from now on. Shortly after crossing the Alps he had left the main party and hastened to Auxerre by means of a series of forced marches. There Suger, who had come to meet him, gave him a full account of the state of the realm. They rode into Paris together, and by way of thanking the loyal counsellor for his devoted service Louis caused it to be proclaimed throughout his lands that Suger deserved to be known as 'father of the nation'.

Eleanor's period of rule was over; from now on Louis would be a respectful husband, full of courtesy and affection, but a firm king. Yet it must have been in the ordinary capacity of husband that he had ceased to appeal to Eleanor, assuming indeed that she had ever loved him; whereas she now felt quite capable of wielding power without, as in the old days, being carried away by womanly whims. She had learned the measure of risk entailed in the exercise of royal authority and the host of responsibilities which go with it. Her counsel was being spurned at the very moment when she might have been able to enact the role of queen to the full. However dangerous and physically taxing it had been, Eleanor must still have regarded her visit to the East as the dazzling vision of a life which might have been hers. Oh, why had she not given her hand to a monarch such as Manuel Comnenus? She felt that she was infinitely better qualified than the present empress to captivate and maintain a hold over that giant among men; better still, she could have carried on at his side the subtle diplomatic game which had enabled Byzantium to remain Byzantium in defiance of the Arabs and the Turks and the Latin kingdoms. Why could she not at least summon the troubadours who had been the delight of her youth? Then, following the example of her grandfather, she could have had them devote their skills to perpetuating her experiences in the east.

But the French court was growing more and more austere. On his return, Louis had made a pilgrimage of atonement to the town of Vitry, henceforth known as Vitry-le-Brûlé—Vitry-the-Burned; it had been rebuilt and on the hills above he planted some cedars from the Holy Land; their offshoots, even today, are an amazing sight in the midst of the Champagne landscape. His days slipped by, divided between acts of worship and the manifold tasks of feudal life: supervising the accounts, meting out justice and even engaging in occasional armed ventures, but these were too unenterprising to awaken much interest in Eleanor. It seemed dull to bicker over a few wretched acres, after the magnificent stakes which had eluded them in the East.

And yet a time was soon to come when she would show a far livelier concern for such matters than she had ever dreamed possible. Louis had fallen out with one of his most powerful vassals, Geoffrey the Fair, count of Anjou. In the month of August 1150 their quarrel reached a crisis and the king started massing men along the banks of the Seine, between Mantes and Meulan. To anyone unfamiliar with the affairs of the realm it might seem strange that a dispute with the count of Anjou should lead to an attack in the direction of Normandy. In fact, the king was determined to carry out a large-scale campaign at the expense of his vassal, one which would thwart him in his dearest designs. Geoffrey the Fair, nicknamed Plantagenet on account of the sprig of broom which he wore pinned to his hood when he went out hunting, had married Matilda, daughter of Henry I of England's still called empress because she had formerly been married to the emperor of Germany, Henry V. Fifteen years older than Geoffrey, this woman— a really remarkable figure whose energy and resourcefulness knew no bounds—had brought to him in marriage her claims to her father's inheritance as king of England and duke of Normandy. She was sole descendant of the king of England, but this had not discouraged someone else from staking a claim to her heritage: Stephen, count of Blois, who through his mother Adela was likewise a grandchild of William the Conqueror. Indeed, Stephen had forestalled Matilda to the extent of actually seizing power. He was now residing in England, where a few of the barons had espoused his cause while others sided with Matilda. As a result of their rivalry, the country was in a state of mounting anarchy, if not civil war, and the quarrel was spreading to the mainland of Europe. Geoffrey had recently (in 1150) made the duchy of Normandy over to his eldest son Henry, who was seventeen at the time. The king of France had hitherto remained in the position of arbiter between his two powerful vassals; by directing his armies towards Mantes, he was coming out in favour of Stephen of Blois. If any further justification were needed for his act, it lay in Henry's failure to do homage to him for the duchy of Normandy.

It was some time, however, before hostilities finally broke out. Abbot Suger might be old, but he expended himself unreservedly in his attempts to achieve a settlement without bloodshed. But this tireless campaigner for peace died a few months later, on January 13th, 1151, to the profound sorrow of the people of France. In the as yet unfinished abbey church, a vast congregation attended the requiem for this remarkable man who had fought so hard to preserve harmony within the realm, drawing on all his energy and ingenuity—qualities which as a rule were devoted to the furtherance of personal ambition. Above his coffin, the new vaults of Saint-Denis, thrusting heavenwards with a boldness never previously attempted, seemed like a foretaste of those visions of glory foretold by the monks as they sang the anthem of the Office for the Dead: 'I know that my redeemer liveth, and that he shall stand at the latter day upon the earth; and though after my skin worms destroy this body, yet in my flesh shall I see God . . .'

Suger's death loosed the tenuous bond which only his stubborn will had maintained between Louis and Eleanor. She simply did not possess the resigned spirit which would have enabled her to bow to the situation confronting her. And no doubt Louis, for his part, was at last beginning to tire of being overshadowed by this woman.

However, hostilities were breaking out again in Normandy. They were complicated by additional personal grievances which the king now felt towards his Angevin vassal. As so often occurred in feudal times, the situation was further complicated by the interplay of personal alliances. For various obscure reasons Geoffrey the Fair was in conflict with Louis's seneschal in Poitou, a certain Giraud Berlai. The latter had spent three years defying him from the powerful battlements of his castle at Montreuil-Bellay. One day Geoffrey decided that he had tolerated this situation long enough: using plenty of boiling oil and red-hot arrows, he concentrated his attack on one of the wooden beams supporting the keep; soon the fire was blazing so fiercely that the Giraud family and their entire garrison came scampering out of every aperture like rats from a sinking ship. Giraud, of course, was taken prisoner. By way of reprisal the king of France attacked the fortress of Arques, in Normandy, and quickly wrested it from its defenders. Eustace, son of Stephen of Blois, hastened across the Channel and lent Louis keen support against his rival, Henry of Normandy. After this, where were hostilities likely to end? Suger was no longer there to reason with the conflicting parties and re-establish harmony between them.

But at this point the illustrious voice of Bernard of Clairvaux was lifted above the fray, exhorting the king and his barons to strive once more for peace. He offered to act as mediator.

81

Events at the court of France that summer were somewhat baffling to those who beheld them. They began with a dramatic scene in the Cité Palace where a large crowd had gathered, attracted by the sudden dramatic comings and goings of Bernard of Clairvaux. When the saintly abbot arrived he was bidden welcome by the king of France with every mark of honour and respect. Then came the Plantagenet, Geoffrey the Fair, accompanied by his son, the young duke of Normandy. Geoffrey fully deserved his nickname, if we are to believe the chronicle which describes him as 'a great knight, strong and handsome, gallant and wise and victorious, as valiant a prince as ever was'. He was in the prime of life —nearly forty—and had proved his valour in the East, for he had accompanied his sovereign on the crusade and conducted himself fearlessly. But he was said to be harsh, overbearing and subject to those fits of black bile which were commonly attributed to the Anjou family. The barons attending this solemn assembly—among them, Raoul of Vermandois—were treated to an astonishing demonstration of this last characteristic. With him Geoffrey had brought Giraud Berlai, chained up like a felon. This was an act of defiance against the Church, as well as against the king, for he had already been excommunicated for laying hands on an officer of the Crown while his sovereign was away on crusade; the quarrel with Giraud had begun before the king's return.

Bernard of Clairvaux spoke first: he offered to lift the ban of excommunication if Geoffrey would agree to release Giraud. Geoffrey's reply was so impious that it horrified every man present: 'I refuse to free my captive, and if it is a sin to hold a prisoner then I refuse to be absolved of that sin!'

'Beware, count of Anjou,' said Bernard, '"with what measure ye mete, it shall be meted unto you".'

But without more ado, the count and his son departed from the hall, to the utter consternation of all who had witnessed the scene. Giraud Berlai went up to Bernard of Clairvaux and asked his blessing. 'It is not for myself I grieve,' he said, 'but for my family who are going to die with me.'

'Fear not,' replied Bernard, 'rest assured that God will help you, and sooner than you would have dared to hope.'

In the days that followed a strange rumour went the rounds:

Geoffrey of Anjou, who had not feared to defy the king and blas-
pheme in the presence of Bernard of Clairvaux, had set Giraud
free. Better still, his son Henry was offering to do homage for the
duchy of Normandy. The situation that had seemed inextricable
was suddenly unravelling itself without the need for any man to
unsheathe his sword. Sure enough, the homage ceremony took
place a few days later. Some people saw this as a miracle resulting
from Abbot Bernard's intervention. Others insinuated that the
queen may well have had a hand in the outcome of the negotiations. The fact remains that peace returned to Normandy even as
Geoffrey and Henry Plantagenet rode back towards the county of
Anjou.

Another event, equally unforeseeable, occurred on the journey
home. When they had got as far as Château-du-Loir, Geoffrey
decided to go for a swim in the river; it was an overpoweringly hot
day. That same evening he went down with fever, and a few days
later—on September 7th—he died, all available remedies having
proved powerless to save him.

In the late autumn Louis and Eleanor set out together on a tour
of Aquitaine, with an imposing retinue of prelates and barons.
There were as many Aquitainians among them as men from the
royal domain: for every Thierry Galeran there was a Geoffrey of
Rancon, for every Guy of Garlande, a Hugh of Lusignan. Some
viewed this as a sign of improved relations between the king and
queen; others, better informed, shook their heads and insisted that
the couple would never again ride forth on a public mission
together. Since the death of Suger, the rift between Louis and
Eleanor had been growing wider all the time. They held court
together in Limoges at Christmas, and in Saint-Jean d'Angély at
Candlemas; slowly but surely, in the estates and castles directly
under Eleanor's authority, Frenchmen were being replaced by
Aquitainians. Then the royal couple proceeded to Beaugency,
where they were destined to spend their last moments of married
life together. For it was here that a synod convened by the archbishop of Sens formally annulled the marriage contracted in
Bordeaux fifteen years earlier.

Eleanor made her farewells and announced her intention of
repairing at once to her own lands, which had been returned to

83

her in accordance with custom. Without further delay, she and a few familiars set out on the road to Poitiers.

It was the first day of spring, March 21st, 1152. Before the season was over, startling news reached the French court. Eleanor had married again. Her new husband was Henry Plantagenet, count of Anjou and duke of Normandy.

VIII

Joves es domna que sap onrar paratge,
Et es joves per bos faitz, quan lo fa;
Joves se te quand a adreit coratge
E ves von pretz avol mestier non a.

Young though she is, she ornaments her breed
And by fair deeds seeks to adorn it still;
Youthful yet prudent, of her name takes heed,
And keeps from thinking, speaking, doing ill.

BERTRAND DE BORN

THERE WERE TIMES during her journey back to Poitiers when Eleanor must have felt all the panic and distress of the hind running before the pack or the fairy-tale maiden chased by giants.

After leaving Beaugency, she and her small party made first of all for Blois. There was a good deal of activity on the outskirts of the city, for it was Saturday in Passion Week and tomorrow was Palm Sunday; people were busily stripping the trees so that there should be enough palms for the church procession and for decorating the fronts of the houses along the route. Eleanor had probably planned to break her journey at one of the local abbeys —St Lomer's, for example. But somehow or other she was forewarned that danger lay in store for her. Some servants from the castle may have gossiped to her retinue, or perhaps her suspicions were aroused by an unusual amount of activity on the part of the garrison; this castle, by the way, had been built by an earlier count of Blois with the unprepossessing nickname of Theobald the Cheat. At all events, she learned that the young count at present residing there, another Theobald, was preparing to kidnap her and make her his wife. Eleanor did not waste her time and energy waxing indignant at the brazen impudence of this young fellow who was not even an eldest son (he was in fact the second son of that Theobald of Champagne with whom she had clashed at the

85

time of her sister's marriage); instead she urged her party forward after dark and left Blois by moonlight—probably telling herself that *this* Theobald was going to be Theobald the Cheated.

But her troubles were not over yet. She was on her guard now and had probably sent a few squires on ahead to act as scouts. Suddenly she was informed that a full-scale ambush was lying in wait at Port-de-Piles, where she had been expecting to cross the Creuse. She had to change her route once more and decided to ford the Vienne at a point downstream from the junction of the two rivers and then make poste-haste for Poitiers, with the prospect of celebrating Easter within the security of its walls.

Once in Poitiers, she could afford to laugh at these two brushes with danger. The villain who had dared conspire against her person and attempted to seize her at Port-de-Piles was young Geoffrey of Anjou, another second son—this time of Geoffrey the Fair, who had so recently and tragically departed the world. A boy of sixteen, he would dearly have loved to reap his father's inheritance; but his elder brother was clearly determined to allow him only a meagre portion.

Twice in quick succession the ex-queen of France had nearly ridden into a trap. How was she going to cope when she began administering her own estates and had to stand up to traditionally turbulent vassals? She might well have to lead armed expeditions against the more intractable . . .

As the festive month of April wore on (for the capital of Poitou was determined to show its delight at the duchess's return) there were mysterious comings and goings of messengers. And spring was in its full splendour when on the morning of May 18th the bells of the cathedral of Saint-Pierre proclaimed to the world that Eleanor, duchess of Guyenne and countess of Poitou, was in the act of becoming countess of Anjou and duchess of Normandy.

The preparations for the ceremony had been carried out in secret, and the wedding itself lacked the splendour which would normally have been warranted by the high station of the bride and groom. In other circumstances, they would have summoned each and every one of their vassals; but only their closest intimates attended the banquet served in the great hall of the palace of the counts of Poitiers. The newly-weds were indeed in a delicate situation, as they were the first to realize: less than two months after the annulment of her first marriage, Eleanor had wilfully allied herself with a vassal of the king whose side she had so recently left; moreover she ought, like any other vassal, to have solicited her sovereign's approval before marrying—and she had good grounds for shirking that formality. At least she and her new husband were wise enough not to parade their act too ostentatiously.

What kind of man was this husband whom Eleanor had chosen for herself? For this time it was she who did the choosing. Everything points to the fact that her mind was set on the marriage and that it was first mooted at the time of the Plantagenets' visit to Paris in August 1151. Only after that visit was there open talk of annulling her marriage to Louis; only then were representations made to the archbishop of Sens, who at first was extremely unresponsive. And one of the best informed chroniclers of the time, William of Newburgh, states categorically that Eleanor *wished* to break with Louis and that the king *gave his consent*.

He would certainly not have given it had he realized the nature of the sequel which Eleanor was planning. That she acted with extreme caution is obvious from the surprise afterwards evinced by her contemporaries. Some even go so far as to aver that her underhand dealings with the Angevins had begun much earlier than the peace-talks conducted by St Bernard at the height of that stormy summer; they insinuate that she had already 'known' Geoffrey the Fair. She may indeed have met him in the East—after all, he had been a member of his sovereign's crusade. But this, it need hardly be said, is not sufficient grounds for alleging intimacy. The accusation, without a shred of evidence to support it, seems nothing but a smear.

On the other hand there seems no reason to doubt that she had deliberately set her cap at Geoffrey's son.

He was ten years younger than she. Eleanor was nearing her thirties; Henry, born on March 5th, 1133, was not yet twenty. But we know that the queen had never looked quite so radiantly beautiful as she did now, and at the same time Henry most likely

87

looked older than his years; even at this period he was patently acting like a mature man, carrying on wars and governing in his own right. As for his private life, he had already sired two bastards; these were being carefully nurtured in the royal household, as was the general practice then. Henry was a fine-looking man, not tall but of strong muscular build with, like all the Angevins, sandy hair and rather prominent grey eyes which grew bloodshot when his temper was up; for—again like the rest of the family—he had 'fits of black bile' which it was unwise to provoke. Though a hardened athlete, he was also a man of great culture. This was another family trait. One of his ancestors, Fulke the Good, was renowned for the missive which he had addressed to the king of France:

> To the king of the Franks, the count of the Angevins:
> Know this, lord: an unlettered king is a crowned ass.

For it had come to Fulke's notice that there was much jeering in royal circles at his clerkly scholarship and his habit of spouting Latin like a monk.

Geoffrey the Fair, Henry's father, had derived his knowledge of the art of war directly from his readings of Vegetius. Henry could read Latin too and spoke several foreign languages—'all the languages in use between the sea of France and the Jordan', as his intimates claimed, not without exaggeration; well, at least he spoke *langue d'oc*. As a child he had been taught by famous men: first by a certain Master Peter of Saintes who, it was said, knew more about versification than any of his contemporaries; and when Henry was nine his father, still dominated by his ambitions concerning England, sent him to Bristol where he was instructed by another cleric, Master Matthew, chancellor to his mother Matilda. With Henry as her husband, Eleanor would be able to indulge her taste for poetry and the arts.

Finally he was of illustrious descent—no small consideration in an age when the individual was seldom considered in isolation from the group, and when it was thought impossible to judge a man without reference to his antecedents. Henry was the grandson of Fulke of Anjou, a man whose career had been truly remarkable. When he was forty and at the height of his powers, Fulke—lord and master of one of the richest counties in the kingdom, who had

88

just married his son to the heiress to the English throne—had handed his estates over to that son in order that he might devote himself fully to the task of defending the Holy Land. He had married Queen Melisande, that same Melisande who had welcomed the crusaders to Jerusalem in 1148, and young Baldwin III—on whom the hopes of the Latin kingdoms now depended—was their son. A hunting accident brought his exploits to a brutal end in 1143, and it was not until the following year that Zengi dared to attack Edessa.

Fulke B d anjou d 1143

For the sake of fairness, however, it has to be admitted that among Henry's other forebears was the notorious Fulke the Black, or Nerra. This Fulke, active in the early eleventh century, was one of the few men who fully lived up to the portrait of the feudal lord generally given in the history books. He was brutal and ferocious, with a reputation for slaughtering anyone who got in his way; he was always sacking towns and despoiling monasteries. Three times he did penance by making the pilgrimage to the Holy Land. His remorse was as immoderate as the horrors he had perpetrated. On his last visit to Jerusalem he betook himself to the Holy Sepulchre, stripped to the waist, and had two of his attendants flog him and cry: 'Lord, receive the wicked Fulke, count of Anjou, who has betrayed and denied thee. Gaze, O Christ, upon his penitent soul...' The crowd of Moslem onlookers was amazed at the sight.

So much for the appearance and background of Henry Plantagenet. In choosing him as a husband, to what extent had Eleanor been guided solely by political considerations? That she could not remain unattached for long had been made abundantly clear by the attempts to ambush her on the journey from Beaugency to Poitiers. Defending a fief in those days, when a feudal lord was required to police his own estate, called for a man who could don a coat of mail and wield a sword. The lands of the counts of Anjou abutted on those of the dukes of Aquitaine, and this would very likely have played a part in her decision; her ambitious imagination must surely have been fired by the thought that, between them, they would govern almost the whole of western France, from the Channel to the Pyrenees, since Henry was also duke of Normandy.

But Eleanor cannot have failed to be drawn to him as a man; she was too much of a woman not to be stirred by his air of virility.

89

She was in love with him—so many different details prove that she was, and her love is attested to an even greater degree by the general tenor of her life.

As for Henry, he may well have been swayed by the magnificence of her dowry, in terms of territorial power, but it would obviously be quite wrong to see his decision as the calculated act of an ambitious man. A passionate nature such as his was bound to respond to the beauty of this queen whose eventful history seemed to invest her with a special aura, and the difference in their ages is unlikely to have weighed with him at the time of the wedding. Far from it: a precocious young man like Henry would be inclined to rate an experienced woman higher than an artless girl. Moreover, his ambition matched Eleanor's, and in this too their understanding was complete: Henry prized his domains just as she prized hers; each supported the other's urge to extend those domains; throughout the long years in which their hearts and wills were joined they were destined to form a perfect, complementary pair, always striving for the same ends, combining to achieve a pattern of living which was active and fruitful in every sense of the word; and Eleanor would not have wished it otherwise. She was no longer a light-headed girl but a woman bent on leading a full life. When William of Newburgh tells us that she sought this second marriage because it was better suited to her personality than the first, his statement gains strength from the fact that here was a chronicler capable of choosing words with precision. *Magis congruus.* In Henry she had found the husband she needed.

Such documents as have survived concerning Eleanor at the time of her second marriage are highly revealing: they disclose an Eleanor eager to forget the past and enter joyously into the future which seemed to beckon. Here she was, joining the Anjou family even as she returned to being duchess of Aquitaine. The documents show her distributing favours to several of her knights— obviously those who had helped her gain her freedom and brought her, ambushes or no, safe and sound to Poitiers. Among them was Saldebreuil of Sanzay, constable of Aquitaine, whom she nominated as her seneschal: the function of seneschal was never a sharply defined one, but in general it consisted of deputizing for the feudal lord

90

whenever the latter was unable to be present in person; the sene-schal was the 'old man' (*senescallus*) among the lord's familiars—the lord himself being the 'elder' (*seigneur, senior*). Nor is it surprising to discover that another beneficiary at the time of her marriage was her uncle, the ever-devoted Raoul of Faye, brother of the viscount of Châtellerault.

In addition, she showered gifts upon the abbeys within her domain. Paying a visit to Montierneuf on May 26th, 1152, a week after her marriage, she went out of her way to remark that she was re-extending all the privileges accorded by 'my great-grandfather, my grandfather and my father'. Her ex-husband, the king of France, had also been generous to the monks of Montierneuf, but of this she makes no mention . . . Next day she was at Saint-Maixent—and here again, itemizing the various concessions she was making to the abbey, she carefully referred to herself as 'Eleanor, by the grace of God duchess of Aquitaine and Normandy, joined in wedlock to the duke of Normandy, Henry, count of Anjou.' And this is what she said: 'When I was queen to the king of France, the king donated the Sèvre-side woods to the abbey, and I too gave and conceded those woods; then, separated from the king by the judgment of the Church, I took the gift back into my own keeping; but on the advice of wise men, and at the entreaty of Abbot Peter, this gift which I at first made almost reluctantly I have now renewed with a glad heart . . . now that I am joined in wedlock to Henry, duke of Normandy and count of Anjou.'

But nothing tells us more about Eleanor and the feelings that animated her at the time of this second marriage than the charter which she dictated a few days later for the abbey of Fontevrault. Like many other documents given under Eleanor's hand, this charter has a distinctive personal tone: the stiff, undemonstrative style favoured in the old chancelleries obviously made no appeal to her. What makes this a moving document is the fact that Eleanor displays visible signs of emotion in it, and it is the first time—except perhaps on the occasion of her audience with St Bernard in the abbey of Saint-Denis—that she has displayed so much feeling. So it may well be that her capacity for loving had not been awakened until then. The phrasing of the charter surely proclaims how happy she was and how exhilarated by the prospects which now

Fontevrault Charter

91

lay before her: 'After separating, for reasons of kinship, from my lord Louis, the very illustrious king of France, and being united in wedlock to my very noble lord Henry, count of Anjou, divine inspiration led me to want to visit the sacred congregation of the virgins of Fontevrault, and by the grace of God I have been able to realize this intention. Thus I have come to Fontevrault guided by God; I have crossed the threshold where the sisters are gathered; and here, with heartfelt emotion, I have approved, conceded and confirmed all that my father and forebears have given to God and to the church of Fontevrault, and in particular this gift of five hundred sous, in the coinage of Poitou, made by myself and my lord Louis, king of France, in the days when he was my husband.'

This abbey of Fontevrault—and its abbess, Matilda, who is named in the charter—were of special significance in the pattern of Eleanor's existence. The least we can do is devote a little time, as she herself did in the early days of her marriage, to an abbey whose history was to be closely linked with her own—and to the abbess who was then presiding over its fortunes.

At the time of Eleanor's visit, the order of Fontevrault was still quite young. Its founder, Robert of Arbrissel, had died only about thirty years previously, one of the most engaging figures of the late eleventh century—a period marked by an extraordinary religious reawakening. Robert began his career as a hermit in the forest of Craon, like so many other ecclesiasts of the time; it was not long before he attracted disciples and eventually great multitudes were converted by his powers as a preacher. The order of Fontevrault was characterized by the same fervour as went into the radicalism of Robert of Moslesme and many others, but it stood out owing to the profound originality of the foundation to which it gave rise. Robert founded cloisters for men and for women too, usually on the same site, though the two were rigidly segregated except when they assembled in chapel. When a nun was in need of the last rites, she had to be carried into the church on a stretcher before she could be anointed with oil. These two cloisters, existing side by side, were placed under the general supervision of an abbess. In their dealings with her, the monks were expected to model themselves on St John the Evangelist to whom Jesus, from the Cross, entrusted the Virgin Mary, bidding him look upon her as a mother.

In our own day, this subordination of a men's cloister to a woman would be considered quite unacceptable; but it does not seem to have created any difficulties then. Robert's avowed aim was that, wherever possible, the abbess in charge should be a widow capable of playing a maternal role. The abbess was intended to be the *domina*, the Lady—in general terms, the religious counterpart of that secular Lady to whom generations of troubadours had paid, and would continue to pay, homage. The first abbess chosen by Robert was Petronilla of Chemillé, widowed at twenty and as renowned for her beauty as for the quality of her mind. A host of other high-born ladies had rallied to her. Among them (this was in 1114, forty years prior to Eleanor's visit, and one or two of the sisters clustering round her may well have known the illustrious penitent) was Bertrada of Montfort, countess of Anjou, whose scandalous relationship with Philip I of France had resulted in the kingdom's being laid under an interdict.

In 1148 Petronilla was succeeded by this same Matilda of Anjou who welcomed Eleanor to the abbey at the time of her official visit in 1152. Matilda's previous history was a sad one. She was the aunt of Henry Plantagenet and daughter of the Fulke who gave up his lands in Anjou and became king of Jerusalem. She was still only a child when she first sensed that she might have a vocation, and at the age of eleven she became a novice at Fontevrault. However, in response to her father's wishes she left the convent in order to marry William Atheling, son and heir of Henry I of England. Shortly afterwards, in 1120, her husband was drowned in the tragic sinking of the White Ship off Barfleur. Drowned with him were his brother and sister and a sizeable party of gay young courtiers. The vessel was piloted by an ex-helmsman of William the Conqueror who had requested the honour of being allowed to steer. Meanwhile, Matilda sailed aboard another vessel with her husband's parents. The two ships were on their way to England when shouts rang out in the dark. The king and his companions were not unduly alarmed, for they knew that the young people had made up their minds to give the crew a drink and thoroughly enjoy themselves during the crossing. But the real cause of the shouting was that the White Ship had struck a reef and gone down like a stone. When the helmsman broke surface and realized that all the

93

royal children had perished, he deliberately plunged back into the deep. Of all those who had gone aboard, only one lived to tell the tale. Henry Beauclerk never got over it; no one ever saw him smile again. As for Matilda, she went back to Fontevrault, where a few years later the nuns chose her as abbess.

In the terms of this charter of 1152 Eleanor showed a preference for Fontevrault over other abbeys which she was to feel all her life long. In later documents she was to refer to Matilda affectionately as 'my aunt', *amita mea*, thereby adopting her husband's kinswoman as her own. Moreover, the charter testifies to the deep impression which her visit to Fontevrault must have made on her. After the terrible circumstances which had resulted in Matilda's becoming the handmaiden of the Lord (a contemporary remarks that she had gone from the king of the Angles to the King of the Angels), she emerged as fully equal to the task confronting her as abbess. She was in charge of the foundation for twenty years or so, and in the course of those years the abbey church must have looked to Eleanor, architecturally at least, more or less as we see it today; for the light from the four cupolas still pours down on to the majestic nave with its splendid crowned columns. She was also able to admire the famous kitchen, a masterpiece of 'functional' design. The grouping of twenty subsidiary chimneys round one large central chimney ensured perfect ventilation and made it possible for the various separate kitchens to be fuelled from a central furnace without the disadvantages of smokiness and excessive heat. There were three such kitchens—one for the monks, one for the nuns and one for the sick and visiting. The guest quarters could accommodate five hundred persons, and on some days it was too small for the multitude of visitors and pilgrims to whom it regularly gave shelter.

IX

Quar de guerra ven tart pro et tost dan
E guerra fai mal tornar en peior;
En guerra trop, per qu'ieu non la volria,
Viutat de mal, et de ben carestia.

From war comes tardy gain and speedy loss;
What's bad war swiftly turns to what is worse;
A host of evils follow war, but not
A single benefaction; war's a curse.

AIMERIC DE PEGULHAN

IT TOOK LOUIS SOME TIME to recover from the affront to his
authority—at first he was utterly bewildered by the very scale of
the calamity which had befallen him. As a husband, he was deeply
humiliated that the woman whom he had loved so greatly should
marry again within two months of parting from him. But as king
he found it quite intolerable that she should have married Henry
Plantagenet. Almost the whole western side of the realm was now
in the same hands, and those hands were renowned for maintaining a tight grip on whatever they held. His forefathers had striven
ceaselessly to maintain a balance of power between the vassals, so
as to fulfil the role of arbitrator. Until now the two great powers
had been the house of Anjou and the alliance formed between the
houses of Champagne and Blois. The kings of France had always
taken good care to ensure that the scales were never tipped in
favour of one rather than the other. And now suddenly these
terrible Angevins were masters not only of Normandy but of
Poitou and Guyenne, lands of which he had been titular head only
a short time ago. With what sadness Louis must have contemplated
his isolation: everyone had gone; his most trusted advisers were
dead; in succession he had lost Theobald of Champagne, Raoul of
Vermandois, Abbot Suger . . . Suger he missed most of all, as an
irreplaceable mentor, father of the kingdom. Why had he not

95

followed the advice which the abbot had dispensed so frequently during his latter years—to close his mind to all bitterness and resentment and put the interests of the state above his own? Of his fifteen years with Eleanor, years which had begun on a note of such brilliant promise, nothing was left to him except his two daughters Marie and Alix. Two daughters. If only Eleanor had given him a son, he would have moved heaven and earth to keep her on the throne of France. Would he ever have fallen in with her wish for an annulment but for the fear that he might never be granted a son and heir?

Louis hurriedly called a meeting of counsellors and it was declared officially that feudal law had been infringed: Eleanor could not contract a marriage without seeking permission from her sovereign. She and Henry were summoned to appear before the king's court. Predictably, they did not trouble to answer this summons. Henry was shortly intending to join his mother Matilda in England, and by Midsummer Day he was ready to embark at Barfleur. And then, suddenly and dramatically, Louis invaded Normandy. Furious at this flouting of his authority by his Norman vassal, he had solicited the active support of Henry's younger brother, Geoffrey. The latter was only too willing to oblige; indeed, he was already fomenting uprisings throughout Anjou in a bid to wrest the county from Henry—for he claimed Anjou as his own.

It was immediately apparent that Henry was going to be a worthy successor to his ancestors on the battlefield. He at once left Barfleur and, with the help of the Norman barons who had remained loyal to him, achieved victory after victory within the six-week period from mid-July until late August. He recaptured Neufmarché after it had fallen to the royal armies; he took Pacy, where the two foes briefly came to grips; and then he swept the board by striking out and seizing the townships of Brezolles, Marcouville and Bonmoulins so that he could garrison the area between his own border and the king's. Next day he dealt with his brother, swiftly subduing the rebellion in Anjou; Geoffrey, entrenched in the fortress of Montsoreau, had no choice but to cry quarter. Meanwhile Louis VII—assisted by his brother, the count of Dreux—was attempting a diversionary thrust towards Verneuil. Operations dragged on for

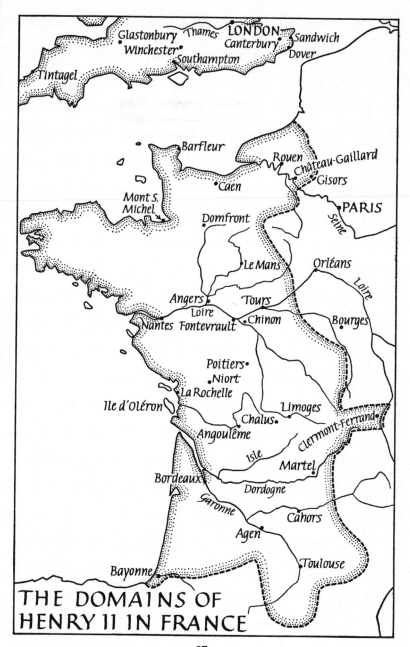

Glastonbury
Winchester
Tintagel
Southampton
Thames LONDON
Canterbury Sandwich
Dover

Barfleur
Rouen
Château-Gaillard
Gisors
Caen
PARIS
Mont S. Michel
Domfront
Seine

Le Mans
Orléans
Loire

Angers
Tours
Bourges
Loire
Chinon
Nantes Fontevrault

Poitiers
Niort
La Rochelle
Limoges
Ile d'Oléron
Chalus
Clermont-Ferrand
Angoulême

Isle
Martel
Bordeaux
Dordogne
Garonne
Cahors
Agen
Bayonne
Toulouse

THE DOMAINS OF
HENRY II IN FRANCE

a while; then, tired and physically unwell, Louis put out feelers for a settlement. Everyone was impatient for peace—not least the borderland bishops, whose dioceses were being held to ransom and laid waste.

Now Henry's hands were free. He returned to his wife until the following January, when he set out for England again, more than ever determined to make good the claims which his mother, Matilda, had gone on staking with such extraordinary tenacity. He was still away when a wonderful piece of news reached him: on August 17th, 1153, Eleanor had given birth to a child, a son whom in accordance with Poitevin tradition she called William after her father and his fathers before him.

And Henry could scarcely object to the name, which had been that of the Conqueror as well.

———————◆———————

The rain pelted down and the waves were pounding the shore, lashed by the gale. The storm had been blowing almost without a break for the best part of a month, and Barfleur harbour was full of tossing, heaving vessels, which had been unable to put to sea. The harbour town was crowded with animals and men; knights and squires, clergy and military, sailors and dockers, all were sheltering as best they could until they could reasonably load their provisions and merchandise, put their beasts of burden aboard and set sail. They spent their time scanning the sky for signs of improvement, but the outlook remained unrelievedly grey. The shore was still covered by a heavy mist, the rain struck at the granite houses, the sea was as menacing as ever.

For Henry Plantagenet the bad weather was infuriating. Coming when he had almost reached his goal and when he was so near to wearing the crown of England for which he had waited so long, this unpredictable and insuperable delay seemed like a physical barrier. Everything had gone so smoothly for him in the past two years—it was as though the path had been miraculously cleared to ensure the fulfilment of an ambition which had been so long and so stubbornly pursued by his line. He was emerging victorious from the rivalry which had kept the houses of Anjou and Blois at logger-

98

heads for thirty-five years. Nor indeed had he ever doubted victory since the day when he had first set foot on English soil as Eleanor's husband—January 6th, 1153. As it was the feast of the Epiphany, he and his retinue had gone straight to church after landing. At the very moment when Henry stepped through the door, the priest was intoning the words of the Introit: 'See he comes, our Lord and Ruler, armed with royal power and dominion . . .'

A happy omen which was borne out by all that followed. In next to no time, with only a handful of men behind him, Henry had succeeded in capturing Malmesbury while King Stephen was still trying to rally his men. Stephen was unpopular in England and had to rely chiefly on mercenaries recruited in Flanders; these held the peasants to ransom and were heartily detested by them. For several days the two men and their armies had stared at one another across the Thames while the rain beat down. In the end neither of them had dared to cross the river, which had reached a dangerously high level. Stephen had rather woefully gone back to London while Henry attended to the task of freeing Wallingford Castle, where a few bands of Flemings were besieging one of his supporters. Stephen of Blois found himself so completely outstripped by events that he decided to issue peace proposals: he was a sick man and his son Eustace, next in line to the throne, was a sorry figure, universally loathed; his other son, William, was illegitimate and had no claim to his father's title—moreover, he was as bereft of ambition as of legal claim. The bishop of Winchester (Stephen's brother) and the archbishop of Canterbury agreed to act as mediators. This infuriated Eustace, for negotiation could only be to his disadvantage. He rounded on the archbishop and began to devastate his lands with insane fury, setting fire to everything in his path—churches, priories, peasants' cottages—until he was suddenly taken ill in Bury St Edmunds, where to everyone's relief he died a few days later.

King Stephen was becoming ever more powerless, and he now resolved to make of his own accord the gesture which would soon be mandatory: on November 6th, 1153, he formally acknowledged Henry Plantagenet as his lawful heir. An assembly of English and Norman nobles, meeting in Winchester, set the seal on this decision which would put an end to the state of civil war in which England

99

had been living for so long. A month later Stephen and Henry rode into the City of London side by side, and the cheers that greeted them were ample testimony of the relief felt by men and women of every estate. Now Henry could be sure of succeeding as soon as Stephen died. In the spring he went back to Europe and to Eleanor and made the acquaintance of the heir whom she had borne him. They spent Easter together in Normandy; in Rouen she met her mother-in-law, Queen Matilda, for the first time. Matilda was the kind of woman who commanded admiration, if not instinctive liking, and there must have been quite an aura about her: she had once worn the crown of the Holy Roman Empire and had afterwards dedicated her life wholly to the task of retrieving the inheritance of her grandfather, William the Conqueror. She had spent all these years battling on both sides of the Channel so that Henry might one day be king of England. That day was now at hand. If Henry was about to achieve his goal, he owed it to his mother's ceaseless dedication.

They did not have to wait much longer. At the beginning of November, messengers arrived in Rouen with the news that King Stephen had died on October 25th, 1154. Eleanor would soon be wearing another crown, and on the whole it was no less desirable than the one she had given up two years earlier. Henry immediately instructed that all should be made ready for departure. Leaving his mother behind in Normandy, he and Eleanor set out for Barfleur with young William. Their official escort, summoned in haste, was made up of Henry's two brothers, Geoffrey and William, and the principal Norman barons and bishops.

And now this interminable bad weather was keeping them in Barfleur. The elements stood between the king-to-be and his kingdom.

But Henry was a match for any situation. On the evening of the feast of St Nicholas, protector of sailors and travellers, he suddenly decreed that the convoy should set sail the following morning. After a hectic day and night of rolling about in the dips of the waves and getting lost in the fog, the vessels finally reached land on December 8th; they were scattered all along the south coast of England, but they had arrived safe and sound. Henry and Eleanor landed near Southampton and made first for Winchester, where

100

the royal treasure was. Gradually they were joined by the other members of the convoy. The news that the king had arrived on the wings of the storm quickly spread throughout the land. Everywhere it prompted stupefaction—most likely mingled with fear in the case of those who had upheld the cause of King Stephen to the very end. But the dominant mood was one of enthusiasm. To ordinary people up and down England, Henry's name was synonymous with the coming of peace; and his audacity in braving the elements obviously appealed to a seafaring race. As the new king and queen rode towards London, the welcoming crowds grew daily thicker, and when they rode into the capital the atmosphere was one of unrestrained joy. On Sunday, December 19th, 1154, they were crowned in Westminster Abbey.

Hopes of a solidly established dynasty were strengthened two months later, for on the last day of February a second son was born to the royal couple. He was baptized by the same Archbishop Theobald of Canterbury who had so recently anointed the parents. The child was christened Henry, a name which was already acquiring overtones of glory.

[handwritten marginalia: Henry II + Eleanor of Aq. crowned at Westminster 12-19-1154]

[handwritten marginalia: Feb 28, 1155 Henry b.]

[handwritten marginalia: Henry 22]

X

Domna, vostre sui e serai,
Del vostre servizi garnitz.
Vostr' om sui juratz e plevitz,
E vostre m'era des abans.
E vos etz lo meus jois primers,
E si seretz vos lo derrers,
Tan com la vida m'er durans.

Lady, I'm yours and yours shall be,
Vowed to your service constantly,
This is the oath of fealty
I pledged to you this long time past.
As my first joy was all in you,
So shall my last be found there too,
So long as life in me shall last.

BERNARD DE VENTADOUR

FOR ELEANOR the next ten years were a time of matchless splendour. She was clearly at the height of her powers as a woman and as a queen, and at last she began to live with the fullness and intensity which her extraordinary nature demanded. In youth she had imagined that she might be barren, yet now she presented her husband with half a dozen more children, zestfully withstanding her successive pregnancies. Her first son, William, died in June 1156 when he was only three; he was buried in Reading. Shortly afterwards, in London, she gave birth to a daughter and christened her Matilda out of respect for the queen mother. The following year, on September 8th, 1157, a third son—Richard—was born in Oxford; and the year after that, on September 23rd, 1158, came Geoffrey. Two daughters followed. The first was born in Domfront in 1161; she was named after her mother and became the godchild of Robert of Thorigny, abbot of Mont-Saint-Michel, who speaks affectionately of her in his chronicle. The second daughter, Joanna, was born in Angers in 1165. Last of all came John, born in Oxford on December 27th, 1166.

There is no sign that bearing all these children made Eleanor less active or less mobile. On the contrary, she did an astonishing amount of travelling, continually crossing the Channel for official tours of Normandy and Poitou and Aquitaine and then hurrying back because her presence was needed in Oxford, Winchester or Salisbury. True, all great landowners had to be continually on the move—especially kings, who went from one residence to another, partly in the interests of maintaining law and order and partly to use up the resources of each estate. We still tend to picture the era as static, whereas travel was really very easy and a commonplace experience; this is borne out by the tremendous number of pilgrims on the roads and the manner in which social and political exchanges were effected right across Europe (as far back as the eleventh century, Hugh Capet's grandson married a Russian princess). Furthermore, it was considered simpler and safer to travel by water, so there was nothing extraordinary about crossing the Channel: it was thought of as being literally a channel, a means of transport, and not a barrier. England did not begin to be an 'island' until much later, when feudal times and even mediaeval times were over.

Moreover, the pace of life was bound to quicken when shared with a man like Henry Plantagenet. From personal temperament, as well as the need to safeguard his possessions, the Angevin had led a far more bustling existence than most men. It was generally held that the Angevins were 'unstable'; in his case, this instability was raised almost to the level of a system of government. In the very first months of his reign this young man of twenty-two showed a keen sense of the true nature of power and manifested it by a series of armed patrols, north, south, east and west, which were designed to rouse England from the state of anarchy that had taken hold while Stephen was king. Indeed, even in Stephen's lifetime he had made a spectacular bid to win over the ordinary country people: he had ordered his own troops to hand back the booty which they had taken during a campaign against the barons in the Oxford area. 'I am not here to indulge in looting,' he proclaimed, 'but to safeguard the property of the poor from the depredations of the mighty.' Speeches like this had not been heard in England for a long time. The barons had acquired independent habits under Stephen, and his bands of Flemish mercenaries had lived by pillaging the populace.

Henry was about to take the country vigorously in hand. By March—within three months, that is, of being crowned king—he was conducting a personal inquiry into the question of how the law was administered by his own sheriffs. Always dressed for travel (he soon became known as 'Curtmantle' because he favoured a short cloak that was especially well suited to horseback-riding), seldom wearing gloves except when hawking, he was perpetually on the move. One of his familiars, Peter of Blois, was later to write some highly amusing letters concerning the atmosphere of bustle and commotion which invariably surrounded the king. Henry kept his companions on tenterhooks: they could never be certain where tomorrow would find them. 'If the king has spoken of making an early start for such-and-such a town, then for once in a way he is bound to lie abed till noon. If he proclaims to all and sundry that he proposes to remain in Oxford, say, for several days, be sure that he will leave town at the crack of dawn.' And Peter goes on to describe how the members of the royal party would doze whole mornings away in the castle courtyard, with their horses saddled up and the wagons hitched in readiness, until such time as the familiar figure emerged in his short mantle, long boots and draped hood. The sudden appearance of Henry would unleash a positive frenzy of activity, with the squires leading out the king's horse, the drivers grabbing their reins and the stableboys hurrying noisily from group to group. Alternatively Henry would rise at first cock-crow and plunge the entire household into a whirl; torches would suddenly flare in the dark as the servants scuffled about rousing his companions from slumber; a medley of sounds would ascend from the courtyard, where the grooms were assembling the horses after giving their coats a swift comb.

Henry was so passionately addicted to power that he would busy himself with affairs of state from morning to night, 'Except when riding a horse or eating a meal, he never sits,' records Peter of Blois. 'There are times when he rides four or five times the distance which most men cover in a day.' And as time went by, he found it harder and harder to keep still; even at Mass he could not help getting up at intervals and pacing about. He never stopped moving except when asleep—and he was seldom asleep. As Peter of Blois emphasizes: 'While other kings are in their palaces, resting their limbs, he is able to surprise and disconcert his foes and keep a sharp eye on everything.' And indeed, in all the campaigns which he had conducted in the past three years Henry had persistently stolen a march on the enemy and caught him unawares. Similar methods had brought rewards in more peaceful undertakings. He would arrive unannounced in one or other of the royal cities, demand to see the tax-receipts (taxes were falling behind), summon the sheriff at some unwonted hour and carry out the most stringent personal checks. To make up for these ways, he cultivated popularity by listening with unfailing patience to anyone who had a complaint to lay before him. Sometimes he would rein in his horse and let the poor and lowly gather round. On these occasions he was always gracious and winning.

Such zeal could only delight Eleanor, who had probably found life dull at her first husband's side. Louis had been hardworking too, but much slower, and he had always inclined towards meditation rather than action. Nothing could have been further removed from the almost patriarchal pattern of existence in the irreproachably dull Cité Palace than the methodicism which Henry—breathing new life into the institutions established by his grandfather, Henry Beauclerk, and his Norman ancestors—was applying to England. The kingdom which Henry had acquired was centralized to a far greater degree than Louis's, deriving from the Normans—those born administrators—the forms and practices which had already stood the test of time in their contintental fief. A biannual ceremony, occurring at Easter and Michaelmas, was emblematic of this willingness to systematize which made kings of England more 'modern' than kings of France, even though the latter were their overlords on the mainland of Europe. This ceremony was the meeting of the Exchequer. Such was the name given to the rendering of accounts in either London or Winchester, where a host of minor officials were summoned to appear before a kind of financial tribunal made up of the king's chief vassals, civil and ecclesiastic. The scene was enacted in a large hall containing a

[handwritten margin note: Exchequer meets at Easter & Michaelmas "given to rendering of accounts"]

Meeting of the Exchequer, Easter & Michaelmas

long table covered with a black-and-white chequered cloth which gave it the appearance of a huge chessboard. The most prominent members sat in chairs at the top end of the table. Most of them, it was whispered, were quite incapable of interpreting the operations carried out in their presence—eyes they had, and saw not; they had ears and heard not. However, they looked on as the treasurer and his clerk, assisted by two chamberlains and two knights, used tally-sticks to reckon the sums received and arranged the counters on the exchequer-table. The table was divided into even columns, and depending on where it was placed a counter could represent anything from a penny to ten thousand pounds. In this way the accounts rendered by the sheriffs were checked, and once the check had been completed by the senior officers of the realm—chancellor, justiciar, constable, marshal—the money was put away in coffers while an army of clerks industriously transcribed the results on rolls of parchment. The might of England was founded on the habit of strict accountancy as well as on the close supervision of the great barons. The latter certainly had rebellious instincts, but as a rule they were held in check by the thought of their castles and estates across the Channel in Normandy, which lay in the tireless grasp of old Queen Matilda.

Eleanor can only have enjoyed the solid, well-wrought structure of the English monarchy. And she shared in its administration, issuing official documents either in her own right or on behalf of the king. Indeed, on several occasions she and Henry specifically divided their responsibilities: she would stay in England while he was away in Normandy; or else she would preside in Anjou or Poitiers or Bordeaux while he inspected his island possessions. Some of the bills she issued were drawn up in the name of the queen and the justiciar (the post of justiciar was of a seniority equalled only by that of chancellor, and at the time it was held by Richard de Luci); others, however, bore her name alone. She dispensed justice, and her rulings—drawn up by a chancellor called Master Matthew, probably Henry's tutor as a boy—were of a tone which brooked no reply. When, for instance, the monks of Reading complained of being robbed of some of their lands she dictated the following letter for delivery to the viscount of London, a certain John Fitz-Ralph: 'I have received a complaint from the monks of Reading to the effect that they have been unjustly dis-possessed of certain lands in London, which were bestowed on them by Richard Fitz-B. when he became a monk . . . I command you to look into this without delay and, should it be true, to ensure that these lands are returned to the monks without delay so that in future I shall hear no more complaints about deficiencies in law and justice; I will not tolerate their being unjustly deprived of anything that belongs to them. Greetings.'

Another time, the abbot of Abingdon complained that certain services owing to him had not been performed—presumably this was a quarrel about statute labour. Eleanor dealt with the matter in these terms: 'To the knights and men holding lands and tenures from Abingdon Abbey, greetings. I command that in all equity and without delay you provide Vauquelin, abbot of Abingdon, with those same services which your ancestors provided in the days of King Henry, grandfather of our sovereign lord; and if you do not do so, then the king's justice and my own will make you do so.'

As always in those days, her duties as sovereign were manifold. At Henry's side she meted out judgment at the official courts which were held every year, usually at Christmas, in one or other of their cities; often Westminster was chosen, but they were also held in Bordeaux, Cherbourg, Falaise or Bayeux. Also she would carefully supervise certain accounts—those of Oxford market, for instance, or of the tin-mines (from which the king was entitled to a due), or of a mill which she owned in Woodstock, and so on.

These accounts have survived to this day, in the shape of the priceless Pipe Rolls lovingly preserved in the Public Record Office, London. They provide, in addition, many invaluable hints as to the nature of the queen's expenditure, invaluable because they are direct pointers to her tastes and personality. Often the records merely show that a certain sum was paid for what is referred to, with exasperating imprecision, as the queen's *corredium*—a vague term which might be translated as 'general requisites'. This could apply to food for heself and her retinue; but it could equally well apply to the acquisition of pack-horses, harnesses, etc. Occasionally this *corredium* is itemized in terms such as wine or flour, but there are times when the cataloguing is more specific. For instance, one of the earliest accounts to refer to the queen by name makes particular mention of a purchase of 'oil for her lamps'. The same item reappears several times in the rolls covering her reign. Eleanor was clearly horrified by the general reliance on candles in England—tallow dips in poor homes, wax candles in wealthy ones; hence her eagerness to import oil from the civilized south, so that she could once more enjoy the soft, twinkling light which brought no unpleasant smells. Similarly, purchases of wine are often associated with the queen herself. No daughter of Aquitaine was ever likely to reconcile herself to beer. 'Cervisia can never hope to beat wine'—it was a common saying in those days. It was probably owing to her influence that the wine merchants of Guyenne made, from that time forward, such frequent trips to English harbours for the greater profit of the Bordeaux wine-growers and the greater enjoyment of the islanders. Calculations reveal that in thirteenth-century England more wine was consumed per head of population than is consumed there today.

Another of her early purchases was linen, for making table-cloths; likewise brass bowls, cushions, tapestries . . . she must have transformed the old royal residences, making them more comfortable and pleasing to the eye. At the time of their accession, the palace of Westminster was in such a dilapidated condition that she and Henry were unable to move in; so their first Christmas court, beginning a few days later, had to be held in another royal residence, Bermondsey. Today the name is still applied to the area of London directly across the river from the Tower, sprawling beside London Bridge, which was for a long time the only link between the north and south banks of the Thames. Eleanor was clearly impatient for her own court to wine and dine in the style for which she had yearned ever since her visit to Constantinople. We know that she imported gold for her plate and received regular shipments of the spices which were so enthusiastically employed for seasoning: pepper, caraway, cinnamon, almonds. These last were used in the baking of succulent pastries, and milk of almonds was also highly thought of as an aid to beauty. Eleanor ordered plenty of incense too, for burning in her chapel and staving off the smells which hugged the ground in time of fog.

What did she make of England? How did her southern temperament respond to this kingdom, acquired after such a strenuous battle against wind and rain? Did her mind turn sadly to the smiling landscapes beside the Garonne or even along the Seine? Sadness was not in her nature, whereas the urge to rule was always strong in her and may have been attended by an unformulated desire to even things up; after all, she had given away one crown without being altogether certain of securing another. As the whole course of her life attests, she was never a woman to shrink from difficulties that had to be faced. On the contrary, she may even—like Henry Plantagenet—have taken pride in the fact that she had triumphed over storms. And from the calm of Bermondsey, where she spent the winter awaiting the birth of young Henry, she must have relished the promise of richness and power held out by all the trading activity on the river around London Bridge, where the slow, cumbersome Flemish ships were piled high with bales of wool and untrimmed fleeces, and where barks took on tin ore and set sail along the ancient routes leading to the cities of the Mediterranean. The banks of the Thames, with their yards and warehouses, smelt of tar and dried fish. How different from the harbour at Bordeaux, which received costly and delicate wares from the east: spices, scents, rich fabrics . . . But the English traders were of an adventurous spirit, and even in those days some of them were not afraid to venture as far as Asia Minor. England was exactly the opposite of Guyenne: sparsely wooded, with plenty of sheep and plenty of mines but only a poor offering of orchards and vineyards. Thus her territories complemented one another and when, after the birth of Henry, she was free to savour the delights of the English spring among the rich green hills of Surrey, its deep lanes alive with birdsong, she must have had high hopes of this kingdom which harboured so many and such varied riches, all the way from Scotland in the north to the Pyrenees in the south.

And the local inhabitants probably appealed to her as well. The English of that day had the reputation of being good company, drinkers and dreamers. Yet something must have been missing. Their women were very beautiful, but the men had not yet learned the courtly ways which had long ago transformed life in Poitou. There were some splendid story-tellers among them, but they were still quite ignorant of the troubadours and the love-lyric, of the poetic convention of paying homage to the Lady, of *Fin Amor* and its subtle laws. English barons were renowned for their valour and undaunted in the face of the most perilous exploits, but if they were ever to resemble the Alexander visualized by the poets in the queen's entourage they would first have to learn to 'speak to ladies courteously of love'. The possession of this delicate skill separated the true knight from the mere brawler, and Eleanor was confident that she could instil it anywhere—even by the foggy Thames.

XI

E s'eu sai ren dir ni faire
Ilh n'aja.l grat, que sciensa
M'a donat, e conoissensa,
Per qu'eu suis gais echantaire
E tot quan fauc d'avinen
Ai del sue bel cors plazen.

If I know how to turn a rhyme
It's due to her; she can instil
Such knowledge and bestow such skill,
I carol blithely all the time;
And what I have of wit and grace
Comes from her lovely form and face.

PEIRE VIDAL

IF EVER A MAN knew how to 'speak to ladies courteously of love',
it was Bernard de Ventadour. His is a high-sounding name, but it
would be quite wrong to imagine some great noble or even the
variety of petty knight in which Poitou and Gascony abounded; for
in those two provinces the castles were seldom more than ten
miles apart, so that a claim to nobility could be entered even by
someone with an income not much higher than that of a middling
cultivator of land in our own day. And indeed the inclusion of
'de' or 'of' in a name has never signified nobility, least of all in the
Middle Ages when it simply indicated the town or district from
which a person came. Bernard de Ventadour was certainly born in
Ventadour Castle, but his father was most likely a mere serf and
his mother was an 'oven-woman'—in other words she was employed in the bakehouse of the lords of Ventadour. Their estate
was an excellent background for a poet. One count of Ventadour
(they were all called Eble, the name being handed down from
father to son) became known as 'The Singer'; he was a contemporary of William of Aquitaine, but fate was less kind to him—none

111

of his poems has survived. However, his successors inherited his feeling for the poetry of courtly love, if not his creative impulse, and one after another they extended a welcome to such fashionable troubadours as Bertrand de Born and Bernard Marti. Nor were their wives any less eager to entertain poets: one was destined to become a poet herself and exchange *coblas* with the troubadour Guy d'Ussel. This was the celebrated Marie of Turenne, wife of Eble V, one of the *tres de Torena*, three sisters who—according to Bertrand de Born—had between them monopolized all earthly beauty.

In these urbane and cultivated surroundings, young Bernard could not fail to give early proof of his poetic gifts, and his humble station did not debar him from the close circle surrounding the count and countess—Eble III and his wife, Alaïz of Montpellier. Like any other troubadour, he addressed his verses to the chatelaine, the Lady; they were splendid verses, for Bernard was undoubtedly the greatest of all the twelfth-century lyric poets writing in the language of western France, and they burned with loving ardour. Was this ardour purely literary? Whatever the answer, the count took umbrage and one fine day Bernard was obliged to leave his native Limousin. This was at about the time of Eleanor's second marriage. By then he was a troubadour of considerable reputation, perhaps the most stirring apostle of the courtly ideal. He sang of nothing but love and, like Marcabru and others, he acknowledged only *Fin Amor* in his verses—not physical passion but the courtly love which prompts the lover to reach beyond himself and attain that ennobling joy to which he is roused exclusively by the sight or memory of the Lady.

Where was he to make for after leaving Ventadour? Eleanor had just returned to Poitiers. No poet could ask for a more exalted Lady than this queen of France who had become, by marriage, 'queen of the Normans'; and she, on her side, must have extended an eager welcome to a man who did not hesitate to proclaim himself the most gifted of the troubadours. Hereafter—and to this practice we owe some of the most beautiful *chansons* in all Provençal poetry— Bernard addressed all his verses to the woman who was indeed establishing herself as the most illustrious Lady of the West, to this queen of England who gave rise, simultaneously, to such a rich harvest of romances and poems. Was it really she whose praises he sang when he wrote of '*Mos Aziman*—my Magnet'? The troubadours preferred to disguise the identity of the Lady to whom they were paying homage by the use of a *senhal*, a sobriquet—for discretion was an inseparable part of courtliness. The name of one's Lady must not be betrayed to the reader; rather it must remain buried like a treasure in the poet's heart. Eleanor was certainly magnetic enough; a few of the *chansons* addressed to the bearer of this mysterious *senhal* suggest that the poet was detained in England at the time, on the king's service, and thereby separated from his Lady, who was 'beyond the Norman region, across the wild, deep sea'. Her absence makes him sigh and exclaim: 'Dear God, why am I not a swallow!'

Can it be that Henry, like Eble of Ventadour before him, became somewhat nettled by the expressions of homage which the troubadour laid before the queen? Was this why he took Bernard to England—because he wanted to put the Channel between them? Such at least was the story put about by the poet's thirteenth-century biographer, Uc of Saint-Circ.

Bernard was certainly a trifle bold at times in the way he addressed '*Mos Aziman*'. In one of his *chansons* he entreats that she shall bid him come to her chamber ('where one disrobes'). True, he immediately goes on to say that he is merely hoping that she will allow him to abase himself before her and take off her shoe. But this somewhat questionable touch of humour may not have been to the taste of the proud and assertive prince.

Bernard was a man never out of love; Eleanor, to a greater degree than any other woman, embodied the spirit of the Lady, the bringer of joy. Are there really grounds for assuming that his passionate verses were anything more than the conventional expression of the type of feeling which was then demanded of a poet? We shall never know the truth, but we may wonder whether even the protagonists themselves could have said for certain whether they were in the grip of a true and intense love or trifling with one another in a most delightful way.

What is *not* in doubt, from either the historical or the literary point of view, is that the poems of Bernard de Ventadour contain echoes of the Celtic past. He likens himself to Tristan, 'who suffered many sorrows for Iseult the Fair'.

113

Tristan and Iseult—they are among the small handful of names which have survived the long centuries of neglect and been handed down to us from feudal times. Their appearance in the work of Bernard de Ventadour is indicative of the forces of change which were at work in literature during Eleanor's reign. Her coronation as queen of England took her into that 'Breton' world to which her mind had first been opened years ago by the tales of Bledhri, Celtic bard at her father's court, for did not her new realm include distant Cornwall, that county lashed by wind and sea which had been the setting of King Arthur's exploits? And indeed, it was one of her husband's supporters against Stephen of Blois (Renaud of Cornwall, a bastard son of Henry Beauclerk) who now, in the middle of the twelfth century, set about building Tintagel Castle. Relics of that castle still survive: its gaping arches and walls of burnished steel are an imposing spectacle on the Cornish coastline, which is as sheer and wild as anyone could ask. The principal structure discernible today must have been a tall keep connected to the outer walls by means of a drawbridge; now it can be reached only by scaling a precipitous flight of steps hewn in the cliff. On misty days these ruins—seemingly an integral part of the rocks, which in turn have been rough-hewn by the storms of the ages— are disquieting. But in a region where clouds gather and disperse with the same rapidity, a shaft of sunlight on the grass-grown slopes of the promontory is enough to re-establish the castle's claim to be the setting of the familiar old legends.

Even before Renaud's walls went up, Tintagel was generally thought of as the birthplace of King Arthur: it was, reputedly, in the castle of Tintagel that he held court and assembled his knights at the famous Round Table which accorded neither precedence nor place of honour.

Although no trace of an earlier castle has come to light on the promontory, the remains of an ancient monastery have been unearthed. These, dating back to the Celtic era (5th–9th century), show that Tintagel was once a remote and secluded place of worship, like many another in Wales and Ireland, which an imaginative populace invested with the legends put about by the poets and story-tellers.

During the years when Matilda Empress was still trying to wrest her kingdom from Stephen of Blois, these legends began to assume an unexpectedly prominent role in literature; by a direct reversal of what might seem the logical process, they were passing from folklore into history. This was mainly due to the industry and inventive powers of a Welshman, Geoffrey of Monmouth, perhaps the most weird and wonderful historian of all time. Geoffrey's history of the kings of Britain—*Historia Regium Britanniæ*—contained the first clear compilation of the fantastic assortment of adventures attributed to King Arthur.

For the historian, Arthur remains as intangible a figure as, say, Roland; yet his fame outshines even that of Charlemagne. And this fame was assured in a host of poetic works written during Eleanor's era, and in her entourage. As a result of the extraordinary osmosis which was to occur between the great themes of chivalry (*matière de Bretagne*) and courtly love, Arthur and his knights were destined for immortality; and this transmutation was the literary marvel of the twelfth century. The Arthurian legend was at the root of so many developments—not least the blossoming of the entirely new genre of the romance, which was to enjoy such a long and illustrious future. For the mood of the age is expressed in the romance which tells of chivalry, just as it is blazoned upon the wonderful tympana and frescoes and capitals in Romanesque cathedrals. And each and every attempt to trace the origin of this fusion between the elements of chivalry, courtly love and Celtic myth leads one back to the court of Eleanor. It was the poets directly associated with her who spread the fame not only of Tristan and Iseult, but of Perceval and Lancelot, King Arthur and Morgan le Fay, Queen Guinevere and Merlin the Magician.

There was Marie of France, who may have been a natural child of Geoffrey Plantagenet and who became abbess of Shaftesbury. An even more eminent example is Chrétien de Troyes, who brought genius to the writing of romances and whose work was subsequently imitated in every country of the West. And in addition there were all those writers who have remained more or less unknown to the general public in our own day, for lack of any intellectual curiosity as to what might have preceded the immoderately celebrated 'Renaissance'. In the forefront of these was Wace of Jersey, an Anglo-Norman poet who was 'reading-clerk'

115

(reader) at the English court in Eleanor's day and whose *Roman de Brut* was substantially a verse rendering of Geoffrey of Monmouth's history, though he inflected it with delicate nuances learned from Bernard de Ventadour and his disciples; in his version, the violent passions of Celtic mythology were softened to courtly love. Nor ought we to forget the Bérouls and Thomases and the countless anonymous bards who sang of Tristan's love and sorrow, all of them showing a greater or smaller degree of Anglo-Norman influence.

Eleanor's own influence on literature extended further. Benoît de Sainte-Maure dedicated his *Roman de Troie* to the woman whom he calls 'Rich Lady of Rich King'; the classical subject-matter of the poem is totally transformed, becoming a mere excuse for parading knights and ladies. Philip de Thaon pays tribute to Eleanor in some lines at the beginning of his *Bestiaire*, that quintessentially 'romanesque' work in which the animal world becomes a 'forest of symbols'; the whole universe is shown as one vast riddle, and by reading between the lines one can discern the history of man and his redemption. Allusions to the story of Eleanor's own life have even been read into *Girart de Roussillon*, an epic poem written at about the time of her second marriage; in this work a king, allegedly recognizable as her first husband, exclaims with a sigh: 'O Queen, how often have you caught me in your toils!'

But it is first and foremost for spreading the legends associated with Arthur, and investing them with the ideals of courtly love, that Eleanor and those about her deserve the gratitude of anyone who has ever responded to the intense poetic power contained in such themes as those of Tristan and the quest for the Grail.

Whether or not her husband took offence at the warm feelings expressed by Bernard de Ventadour, he certainly contributed to the Arthurian revival; no doubt it occurred to him that some of Arthur's glory might rub off on to himself. And indeed the latter, in the hands of Geoffrey of Monmouth, had become an almost messianic figure. The story was that, after beating the Saxons and Gauls and Vikings and occasioning fear and alarm even in imperial Rome, Arthur had vanished from human sight during the struggle against his nephew Mordred; one day he would reappear in response to a signal from Merlin, that stage-manager of the history of the world, and win back his native land with the help of the last Bretons, who had taken refuge in Armorica. Out of these tales, with their all-wise astrologers, fiery kings and peerlessly beautiful women for ever feasting in enchanted castles or watching prodigious tournaments, arose the expectations of some great king who would restore Britain to the splendour which had been hers before the Roman invasion, by establishing peace in the land and instilling the virtues of chivalry. A great king ... Henry might be practical and down-to-earth, but at this point he could not fail to lend an ear to the legend. An enthusiastic student of history, he ordered excavations to be made in the vicinity of Glastonbury, where there was a royal abbey popularly identified with Avalon, resting-place of King Arthur. Sure enough it turned out to be an ancient Celtic site, and some prehistoric tombs were also discovered there. The rumour spread that Arthur's sword, Excalibur, had been found in the very tomb where he and Queen Guinevere were buried side by side. The legends surrounding Arthur's reign, and deriving from the mythical figure of Merlin the enchanter, gradually took root in this venerable soil; even today it is a shrine for tourists, who pour in to gaze at the ruined side-chapels and imposing lengths of wall (the abbey was destroyed at the time of the Reformation). It was here, allegedly, that Joseph of Arimathaea first initiated the Celts into the Christian faith, planting a thornbush which was destined to blossom twice a year, at Christmas and Easter. Here too, concealed from all eyes, or so the story ran, was the famous vessel from which Christ had drunk at the Last Supper and in which had been caught a few drops of the blood which He had shed on the Cross.

Thus the soil on which the old abbey stood nourished the idea which took root throughout the West that—impelled by that love for their Lady which had now turned into an almost mystical feeling—knights would roam the world in quest of adventure, eager to brave those ordeals which would eventually lead them to the Holy Grail.

Glastonbury identified with Avalon, resting place of K Arthur

117

XII

Et qui le voir dire an voldroit,
Des se retient devers le droit,
Et Des et droiz a un se tienent;
Et quant il devers moi s'an vienent,
Donc ai je meillor conpagnie,
Que tu n'as, et meillor aïe.

And whosoe'er the truth would say
Must grant that God inclines alway
To what is just, for just is He;
When God and justice join with me,
Then better company have I
Than you can boast, and aid thereby.

CHRETIEN DE TROYES

THERE WAS A RARE MAGNIFICENCE about the procession filing across the larger of the bridges leading to the Ile de la Cité on that June day in 1158. People had congregated from all over Paris to watch it go by, and each successive group was greeted with cries of wonder. First came those on foot: two hundred and fifty pages and squires, in squads of sixteen, marching to the tune of English or Welsh songs. After these came the hunting-train: kennel-lads leashing in the hounds, falconers bearing splendid birds on their leather-gloved forearms—not only falcons but goshawks and sparrow-hawks, all carefully jessed and hooded. Then the heavy wagons with stout leather awnings, their iron wheels rumbling over the cobbles; each wagon was drawn by five horses, led by an impeccably attired groom with an enormous mastiff trotting beside him, large and powerful enough to overwhelm a bear. The leading wagon—sumptuously decorated, with gilt axles and scarlet hangings—obviously contained the portable chapel, while the last two wagons were open and loaded with barrels of beer.

After the wagons came a dozen pack-mules, each with a chest

118

roped to either side and a long-tailed monkey gambolling in between. These chests contained the gold and silver plate which was brought out at every halting-place: spoons, ewers, goblets. The ostlers holding the mules by the halter were all dressed identically, in the livery of the king of England. Next came the men-at-arms, carrying shields and leading the horses ridden by the various dignitaries: clerics, knights, officers of the royal household and—last of all, surrounded by a few familiars—the king of England's chancellor, Thomas Becket.

Thomas Becket

Never in living memory had an envoy brought such a party with him, and the procession was talked about long after the trumpets of the heralds had faded.

Henry and Eleanor had decided to treat with the king of France; and the chancellor, to whom they were leaving the negotiations, had, as always, laid the foundation's for total success. Thomas Becket was a great believer in success and in the task well done, and when the nature of the task tallied with his personal inclinations, which were towards outward show and munificence, he had no equal. Henry was well aware of the fact and congratulated himself daily on his good fortune in having appointed as chancellor, soon after his coronation, this son of an ordinary London burgher, a Norman who had been brought to his notice by Theobald, archbishop of Canterbury. But the influence exerted over her husband by a man fifteen years his senior was not altogether welcome to Eleanor. She felt a sort of jealous rivalry towards him: a wife seldom warms to her husband's best friend, and it was not long before the chancellor became the king's best friend. She had to resign herself to sharing a power over Henry which she would have preferred to exercise alone. Still, she could not help admiring his efficiency and zeal, qualities which did not prevent him from being a man of style, even of grandeur. When Thomas was entrusted with the task of restoring the palace of Westminster, the commission—which would have taken anyone else several years—took him fifty days, from Easter to Whitsun. Craftsmen of every guild worked side by side on the scaffolding, making such a din and shout that it was like the tower of Babel.

His present task was to bedazzle the king of France and impress upon him that his vassal for Normandy, Anjou, Poitou and

119

Guyenne was magnanimously going to a great deal of trouble for the sake of assuring peace between the two houses. And Thomas had not missed a trick in his efforts to spellbind the ordinary people of France as he journeyed down from Normandy to Paris. Throughout his visit he was openhanded in the extreme, showering gifts upon the king and those about him, providing good English beer for the lower classes who came to gape at the Temple buildings, where he and his retinue were officially lodged, buying up all the meat, fish and bread that were available in the markets outside Paris—for the king had been careful to warn him that he could not revictual his entourage in the city itself—and instructing his buyers not to haggle but to pay generous prices.

This opulent cavalcade produced the desired effect. By the time he returned to Normandy, Becket had secured a promise from Louis that his daughter Marguerite, still only a six-months-old baby, would marry the king of England's son, Henry.

For the king of France had likewise married again. In 1154 he had resolved to make the pilgrimage to the shrine of St James, at Compostela. His journey took him through Eleanor's domain and he set out without seeking his vassal's permission; but it would have been in bad taste for her to protest and she had carefully refrained from doing so. On his return he had announced his intention of marrying Constance, daughter of the king of Castile.

Two years after the wedding, Constance was with child. It was a time of keen anticipation for the royal house of France, since Louis still had no heirs apart from Eleanor's daughters, Marie and Alix. But heaven chose to send him another daughter—little Marguerite. It is not easy for us to realize how great a value used to be placed upon a male heir, when today a queen can govern without ever, or hardly ever, needing to step outside her own palace. In Eleanor's time, the administration of a fief or kingdom required that the ruler should maintain and administer the law in person; he had to be capable of wielding a sword, donning a coat of mail and riding at the head of his troops whenever a vassal needed to be punished for looting or brought to heel after refusing to do homage. Hence the disadvantageous position of any fief which had a girl for heir: she had only to pick an incompetent husband, and her subjects' worst fears were liable to be realized. Ample demon-

120

stration of this truth was shortly to be given in the kingdom of Jerusalem. Sybil, who inherited the throne, capriciously disregarded the advice of her barons and married—for his looks, presumably—the worthless Guy of Lusignan, one of Eleanor's vassals. This afterwards resulted in the loss of the Holy City, which had been reconquered at the cost of so much blood, sweat and tears.

So Louis was distressed to find himself with another daughter. How bitter the poor man must have been at the news that Eleanor had produced a son so soon after marrying Henry, to be followed not long afterwards by a second and third. And by the time Becket set out on his mission, Eleanor was pregnant again. In September, Louis was informed that she had given birth to yet another son— Geoffrey. For all his piety, he can hardly have failed to reflect that God was on the Angevin's side and no mistake!

Indeed, Henry and Eleanor seemed unable to do anything wrong. When, two years earlier, they had jointly presided over a plenary court in Bordeaux, their authority had been recognized without any cavilling on the part of the habitually truculent vassals of the duchy of Aquitaine; and in the spring of the present year—at Easter 1158—a second coronation service, even more solemn than the one at Westminster, had been held at Worcester before the assembled nobles of England and Wales. Henry was on his way to becoming the most powerful king in all the West. One after another, the last adherents of the house of Blois were surrendering their castles and paying tribute; King Malcolm of Scotland had held back at first, but now even he had finally done homage for his estates in England. The Welsh barons, always liable to be swept away by a spirit of rebellion, had been promptly brought to their senses. Henry, whose gifts as an administrator were on a par with his military skill, had just ordered the minting of a new coinage, stronger and sounder than any which had been known up to that time; this inspired confidence in the merchants of the City of London, who could be certain from now on that they really *were* being paid in hard cash. His fame spread far beyond his own borders: when Thierry of Alsace, count of Flanders, set out for the Holy Land, he first entrusted his lands and his young son to the king's safekeeping.

Eleanor continued to play a full part in their joint affairs. Whenever his duties kept him in the county of Anjou or the duchy of Normandy, she was queen of England; as soon as he was recalled, she reverted to being duchess of Aquitaine and countess of Poitou. It was exactly the life she had longed for: active, fruitful, victorious. And that summer of 1158, which had opened with a diplomatic success, was to be marked by a further triumph. Henry's troublesome brother Geoffrey had at long last found an outlet for his ambition; the Bretons, having driven out their overlord, had appealed to him—and Geoffrey had accordingly taken possession of the duchy of Brittany. But scarcely had the poor man moved to Nantes and begun to wield power, as he had always dreamed of doing, than death claimed him. This event, on July 26th, 1158, gave Henry an excuse to ask the king of France for the title of seneschal of Brittany which, he claimed, had always been borne by his forefathers. Louis bestowed it, in a mood of resignation. What else could he do? The estates of his mighty vassal lay between the royal domain and this remote, unfamiliar region which was utterly alien to the court of France in customs, language and history. So Henry and Eleanor were now able to talk as masters of the whole western side of his kingdom.

This series of events served to confirm the prospects opened up by Becket's mission to Paris. Henry and Eleanor must surely have exchanged a smile of complicity whenever they talked in private about the kingdom of France. Now they could negotiate as equals with the man who was still their 'overlord' on the mainland of Europe. And perhaps some day both crowns, those of England and France, might be conferred on young Henry, their son, now betrothed to Princess Marguerite. This would certainly appear to have been Eleanor's dominant ambition. She may have chosen to step down from the French throne, but she had never resigned herself to surrendering it for good and all. And now, six years after the separation at Beaugency, she and her new husband were in a position to draft a long-term policy. The aim of that policy was nothing less than the acquisition of the kingdom of France.

Marguerite's betrothal to Henry seemed to make the union of the two crowns a foregone conclusion. Thus, by marrying the Plantagenet, Eleanor would have given birth to a new empire; the whole of western Europe would be in the hands of a dynasty with an assured future, stemming from Aquitaine and taking over where the Capetians left off.

What obstacles were there to these grandiose dreams? None save the presence of Eleanor's own daughters, Marie and Alix, who took precedence through age over little Marguerite. In early infancy (at the time of the departure for the Holy Land, when she was only two) Marie had been betrothed to Count Henry of Champagne—son of Count Theobald, whom Eleanor had defied when she was still queen of France. In the meantime, Alix had likewise been betrothed to a prince of the house of Champagne: Henry's brother, Theobald of Blois, the young man who had audaciously plotted to kidnap Eleanor while she was journeying through his estates. By strengthening his ties with the house of Blois-Champagne, the king of France was doubtless hoping to thwart the ambitions of the Angevins. It would not be the first time that Capetian wariness had maintained peace between the two rival powers. But on this occasion the ultimate future of the kingdom itself was at stake. Would it fall into the hands of a count of Champagne, or of the Angevin who was already master of England and a considerable area of France? Would the next king to rule in Paris come from east or west of the royal domain?

As Henry and Eleanor saw it, there could be little doubt as to the answer. Between them, they were quite capable of checkmating the rival group; the important thing was to deploy their pawns carefully, in preparation for the final victory. And the key-piece in their game was obviously little Marguerite. The customs of the time required that she be brought up as a member of her future husband's family. Some time after Becket's departure, therefore, the king of France received a personal visit from the king of England: he had come to collect his future daughter-in-law, still in swaddling-clothes. Louis made it a condition that she should not be brought up by Eleanor. This came as no surprise to the queen, who had resolved in advance to agree to whatever concessions were demanded of her. It was mutually decided that the child should be placed in the care of a knight who fully satisfied the requirements of both parties: Robert of Newburgh, a man of unimpeachable character and piety. He agreed to look after the girl,

123

though it meant postponing his intention of becoming a monk and entering the abbey of Bec.

A few weeks later, Louis announced that he had decided to make a pilgrimage to Mont-Saint-Michel. Not only did Henry agree to his request for free passage through Normandy: he extended an eager welcome to his overlord, who was given ample opportunity to set his mind at rest as to how his daughter was being looked after. And this was not all. Now that a definite mood of conciliation was abroad, Henry allowed Louis to talk him into making peace with his traditional enemies, the counts of Blois-Champagne. A settlement was reached by exchanging a few castles along their respective borders.

Thus the year 1158 saw the clearing-up of ancient quarrels and the emergence of a practical policy. In Cherbourg, where they held their Christmas court, Henry and Eleanor could look back in contentment on the long road which they had travelled since that day at Barfleur, four years earlier, when they had braved the stormy sea together so that they might at last take possession of their new kingdom. Now they were firmly in control of their possessions on either side of the Channel; they were surrounded by their vassals, some from England in the north, others from Poitou in the south; and their four children were the embodiment of four strong hopes for the future. The eldest, Henry, would one day be king of England —and of France too, perhaps. In Richard were vested the aspirations which Eleanor had once nourished for William, her firstborn; already he was looked upon as count of Poitiers. As for Geoffrey, why should he not inherit the fief of Brittany from the uncle whose name he bore? And only the highest-born could entertain ambitions of marrying little Matilda.

Eleanor's will appears to have triumphed in all that the royal couple had planned and achieved during those years of glory; everything which had been fulfilled, or even attempted, was in accord with her personal views. As soon as England was securely in their grasp, they had both turned their eyes towards her domain. Quite apart from his manœuvres concerning the French crown, Henry Plantagenet had in this same year (1158) swooped as far south as Limousin for the purpose of bringing to heel Viscount Guy of Thouars, who for a long time had insolently asserted his independence from his overlords, the counts of Poitou. Yet, for all the regal magnificence with which he held court to his own vassals, he had been forced to yield. His reputedly impregnable castle had been captured in three days.

And now once again, as in the early years of her marriage to the king of France, Eleanor was directing ambitious glances at Toulouse. She had never renounced her claim to the province, which had formerly belonged to her grandmother, Philippa. With the pressure on the borders of Anjou and Normandy eased by Henry's peace settlement with the house of Blois-Champagne, was the time not ripe for a reassertion of her rights? The present count of Toulouse, Raymond V, was a poor specimen, unscrupulously trying to enlarge his feudal area at the expense of Provence. If only he could be made to accept the overlordship of the dukes of Aquitaine, they would enjoy free access to the Mediterranean and hence to the East, which had cast so strong a spell over Eleanor. The only difficulty lay in the fact that Raymond had married the king of France's sister, and nothing must be done at this early juncture to jeopardize an alliance which held out such dazzling prospects for the Plantagenet heir. On the other hand everybody was aware that Raymond misused poor Constance of France in the most despicable way, and it was debatable whether Louis would be much concerned to defend his disagreeable vassal and brother-in-law. The latter saw a veritable league assembling in opposition to him. The count of Barcelona, the count of Montpellier, the viscountess of Narbonne (the famous Ermengarde, a beauty constantly celebrated by the troubadours): all these were attempting to shake off an overlordship which was a sheer burden to them. Henry and Eleanor had picked a favourable moment.

In January 1159 they set out from Normandy together to make a round of visits in Aquitaine. England was sufficiently peaceful to be left in the hands of the king's justiciar, the earl of Leicester. At Blaye the sovereigns met the count of Barcelona, Raymond-Berengar V; there was talk of betrothing his daughter, Berengaria, to young Richard; at all events it emerged that the house of Barcelona had grounds for complaint against the house of Toulouse and was prepared to join in the fight. Support could also be relied on from the viscount of Carcassonne, Raymond Trencavel, who was likewise hostile towards the count of Toulouse.

All these attendant circumstances weighed in favour of Eleanor's schemes. So Henry proceeded to levy a war-tax in England and Normandy: in Normandy he demanded sixty sous of every knight, and in England the amount rose to two marks. The ease with which the sums were raised must have afforded him considerable pride and satisfaction: his highly organized administrative system was certainly proving effective. The funds that were gathered in enabled him to assemble a strong army of mercenaries. By now Henry had sufficient experience of war not to rely on the contingents supplied by his vassals; such troops were under no obligation to give more than forty days' service a year and might well desert half-way through the campaign. Toulouse was a long way off, and the siege might take a considerable time.

On reaching Poitiers, he sent orders to all his senior vassals that they and their forces were to rally to him on Midsummer Day, June 24th. However, before finally committing himself he thought it wise to seek an audience of the king of France. They had two discussions, the first in Tours, the second at Heudicourt in Normandy. And on both occasions Henry was taken aback by the degree of stubbornness shown by this man whom he had thought of as weak and retiring. Louis announced that he would most certainly defend the count of Toulouse against any act of aggression: quite apart from being his brother-in-law, the count was his vassal, and as such entitled to royal protection; no power on earth would deter the king from doing all in his capacity to maintain justice within his borders.

Henry was discovering a side to Louis's nature which had hitherto been entirely concealed from him. Until now he had known him solely as Eleanor's former husband—a gullible man, lacking in self-confidence and easily discouraged, in contrast to whom he had fancied himself as the dashing young hero. But now Louis addressed him in the tones of a king, of an overlord determined to stand by feudal tradition and undertake the defence of his vassal. Henry was a king himself and certainly had nothing to gain from establishing a precedent for the violation of feudal customs. When he got back to Poitiers, he might well have been only too glad to undo all the preparations which he had made for the attack. But word now reached him that King Malcolm of Scotland, his once truculent vassal, had decided to join in the expedition and was already on his way with a fleet of forty ships. Then again, his chancellor—Thomas Becket—had just equipped seven hundred knights, and they were about to cross the Channel. Even Stephen of Blois's son, William the Bastard, was making ready to join him. There was no escaping the truth: it was too late to turn back.

People could hardly believe their ears when, a little while later, they learned the outcome of the operation. Henry had marched his troops all the way to the walls of Toulouse and then withdrawn without a fight, declaring that he could not possibly lay siege to a city containing his sovereign lord. For at the outbreak of hostilities, on June 24th, Louis had journeyed to Toulouse with a handful of men. Henry's own movements, as a rule so rapid, had been exceptionally slow. After massing his forces at Périgueux he had held a spectacular military parade, conceivably hoping to intimidate the French king by a show of force. Before the assembled host of feudal supporters and Brabantine mercenaries he had conferred a knighthood on King Malcolm of Scotland who, in turn, had immediately knighted thirty young nobles from among his own vassals. In the midst of all this, it was learned that Cahors had risen in support of the king of England and that the count of Barcelona was on the move, having joined forces with Raymond Trencavel. Victory seemed a foregone conclusion.

And yet the siege never took place. The count of Barcelona need not have stirred, the count of Toulouse need not have lost a moment's sleep.

What exactly occurred? The historians generally admit to being puzzled. Some seek to explain it in terms of strategical considerations: Henry, they suggest, had decided that the campaign was causing him to stray too far from base; but anyone who compares the Toulouse expedition with the conquest of Ireland a few years later must surely reject the explanation as inadequate. Others have conjectured at possible acts of treachery and devised all sorts of complicated theories. In their own accounts of what happened, Henry's contemporaries adhere to the reason which he himself gave—that he had no wish to besiege a stronghold where his overlord was in residence, for such an act would have been in clear

127

defiance of his feudal obligations. Naturally the historian of today, so used to judging everything in the light of his own mental attitudes, will reject any motive which is not based on military or economic considerations; such a person would think it extremely naïve of anyone to accept reasons compatible with the mental attitudes of the twelfth century, and would point to occasions when Henry was prepared to make light of the feudal oath.

But there is surely something even more naïve about a historian unwilling to allow that a man may act in different ways at different times. Surprisingly, the obsession with good and bad, with the wicked wolf and the guileless lamb, with cowboys and Indians, remains deep-rooted in most of us and is the enduring cause of a great many mistakes, which could probably be avoided if only people were to refer more often to everyday life. Is it really so unusual to see a given person behave 'well' in circumstance A and 'badly' in circumstance B?

What cannot be questioned is the historical fact that Henry withdrew on the grounds that to pursue the matter further would have been to infringe his feudal oath. And if it is compulsory to ascribe self-interest to his decision, was it not to his advantage to avoid creating a precedent which might afterwards cost him dear, as a king and overlord in his own right? Perhaps Louis's firmness during their talks together had borne fruit. Henry's kingdom was not yet unshakable, and he had everything to gain from setting his numerous vassals an example of loyalty to feudal tradition. Besides, it would take a blind man to regard the Plantagenet as 'all of a piece', for he was blatantly full of contradictions. This sudden dramatic change of plan at Toulouse had very likely saved the French crown, but Henry was well aware of the troubles which he would have brought upon himself by laying hold of the king of France.

Entrusting his chancellor with the task of leading the army back to Cahors, he himself went first to Limoges and then to Normandy, where the king of France's brother, Robert of Dreux, had in the meantime launched a diversionary attack. This time the king of England fought with a vengeance. He meant to keep Normandy intact, and at the same time he was determined to show that his military prowess was as great as ever, even though he had not

128

Exterior and interior of the great hall of Eleanor's palace at Poitiers, now the Palais de Justice, which she watched being built

The façade of Notre Dame la Grande, Poitiers, and the remains of the city's ramparts

Interior of the abbey
church of Fontevrault

The 12th c. kitchens of
the abbey, and the
refectory

A knight does homage to his lady, from a 12th c. seal in the Bibliothèque Nationale. Right, the troubadour Bernard de Ventadour, from a 14th c. manuscript in the Bibliothèque Nationale.

Below, the murder of Thomas Becket, from a Latin psalter executed in England *ca.* 1200

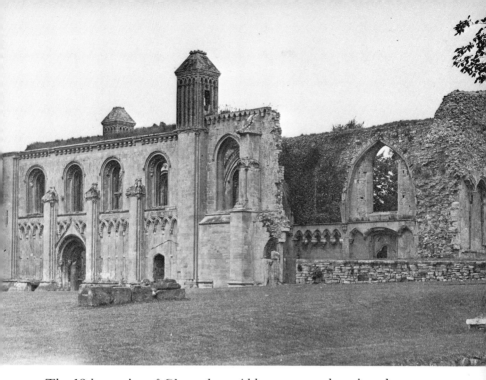

The 12th c. ruins of Glastonbury Abbey, supposed resting-place
of King Arthur

Tintagel Castle, associated with Tristan and Iseult

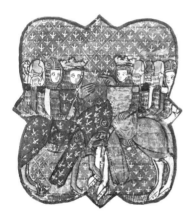

The seal of Richard I

The Kings of France and England
set off on the Third Crusade,
from a 14th c. manuscript
in the Bibliothèque Nationale

The ruins of
Château Gaillard—
Richard's 'Saucy Castle'

The castle of Niort

The ruined keep of
the castle of Gisors

The tombs of three of Eleanor's children: John in Worcester Cathedral;
Matilda in Brunswick Cathedral; Richard in Fontrevault

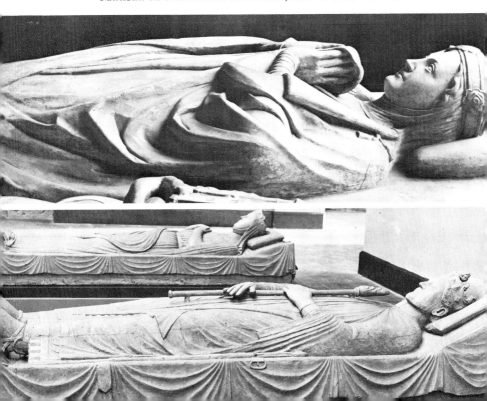

* See "My Lord Brother, the
~~Lion~~ Lion Heart" for development of this.

chosen to display it of late. If his prestige had been in any way
tarnished by that unfortunate business at Toulouse, he soon put
matters to rights. In swift succession he raided Beauvaisis, destroyed
the fortress at Gerberoy and forced the count of Evreux to do
homage to him, by which time it was obvious to everybody that the
king of France would no longer be able to journey in safety from
Paris to his old fief of Etampes, which had always been in the hands
of his family. So Louis requested a truce, and it was immediately
granted.

Eleanor may have been somewhat nettled at the failure of the
Toulouse expedition, but her feelings were as nothing compared to
those of Raymond V. The incident filled him with a deep and lasting bitterness towards her, as subsequent events were to show.

For the present, however, the episode had little effect on the
Plantagenet's career. The opening days of the year 1160 found
Eleanor on her way back to England; she was to fulfil her husband's
duties there while he stayed in Normandy, carrying out those
administrative reforms which had already yielded such good
results in his island possessions. She began to lead a wanderer's life
again: the Rolls, and the official documents issued in her name,
show her journeying about the country, moving from residence to
residence, taking good care to ensure that wine was delivered for
her table and oil for her lamps. The roads were safe in England
now; the sheriffs devoted themselves conscientiously to the task of
raising taxes and administering justice. The sheep grazing on the
green hills became more numerous with every passing year,
thanks to the methods of rational breeding introduced by the
Cistercian monasteries; the bales of wool rose higher and higher at
the port of London, where the Flemish merchants came to collect
them. Shipments of wine were on the increase too: casks were
regularly stacked in pyramids at the Channel ports, while across
the sea in Aquitaine the vine-growers ploughed deeper and deeper
into the surrounding wasteland to satisfy the demand for more
grapes. The wines of Bordeaux were finding their way into the inns
and offering serious competition to English beer.

Many of England's roads follow much the same course as in
Eleanor's day, and those who travel along them will continually
meet with the landscapes, castles and towns which Eleanor must

Henry
campaigns
in Limoges,
then Nor-
mandy.

Truce between
H II & L VII

Eleanor &
Raymond of
Toulouse
now enemies

1160

England
thriving.

have visited in her excursions among the sweet and tuneful English springtime. It is easy to picture her setting out from Bermondsey and crossing the river to the borough of Westminster, where the walls of the new palace provided a glittering patch of colour, while away to her right—beyond that shoreline still known as the Strand—rose the walls of the City. Farther westward, on the other side of Oxford, where famous teachers were already giving education, she frequently went to stay at Woodstock in a broadly undulating landscape framed by large woods. We find her again at Sherborne, where the ochreous stone employed in building the roofs of houses as well as the walls contrasted strongly with the stern hues of Cornwall or the red battlements of the castles in Devon. And everywhere, dotted about beside the streams and meadows, were the small limewashed cottages such as are still occasionally to be found along the byways of England and, more particularly, Ireland. There were a great many abbeys, and some of them—those of St Albans and Tewkesbury, for instance—still bear traces of Eleanor's day, with their mighty pillars and high semicircular arches. The king and queen devoted considerable attention to these abbeys, establishing or authorizing new foundations and contributing to reforms. The order of Fontevrault was a particular favourite with Eleanor, and due to her promptings it spread into England; at Eaton and Westwood were to be found the spiritual daughters of Robert of Arbrissel, and it was to them that the sovereigns turned when replacements had to be selected for the nuns at Amesbury Abbey, after the scandals there. And there are likewise many keeps dating back to the time of Henry and Eleanor, from Dover Castle and the Tower of London itself to Porchester, Farnham or Carisbrooke in the Isle of Wight, to which Eleanor paid several visits with her children—enjoying, perhaps, what we would nowadays call a seaside holiday.

On the continent, too, this was an expanding period. Henry had a great enthusiasm for building, and there can be no doubt but that his achievements in this field brought realization to Eleanor's own wishes. Together, they set about constructing a new residence in Poitiers and built the great hall of the palace there; they added to their castles at Angers and Rouen, and on the outskirts of the latter city—at Quevilly—they commissioned what one might call a country house, surrounded by a large leafy park; all these were in addition to fortifications, of primarily strategic importance, along the borders of Normandy and Maine, at Amboise and Fréteval. At Bures they erected a full-size palace, so large that a thousand oaks had to be felled. Finally, as was customary at the time, they founded numerous hospitals both in France and England—the leper-house at Caen, for instance. In short, everything bears witness to the prosperity of this kingdom of the West, which was growing and developing at a rate well-suited to their mutual ambitions.

1160

XIII

Deu pri e le martir, que j'ai servi maint jur,
Qu'il mette pes el regne, e tienge en bon' amur
E le pere e le fiz e la broiz e l'oisour.

May God and that martyr I've served all my life
Give peace to this reign, and put an end to strife
Between father and son, between mother-in-law and wife.

GUERNES DU PONT-SAINTE-MAXENCE

A HOT AUGUST NIGHT in the year 1165. In the small room where
he was lodging as a student in the Latin Quarter of Paris, a young
man, known to history as Giraldus Cambrensis, had but recently
blown out his candle. After sitting up late over his books, he had
fallen asleep as soon as his head touched the pillow; but in his sleep
he was dimly aware of a mounting tumult. How noisy these French
were! The noise grew until it carried through the wide-open
windows to the little room where the student lay. Still only half-
awake, he heard bells tolling and saw lights moving about: he
began to think there must be a fire, the great scourge of the time.
This notion finally overcame his drowsiness and sent him rushing
to the window. The street below was full of people waving and
shouting, and the bells of the dozen parish churches—not to
mention those of the old cathedral, already being rebuilt—were
vying with one another. They were not sounding the alarm, they
were pealing for joy.

'What is it? Why all this noise?' he called down to a pair of old
ladies as they hurried along the opposite pavement, holding their
hands up to shield the candles with which they were lighting their
way.

'An Englishman!' cried one of the women, while the other
called back exultantly: 'A king has been born to us. God has given
us an heir to the throne, and your own king will rue it!'

132

The remainder of her speech was lost among shouts of happiness and the general hubbub of the surging crowd.

Sure enough, a few hours earlier Louis VII had been urgently awakened by one of his equerries. The queen, who was at Gonesse, had just given birth to a son. Beside himself with happiness, the king had immediately given orders for the news to be proclaimed in the streets of Paris. Then, after dictating a deed whereby the bearer of the glad tidings was to receive three bushels of corn each year from the royal granaries, he had hurried off to Gonesse to feast his eyes on the heir for whom he had ceased to hope—Philip the God-given.

Whatever might come of the words of ill-omen which the old woman had addressed to Giraldus Cambrensis, the very fact of the child's birth put an end to the hope, long entertained by Henry and Eleanor, that their eldest son would one day inherit the crown of France, as well as the crown of England. This hope had been in jeopardy for some time past—ever since Louis's marriage to Adela of Champagne. For in the year 1160 his second wife, Constance, had died immediately after giving birth to a daughter. Only a fortnight later came the astonishing news that he had decided to marry for a third time, and that his choice had fallen on Adela of Champagne. By choosing her he brought about a strange and intricate pattern of kinship within the French royal family, for Adela was sister to Count Henry of Champagne and Count Theobald of Blois, who were Louis's sons-in-law elect. This, however, was but a minor detail; it might make life somewhat difficult for the genealogists, but it was as nothing to the sharp, direct blow dealt to the house of Anjou. The kingdom of France was now securely in the hands of the rival claimants. *a retaliatory action.*

Henry and Eleanor had immediately riposted by celebrating, in Rouen, the marriage of Prince Henry (aged five) to Princess Marguerite (aged two). By this means they came into possession of the dowry which had been set aside for the royal children: the Vexin region, defended by the fortress of Gisors, an enduring bone of contention between France and Normandy, which, ten years earlier, Geoffrey Plantagenet had voluntarily handed over to the king of France as tangible proof of his desire for peace. The fortress of Gisors had been placed in the care of the Templars at the time of

Marguerite's betrothal to Henry; now that the wedding had taken place there was no longer any reason for them to maintain their hold over it, so they had surrendered the keys to the king of England. Louis felt he had been made a fool of; he forthwith expelled the Templars from their hall in Paris. Subsequently there were a few skirmishes along the borders of the Vexin; but what was done could not be undone and, as so often, Louis had to bow to a situation which had been forced on him.

And now his third wife had presented him with the heir he had always longed for. This at the very time when Henry Plantagenet was extending his ambitions beyond the realm of France and looking towards the Empire, for in the spring of 1165, his eldest daughter Matilda had been betrothed to the duke of Saxony, Henry the Lion. This must have gladdened the heart of his mother, Matilda Empress: she was still alive in Rouen and still publishing decrees (most of them, if the truth be told, witnessed by her doctor—a man called Hugh).

Eleanor herself was with child when Philip of France was born—the Philip who was to go down in history as Philip Augustus. In September 1165 she gave birth to a daughter, Joanna—her third daughter by Henry. A final birth came in the following year: a son called John, known for ever after as John Lackland.

But already an irreparable rift had occurred. Between her and her husband there would always, from now on, stand the figure of Fair Rosamond, whom Henry had taken as his mistress. Gone were the shared, identical hopes and ambitions which had hitherto united them in every deed. By betraying Eleanor, Henry made an enemy of the woman who had been his constant ally in good times and bad—an enemy who was as bent on harming him as she had previously been bent on supporting him.

In England, an endless number of ballads and verse dramas have been written around Fair Rosamond. And her name conjures up a whole series of legends in which Eleanor is usually shown in the least favourable light—not simply as the spurned wife, but as the vindictive and malevolent queen who eventually kills her rival. Poets and dramatists have from the first made Woodstock the setting of Henry's love-affair with Fair Rosamond. They are depicted as meeting now in an arbour, now in an indoor bower. So

134

that the woman he loves may be out of the reach of the queen's vengeance, Henry has constructed a labyrinth whose secret is known only to himself and a trusty manservant. But while he is away on the continent, coping with his rebellious sons, the secret of the labyrinth is penetrated by Queen Eleanor. In her implacable jealousy she reaches Rosamond's retreat and forces her to take her own life, making her choose between a dagger and poison. Fair Rosamond drinks the poison and is buried in the near-by convent of Godstow by nuns whose hearts have been swayed by pity.

The historical realities concealed beneath these legends have been successfully disentangled by the scholars and, as always, fact turns out to be more profoundly dramatic than fiction. Rosamond, daughter of the Norman knight Walter de Clifford, made her appearance in Henry Plantagenet's life round about 1166, the year when John Lackland was born. It may well have been on her return to England, in time for Christmas and her lying-in, that Eleanor became aware of her husband's infidelities. Until that juncture, whatever may have been said to the contrary, Henry had been a relatively faithful husband. It would certainly seem that his lechery has been exaggerated—at least during this period of his life. He may have allowed himself to stray a few times, but only momentarily; on the whole, he had behaved reasonably well. The only story which has been quoted to suggest otherwise concerns a mistress living in Stafford, a lady called Avice. It is at least possible that she was the mother of the two illegitimate sons, Geoffrey and William, whom he had fathered before his marriage. At all events, he had wearied of her. One day Thomas Becket happened to be passing through Stafford and she sent various gifts to him. This aroused the suspicions of the chancellor's host. After dark he stole to the door of Becket's room, expecting to find him with the king's former mistress. Hearing no sound from within, he opened the door and found Becket, all alone, stretched out on the floor where he had fallen asleep while saying his prayers.

However that may be, Eleanor herself does not seem to have had overmuch cause to complain about her husband during these fourteen years of married life. How striking, then, was the change brought about by the advent of Rosamond—whom Giraldus Cambrensis, always a merciless satirist, dubs *Rosa-immundi*—Rose of

Avice, lived in Stafford had 2 sons by Henry II Geoffrey + Wm. before he was married

Unchastity. From that time forward there was to be the sharpest of divisions between husband and wife. Indeed, Eleanor subsequently made only one brief visit to England (in 1167) . . . until, that is, the moment came when she was forced to return against her will.

A link has already been established between Rosamond and Woodstock, and we have touched on the existence of a labyrinth and either an arbour or a sumptuously furnished bower. In reality there is no reason why the royal residence at Woodstock, which Henry and Eleanor had taken pleasure in improving, and which, according to contemporary accounts, was surrounded by an extremely beautiful park, should not have included a maze. The age was well-disposed towards this particular form of whimsy: we have only to think of the labyrinths adorning the mosaic floors of cathedrals or of the intricate interlacing patterns decorating the *Book of Kells* and many other manuscripts, especially in the Celtic regions. Legend has turned this maze into the device whereby Henry sought to keep Fai Rosramond safe from her rival. All of which would suggest, to put it at the lowest, that he had not been afraid to install Rosamond at Woodstock, and it is hardly surprising that Eleanor should have turned her back on England and reverted to being duchess of Aquitaine. Henceforth she resided almost continuously in Poitiers, making occasional rounds of visits within her own borders and taking her vassals and her children in hand. Slowly but surely she acquired sufficient control over both to make them act in accordance with her wishes; and when eventually she achieved this full control, Henry was given ample opportunity to measure the cost of being unfaithful to his wife and violating the marital agreement which had once guaranteed such harmony of thought and action. As the historian E.-R. Labande has written in an excellent study of the matter: 'Eleanor did not take her revenge by murdering Rosamond. She did better than that: she roused Poitou to rebellion.'

All these events have been somewhat overshadowed, for historians as for contemporary witnesses, by the great quarrel which the king of England was conducting at the same time with the prelate who had been, to quote his own words, 'his sole counsellor'—his faithful chancellor and inseparable friend: Thomas Becket.

Henry had considered it a masterstroke on his own part to have secured the archbishopric of Canterbury for the man who had abetted him so wholeheartedly in framing a new policy and administration for the realm of England. The appointment would combine within the same hands the powers ecclesiastical and temporal, with the result that secular authority would no longer be subject to the limitations which the church imposed on it. Becket had shown his mettle at the time of the Toulouse expedition, when he had successfully taxed the clergy to pay for the hire of the Brabantine mercenaries. In the increasingly authoritarian policy which he was pursuing, Henry was continually coming up against the obstacle of ecclesiastical privileges. In Becket he confidently expected to find an ally who would gradually curtail those privileges and thereby strengthen the power of the throne. So a year after the death of Archbishop Theobald, Thomas was ordained a priest—having been only a deacon until then—and on Whit-Sunday 1162 he was consecrated as a bishop in the presence of Henry the Young, who had been entrusted to his supervision at the age of seven.

It might have been expected that following his enthronement the new archbishop would make some solemn demonstration of allegiance to his king. But instead, Thomas had devoted his considerable propensity for solemn ceremonial to the task of instituting the celebration of Trinity Sunday in his diocese. Almost overnight he had entirely changed his way of life. As chancellor, he had always loved personal luxury; yet now he distributed his goods among the poor. He who had daily regaled eminent lords with choice dishes and noble wines now subjected himself to regular fasting; his residence became a home for beggars, who arrived in great numbers clad in their filthy rags. He even changed his style of dress: very soon after his accession to the archbishopric he assumed the garb of the Augustinian monks of Merton, from among whom he had always chosen his confessor—a full-length black habit, made from coarse cloth and trimmed with lambswool, and over it a short white surplice and the stole; not until after his death did it become known that he wore a hairshirt under his habit. Always staunchly dutiful, Thomas had transferred his first allegiance from his king to his God and was, as ever, wholehearted in the performance of his office. Henry could only stand and watch, in sheer bewilderment, a metamorphosis which he himself had brought about.

All Henry's plans and preconceptions were thwarted, and it was not long before he awoke to the fact. Barely a year after Becket's elevation, the first open clash occurred. A cleric had been hauled before the king's justices; Thomas insisted that, in accordance with tradition, the man be judged by an ecclesiastical court. Other disagreements followed, and in 1164 the king and his ex-chancellor found themselves on terms of overt hostility. The king attempted to get the upper hand by ordering the enactment of the famous Constitutions of Clarendon, a document which aimed at nothing less than the establishment of a sort of national church, the withdrawal of the bishops' powers of jurisdiction and a ban on appeals to the pope. In October the two men came face to face in Northampton and there were violent scenes between them. As a result Thomas set out in disguise for Eastry Priory, on the coast. On November 2nd he rose before dawn and took passage from Sandwich to France. He was never again to return to England, except to die.

The ins-and-outs of this dramatic quarrel are of present interest only in so far as they relate to the story of Eleanor's life. She held firmly aloof from the whole business, and we have already seen that she harboured a kind of jealousy towards Becket. Yet it is clear from one of John of Salisbury's letters that she intervened on the archbishop's behalf, as did Matilda Empress. True, another letter—this time written by John of Bellesmains, bishop of Poitiers, towards the end of May 1165—warns Becket that he can hope for neither aid nor counsel from Eleanor, 'especially since she puts all her trust in Raoul of Faye, who is no less hostile towards you than usual.' Raoul of Faye had, in fact, been involved in personal disputations with the prelate; on the other hand he was actively engaged in helping the queen in her campaign against her husband.

Nevertheless, the deeds and deportment of Thomas Becket were destined to have a decisive effect on the behaviour of the queen and her children. For it was at the French court that Becket sought and found asylum; and once again, as at the time of the Toulouse affair, Henry Plantagenet was treated to a lesson by the despised

Louis whom he had so often defied and mocked. After Thomas had slipped away from the confrontation in Northampton, the English king made haste to close his ports and requested the count of Flanders not to receive the archbishop, should he succeed in leaving the island. Then, suspecting that Becket would make for the French court, he promptly sent envoys to Louis. By an extraordinary coincidence, these envoys crossed the Channel at exactly the same time as the archbishop—the night of November 1st-2nd, 1164. They obtained an audience of King Louis in his castle at Compiègne and laid Henry's petition before him, entreating him not to give shelter to the archbishop of Canterbury, who had left his diocese without the king's permission and was on that account dismissed from office.

Envoys from Engl to L VII nov. 1164

'What is this I hear?' cried Louis, feigning astonishment. 'A prelate judged and dismissed from office by the king? How can that be? I am a king too, as much king in my own kingdom as the king of England in his, yet it is wholly outside my powers to dismiss the humblest clerk residing within my realm!'

At this the envoys somewhat basely reminded Louis how, as chancellor, Becket had frequently worked against him—especially at the time of the siege of Toulouse. Louis replied that he could not possibly hold it against Becket that, during his chancellorship, he had served King Henry to the best of his abilities. The envoys had no choice but to leave the castle and make post-haste for Sens, where Pope Alexander III was in residence; in open conflict with the German emperor, he too had sought asylum in France. Some while later it was the turn of Becket's devoted friend Herbert Bosham to be received by the king of France. Louis assured him that he intended to adhere to the ancient royal custom whereby all exiles, especially men of the church, could count on asylum and protection in France. He was as good as his word. From now on France became the setting of the various episodes in the struggle between king and archbishop. Becket was to spend the greater part of his time in the abbey of Pontigny, founded by St Bernard.

Alexander III Pope at Sens

Thus the king of France came to be cast in the role of arbiter between the archbishop, whose zealous concern for the rights of the church were to end in martyrdom, and the most powerful monarch in the West, a king who for a time had even seemed likely to secure possession of the French throne. How many others were to follow in Becket's footsteps and turn to Louis for protection will emerge in due course.

Meanwhile Eleanor was back in Poitiers. She seemed to have made up her mind quite firmly that she was not going to return to England, where there was a risk of encountering her rival, Fair Rosamond. From now on all her actions were those of a mother, not of a wife. From within her own domain she was to implement a policy of her own devising, and the world was soon to see just how hostile that policy was to Henry's.

The king had fondly supposed that he would be able to impose his will on Aquitaine in the same manner as on England and Normandy. But the barons beyond the Loire, especially those in Poitou, were extremely jealous of their independence and had no intention of being ordered about by a foreigner. When Henry went back to England in January 1168—after his Christmas court in Argentan, which Eleanor had attended—he thought it would be a clever move to have the queen deputize for him in Aquitaine, where there had been rebellion after rebellion. He had hoped to put an end to these revolts by razing the fortress of Lusignan; but he thought, not without reason, that Eleanor would be more readily accepted than he in her own domain. With what alacrity she must have agreed to an arrangement which so clearly favoured her own designs! Can it have been because he mistrusted her and was eager for her to be accompanied by a man on whom he could rely that Henry assigned Patrick, earl of Salisbury, to her party? Impossible to say for certain. The unrest in Aquitaine at that time would in any event have demanded that the queen have at her right hand a devoted and dependable aide. Events were to underline this all too soon, for as early as April Eleanor was nearly the victim of an ambush. It had been set by the Lusignans and was to cost the earl of Salisbury his life.

The incident occurred in Easter Week. Eleanor was travelling with the earl and a small escort; she was evidently quite close to Poitiers or one of her other castles—the chroniclers do not specify which one, though they make it clear that the war-horses had been sent on ahead—when all of a sudden she came face to face with an armed troop bearing the banner of the Lusignans. The earl was a brave man and had no intention of fleeing. He bade Eleanor mount the fastest horse and held off the attack while she galloped to safety. He and his men were at a disadvantage, for they were not in armour. He himself was mounted on a mere palfrey; someone hurried away to collect his charger, but it arrived too late to be of any use to him. No sooner had he mounted it (his companions were still donning their coats of mail and putting on their helmets) than one of the Lusignans struck him from behind with a hunting-spear, killing him outright.

The engagement that followed provided a first taste of battle for a young man who was to be closely bound up with the future of Eleanor and her children. This was the earl of Salisbury's nephew, William the Marshal. Brought up by the lord of Tancarville—another William, soon to succeed the earl of Salisbury as governor of Poitou—he was then about twenty-four and had been knighted two years earlier. Long afterwards, one of his descendants celebrated his deeds of valour in a long narrative poem. For he lived, unfalteringly, the life of a perfect knight of his time: he was loyal, he was upright and again and again he was involved in exploits of a singular romantic charm. On the day of this encounter with the Lusignans he fought, says the poem, 'like a famished lion'. His horse was killed under him, but William picked himself up, set his back against a hedge, so that he need fear only frontal attack, and shouted: 'Hither, any man who seeks to try his strength!' If the poem is to be believed, he was outnumbered sixty to one, yet he held them at bay 'like a wild boar besieged by hounds'. He was invincible until at last a knight rode over the hedge and struck him from the rear, thrusting a lance into his thigh. He was taken prisoner and led away by his assailants, now hoisted on a cart (the height of ignominy for any knight), now mounted on an ass or some broken-down old horse. No one showed any concern for his wound; he had to bind it himself with strips of his own clothing. Not until the troop halted for rest at a castle one night did he receive any attention. Noticing this tall young man with his ashen cheeks and heavy limp, a lady guessed the truth of his dilemma and smuggled a bandage to him in a hollowed-out loaf. At this point Eleanor, who had felt great concern as to the fate of her defenders, paid his ransom. When he reached Poitiers she presented him with a suit of armour and a horse and some new clothes, for he was merely a younger son and had no fortune of his own. In addition, she instituted a yearly mass for the repose of the soul of Patrick, earl of Salisbury, making a generous endowment to the monks of the abbey of Saint-Hilaire, in Poitiers, for this purpose.

William the Marshal became knight-at-arms to the royal children and was soon the inseparable jousting companion of Henry the Young. Indeed, the entire episode was chiefly of note in that it gave the queen the opportunity of discerning the perennial characteristic of this young knight: his perfect loyalty.

Eleanor was now free to take her own territories in hand again and win over her rebellious vassals one by one. Henry became increasingly embroiled in the problems arising from his quarrel with the archbishop of Canterbury. His position was more and more isolated. His mother Matilda had died the year before, in 1167, and with her had died the influence of her steadying counsels. In his dealings with the pope, who had at first been well-disposed towards him, he had quickly damaged his cause by entering into negotiations with the schismatic bishop of Cologne, Rainaud of Dassel, who was supporting an antipope at the prompting of Frederick Barbarossa. Henry had done this at the time of his daughter Matilda's marriage to the duke of Saxony in 1167—the occasion of Eleanor's sole voluntary return to England. She had wanted to be with her eldest daughter at the time of her departure for Germany, and they had set sail from Dover together after Eleanor had supervised the packing of the young princess's belongings. Three other vessels departed with the ship in which Matilda was sailing; aboard them were the forty chests and forty-odd leather bags containing her dresses and jewellery and the gifts intended for her bridegroom and his family, together with a regal gift of twenty-eight pounds of gold with which to gild her plate. Eleanor accompanied her as far as Normandy, then let her continue her journey to distant Saxony in the care of the escort sent by her husband-to-be. She herself returned to Poitou.

For it was here that her hopes and ambitions now lay—both

vested in her second son, Richard. Eleanor was re-emerging as duchess of Aquitaine, with her son at her side in lieu of her unworthy husband. Her new purpose was to stand up to the latter in defence of her children's rights. And those rights were drawing her back into the orbit of France, since as duchess of Aquitaine she was King Louis's vassal.

Thus Henry found himself confronted at every turn by the failed monk, the little king whom he had always been ready to despise. More even than he imagined (for he was entirely unaware of his wife's secret ambitions) his conduct resulted in Louis's becoming the touchstone of his own situation. By flaunting his strength, acting with ever greater despotism and exceeding his rights as a king and a husband, he seemed merely to enhance the prestige of the French king, who was such a respecter of justice and legality. For all his grandiose designs (and at the time of his daughter's marriage to one of the mightiest barons in the German empire it had even been possible for him to entertain imperial aspirations) Henry could still, even in the eyes of the people he ruled, be held up to judgment by this little king whom he had so often defeated and humiliated, yet who countered the antics of his haughty vassal with smiling simplicity. It must have been at about this time that in conversation with Walter Map, archdeacon of Oxford, Louis voiced the celebrated rejoinder which Map has handed down to us: 'Many and various are the riches of kings . . . Those of the king of the Indies take the form of precious stones and of lions, leopards and elephants; the emperor of Byzantium and the king of Sicily glory in their gold and silk, but their men are mere talkers and useless in time of war. The Holy Roman Emperor . . . has men gifted at war, and battle-steeds too, but no gold, no silk, no other riches . . . Your own master, the king of England, does not want for anything: he has men, horses, gold, silk, precious stones, fruit, animals and all else. We in France have nothing save bread, wine and gaiety.'

Perhaps it was his awareness of dealing with a power of a different order, and his desire to confront it boldly once and for all, which drove Henry to take a dramatic step early in 1169. On the feast of the Epiphany a formal meeting between the two kings was held in the castle of Montmirail, on the borders of Maine and the Chartres region. Henry brought his three sons with him, so that they might do homage to Louis for the mainland provinces which were to be theirs: Henry the Young for Normandy, Maine and Anjou; Richard for Poitou and Aquitaine; Geoffrey for Brittany.

'Sire,' said the Plantagenet, 'on this feast of the Epiphany, commemorating the day when the three kings came bearing gifts to the King of Kings, I commend my three sons and my lands to your safekeeping.'

'Since the King who received those gifts from the Magi seems to have inspired your words,' replied Louis, 'may your sons, when they take possession of their lands, do so in the sight of God.'

Once again the king of England was being treated to a lesson by the king of France: no clearer reminder could have been laid before him of the duties inherent in an overlord's powers.

While Henry was at Montmirail, an attempt was made to re-establish peace between him and Becket. These talks were the occasion of the archbishop's famous, carefully phrased utterance in which he made his submission to Henry yet distinguished between the duty owed to God and the duty owed to a king: 'In the presence of the king of France, the papal legates and the princes, your sons, I surrender the whole case and all the difficulties which have arisen between us to your royal judgment . . . excepting the honour of God.'

Eleanor did not attend the talks at Montmirail, but she must have rejoiced at them. They marked a first step towards the goal which she had begun to pursue with such stubbornness: the transference of power from her husband's hands to her children's. She therefore joined him at the magnificent Christmas court which he held in Nantes that year. Before the assembled barons and prelates of Brittany, it was announced that nine-year-old Geoffrey was to marry the hereditary heiress of the province—Constance, daughter of the late Duke Conan. All swore fealty to the boy, and Henry must have felt that in this distant western province his sovereignty was not an empty word. But Eleanor was soon to put her own authority to the test. After Henry went back to England (more than ever in danger of being excommunicated) she made plans to have Richard formally installed as her successor the following Easter.

The new duke of Aquitaine and count of Poitou was presented

to his vassals, and received their allegiance at an assembly in Niort. Eleanor toured the duchy at his side, investing him with all her possessions from the Loire to the Pyrenees. On his return to Poitiers, Richard was officially accorded the hereditary and purely honorary title of abbot of Saint-Hilaire. Seated in the ancient abbey, which was of more or less the same significance to counts of Poitiers as Saint-Denis was to kings of France and Westminster to kings of England, he was presented with the insignia of office—lance and standard—by John, bishop of Poitiers, and Bertrand, archbishop of Bordeaux.

But the most richly symbolical of these ceremonies took place in Limoges. Eleanor was shrewd enough to take full advantage of a discovery recently made by the monks of Saint-Martial: from the archives of their abbey they had disinterred an ancient life of the city's patron saint, St Valerie, whose sole surviving relic took the form of a ring. This was an excellent excuse to resuscitate a ceremony which had fallen into disuse but which in the old days had, or so it was said, played a prominent part in the coronation of dukes of Aquitaine; moreover, the legend of St Valerie, one of the early martyrs, was bound up with the supremacy of the bishopric of Limoges. So a long procession of clergy in surplices and white copes came to meet Richard at the door of the cathedral. After blessing him and arraying him in a silk tunic, the bishop slipped St Valerie's ring on to his finger: in this moment, while Eleanor looked on in triumph, Richard was contracting a mystic marriage with the city of Limoges and the whole of Aquitaine. Clutching the standard and wearing a crown of gold, the young duke advanced to the altar at the head of the procession of clergy and received sword and spurs in accordance with the rites prevailing in this age of chivalry. He took the oath on the Gospel and heard mass. Then came feasting and jousting fit to mark the coronation of a king.

Afterwards, Richard and Eleanor together laid the foundation stone of a local monastery which was to be dedicated to St Augustine. In the eyes of the clergy and the common people, as well as in the eyes of the barons of Limousin, Richard was now acknowledged as the rightful heir of the Troubadour and the rest of his forefathers. And there was nothing haphazard about Eleanor's decision to show herself in the city of Limoges. It was here that

Henry had acted most tyrannically; after quarrelling for some reason or other with the abbot of Saint-Martial, he had twice ordered the demolition of the city walls and imposed heavy fines on the inhabitants. Now genuine harmony had been established between the people of Limoges and the prince whom Eleanor had made heir to her heart and lands alike.

Further, she associated his name with one of those bountiful acts in favour of Fontevrault which marked every decisive moment in her life. For in this same year, 1170, acting on behalf of the king and his sons, but also of her own father and forefathers, and for the salvation of their souls, she conferred lands on the monastery, together with the right to draw timber and firewood from one of her forests. The legal document to this effect was witnessed by the loyallest and closest of her attendants: Saldebreuil, her constable; Raoul of Faye; Peter, her chaplain (conceivably the writer Peter of Blois, of whom much will be heard later); and finally her clerk, Jordan, likewise to remain one of the queen's staunchest aides.

And it was with joy, so the record tells, us, that she learned of Henry Plantagenet's personal decision to have his eldest son, Henry the Young, crowned in London in June 1170. True, the king viewed this coronation chiefly as a slap in the face for Becket—for it was the archbishop of Canterbury's privilege to anoint any new king of England, just as the archbishop of Rheims traditionally anointed any new king of France. But Eleanor saw the measure as another step towards the fulfilment of her private plans. Henry was voluntarily casting off power in favour of his children. After this, they would be entitled to take him at his word and demand in full measure the power which he had elected to bestow on them.

Henry the Young was perfectly suited to such a role. At the banquet which followed the coronation (his father had resolved, again as a means of defying Becket, that everything should be done on a magnificent scale; for the goldwork on the crown he had paid his goldsmith, William Cade, the great sum of thirty-eight pounds and six shillings) the young king was seated in the place of honour and his father insisted on serving him, as a clear indication of the exalted rank to which he had elevated the boy. He could not refrain from drawing attention to the oddness of the situation.

146

'It is surely rather unusual,' he observed jestingly to his son, 'to find a king waiting at table.'

'Ah,' retorted Henry the Young, 'but it is not unusual to find the son of a count waiting on the son of a king.'

A rejoinder which left the nobles of the entourage speechless.

Not until long afterwards did Henry II wake to the full significance of what he had done, or realize how greatly it would benefit Eleanor. On the other hand, he found out soon enough that his bold attempt to minimize the importance of the archbishop of Canterbury was adding to the thorniness of his own position vis-à-vis the remainder of Christendom. For it was in defiance of the pope's categorical instructions that the archbishop of York, always hostile to Becket, had agreed to perform the coronation service; and by so doing, writes a contemporary, he had acted 'against the wishes and opinions of practically everyone in the kingdom'. Soon after the ceremony Henry II, back in Normandy, met one of the bishops to whom he had been looking for support—his own cousin, the bishop of Worcester. The encounter occurred in Falaise, where the prelate had remained even though Henry had commanded every bishop in the realm to attend the coronation; the king upbraided him fiercely for failing him both as a church leader and as a member of the family. To which the bishop replied that even as he was making ready for the journey to England his departure had been forbidden by royal mandate.

'What!' exclaimed Henry. 'The queen is in Falaise at present—and with her is my constable, Richard du Hommet. Are you trying to tell me that one or other of them prevented you from making the crossing, in defiance of my orders?'

'Pray do not level any charge at the queen,' replied the bishop; 'if, out of respect or fear for you, she conceals the truth, expend your anger on me. If she admits to the truth, it is upon her that your wrath will fall. And I would rather lose a leg than know that you had addressed a single harsh word to that noble Lady on my account . . . I consider it better,' he continued, 'that things should stand as they do now than that I should have attended a coronation performed unrighteously and contrary to the will of God—not because of him who was crowned, but because of the impudence of him who crowned him.'

147

The tenor of this conversation is a fair guide to the tensions and confusions assailing the bystanders in this tragic duel between king and archbishop. Further, it shows that—for all the joy she may have felt at seeing her son crowned—Eleanor was not willing to support her husband's stand.

Henry had placed Marguerite of France in her care. Marguerite's father, Louis VII, was a fellow-victim of the affront administered to the archbishop of Canterbury: his daughter should by rights have been crowned at the same time as Henry the Young, to whom she was married. Louis therefore exacted certain promises from Henry, as tokens of repentance. In particular he was obliged to give an undertaking that the crown would be conferred on Marguerite as soon as the archbishop of Canterbury returned to his see. It was with this end in view that Louis engineered the final meeting between Henry and Becket. It took place at Fréteval on the feast of St Mary Magdalene, July 22nd, 1170. This time Henry was outwardly as contrite and friendly as could be. He promised that a second coronation would be celebrated shortly. Indeed, he showed every sign of wanting to return to the old warm relationship with Becket, as though there had never been a rift. He even held Becket's stirrup when the time came for them to part.

But the seal would not be set upon these cheering words unless he gave the archbishop the kiss of peace. This Henry refused to do, and neither Louis nor Thomas could be in any doubt as to the meaning of his refusal.

'My lord, I have a feeling that we shall not meet again upon this earth.' It was with these words that Becket took his leave of Henry. Louis, for his part, implored the archbishop to place no reliance upon what the king had said, but to remain within the secure haven of France.

Their reactions may seem hard to understand, when the king of England was manifesting such deep remorse and pouring out promises of peace. But in those days the kiss was looked upon as of greater account than any number of words, written or spoken. Liturgy was the great moulding influence of the age—it was the *gesture* which counted. A vassal displayed fealty by placing his hands within those of his overlord as he vowed homage, and it was this gesture which finally committed him—just as it was the kiss given in return which finally committed the overlord to providing him with protection. Henry might voice oath after oath of friendship; the fact that he was withholding the kiss, the sacred pledge of friendship, made it clear to everyone that his words were so much wind.

On December 1st, 1170, six years after his clandestine escape, Becket stepped ashore at Dover. A great host of the poor and humble escorted him all the way to Canterbury; the entire population of his town was awaiting him in the cathedral, which had been especially decorated for the occasion.

On Henry's instructions Eleanor spent Christmas with him at Bures, in Normandy. It was there she learned that on December 29th the archbishop had been murdered in his own cathedral.

12-29-1170
Becket murdered

XIV

Pel doutz chan que.l rossinhols fai
La noih can me sui adormitz,
Revelh de joi totz esbaïtz,
D'amor pensius e cossirans;
C'aisso es mos melher mesters,
Que tostems aï joi volunters,
Et ab joi comensa mos chans.

The nightingale sings all night long;
To her sweet notes I wake from sleep,
Filled with a love-longing so deep
The joy of it runs in me strong.
My sweetest verses stem from this:
I give myself with bliss to bliss;
In joy begins my every song.

BERNARD DE VENTADOUR

OF ALL THE TOWNS to which Eleanor's eventful life took her, none
holds as many memories of her as Poitiers. This favourite city of the
dukes of Aquitaine, this honoured land which produced the
earliest flourishing of the troubadours' art, has retained the im-
print of its romanesque history. Some of the ramparts have not
altered since the days when they defended the queen of England
from the possibility of attack by rebellious vassals. The baptistery
of Saint-Jean, the church of Saint-Hilaire and at least part of
Sainte-Radegonde, these remain more or less as Eleanor knew
them. The beautiful façade of Notre-Dame la Grande is the one she
must often have gazed at, and she watched the great hall of the
ducal palace going up stone by stone—also the cathedral of Saint-
Pierre, where one of the stained-glass windows is said to include
a likeness of her. Then there are those sudden, brief surprises
which arrest the eye as one rounds a corner or peeps into a court-

150

yard—the belfry of Saint-Porchaire, for instance, or the cloisters of the medical school, formerly the main hospital. All these buildings were part of Eleanor's world, the world of French romanesque architecture in its full glory.

And the city itself was of a splendour unrivalled in any other era when Eleanor was busily establishing her position as duchess of Aquitaine. Granted this setting, it is easy to picture her as she appears on her seal, with a flower clasped in her right hand and a hawk perched on her left. And during these years Poitiers became the home of poetry, the kernel of the courtly and chivalrous ideal. To an even greater degree there than in France or England, Eleanor was queen: she reigned through her children, guarantors of a long line; she reigned over a court of eager vassals and poets; more, she dominated all around her by that intellectual radiance, that love of literature and fine language, which was her hallmark. It was about this time that Chrétien de Troyes frequented the court of Poitiers and there became imbued with the twofold influence which lies behind all his work: Celtic legend and the poetry of courtly love. It may even be that the subject-matter of his earliest romance, *Erec et Enide*, was supplied by Eleanor herself. The poem extols the virtues of the couple, not as self-absorbed but as pursuers of a common goal—the full-fledged Knight and Lady who, as a result of giving themselves to experience and sharing in chivalrous adventure, achieve the full joy of courtly love. For almost fifteen years, this had been the essence of Eleanor's life with Henry. Both had committed themselves, fully and in complete harmony, to the task of leading their huge kingdom to a glorious future. But Henry had broken faith: he had prized lechery above creative sharing, and now the joy of courtly love was gone for ever. Henceforward Eleanor would be alone in her quest for chivalrous adventure, in that 'hunt for the white hart' famed in Arthurian legend. She would pursue it on behalf of her sons, with a mother's passion, now that she had been cheated of her rights as a spouse.

Such was the task which she fulfilled during these years in Poitiers: in the face of the increasingly isolated and tyrannical power of Henry II, she had to assert the rights of her children—even to the point of open rebellion. And all this against the background she could create so well: the playing of the troubadours, feasts worthy of King Arthur and his followers, the keen and subtle arguments of the courts of love. Fortunately, no one in our own day credits the interpretation which, with typical ponderousness, the literary historians of the French classical era felt justified in placing on this delightful expression 'courts of love': they saw such courts as real tribunals, issuing sentences to which lovers were compelled to submit . . . In reality it was all an intellectual game, the exquisite invention of a highly cultured society which delighted in the analysis of love and all its nuances; only in jest was a judgment given after a case had been argued, and these judgments were deliberately given the tone and form of those pronounced at feudal assizes. André le Chapelain's *Traité de l'Amour*, a work which seems so extraordinary to modern readers, successfully preserved the memory of these debates on courtly love presided over by a noble Lady—Ermengarde of Narbonne, Isabella of Flanders, and occasionally Eleanor herself or her daughter Marie of Champagne.

For Eleanor had begun to spend time with her two elder daughters. Both were visitors to Poitiers during this period. There was Alix of Blois: later one of her own daughters was to enter Fontevrault, and the gifts which the queen bestowed on her suggest that she enjoyed a particular place in her grandmother's affections; and there was Marie of Champagne, whose visits were of greater importance, for unquestionably Eleanor felt closer in spirit to her than to any of her other nine children. The poet Rigaud de Barbezieux describes Marie as 'the joyous and gay countess . . . the light of Champagne'. She had inherited her mother's feeling for the arts, her intellectual curiosity and her ability to encourage poetry. Chrétien de Troyes was among her followers—and it was at her prompting that he later wrote the narrative poem entitled *Lancelot* or *Le Chevalier à la Charrette*, which gives fuller expression than any other *roman breton* to the cult of the Lady; Lancelot's love for Guinevere makes him accept even dishonour; for her sake he is willing to be defeated and branded a coward.

It may have been in these same fertile surroundings that Marie of France (was she really, as has been conjectured, a natural

daughter of Geoffrey Plantagenet?) composed her *lais*. Every one of
those bewitching narrative poems is inspired by the ideals of
courtly love and chivalry and is based on some Celtic theme; they
are as inseparable from the atmosphere of Eleanor's court as the
creations of the troubadours themselves. At all events, the court of
Poitiers reclaimed Bernard de Ventadour during these years—and
with him came other poets such as Rigaud de Barbezieux, who
salutes Eleanor in his poems, referring to her as *Plus-que-Dame*, and
Gaucelm Faidit, who exchanged badinage with young Geoffrey of
Brittany in one of those rhyming duologues which were so popular
at the time.

For the princes, too, were engaged in writing poetry. Richard
was well-known as a troubadour and was later to dedicate works
to Marie of Champagne, the 'sister-countess' for whom he would
seem to have felt considerable affection. And it was no accident that
Geoffrey's first-born son was christened Arthur.

Eleanor must have been overjoyed to see her children gathered
about her at the court of Poitiers. Not one of them had failed to live
up to her hopes.

Their contemporaries are unanimous in depicting the eldest,
Henry (the 'Young King' of the history books, *el Jove Rey*), as the
personification of chivalry and the courtly ideal. He had received
a thorough education, largely at the hands of Thomas Becket, to
whose care he had been entrusted at the age of seven. Tall, fair and
as handsome as a young god, he expressed himself with an easy
grace and was a master of the amiable but witty rejoinder; he was
good-natured, affable, forgiving and generous beyond compare.
The traits recorded by those who met him add up to a portrait so
attractive that even the young prince's defects are made to seem
likeable—the reckless extravagance, for instance, which was the
despair of his father. Even Giraldus Cambrensis, so tartly critical of
human beings in general and the Plantagenets in particular, is not
proof against the aura of charm surrounding the Young King:
'His mind was so constituted that he never refused anything
to anyone who was worthy to receive, and never allowed any
deserving person to depart from his presence downcast or dis-
satisfied. Like a second Titus, he would consider his day wasted
unless he had heaped gifts on a great number of people and

had benefited them in heart and body by an abundance of kind actions.'

From 1170 onwards he was always accompanied by William the Marshal, the same whom Eleanor had ransomed from the Lusignans; it was he who, in 1173, was to confer the accolade on the Young King. The poem telling the story of his life abounds in descriptions of tournaments and in anecdotes which conjure up the atmosphere of the festive occasions of that period. There was jousting every other week, the poet tells us, and he goes on to say that quite two hundred knights or more were living as dependents of the Young King. They all tried to outshine one another in the eyes of the ladies and damsels seated beside the lists. One day there was a tournament at Joigny. As soon as they arrived, the knights donned their armour and rode to the tilting-ground, not far from the town; there they dismounted and waited for their opponents. The countess (Aelis, wife of Rainaut of Joigny) came over to them, with the rest of the ladies. Since there was still no sign of the opponents, someone suggested that the company might wish to dance. According to custom, a song had to be improvised as an accompaniment to their steps. So the Marshal, with his usual knightly accomplishment, set himself to compose one. Then a young herald improvised a second song, with the refrain: 'Marshal, I need a good horse!' The Marshal withdrew in silence and made for the lists, where the jousting had at last begun. He challenged one of the opposing party, unseated him in a trice, took possession of his mount (the traditional right of the victor) and led it over to the young herald, whose song was not yet done. Whereupon the youth adjusted the refrain: 'I have a horse! The Marshal gave it to me!' On another occasion the Marshal took possession of the horse belonging to a Fleming called Matthew of Walincourt. The latter was greatly put out and begged the Young King to order the beast's return. The Marshal complied; but later on he fought Matthew a second time and again led the horse away. That evening, while all the knights were banqueting together, Matthew approached the Young King and renewed his request that the horse be returned. Henry was considerably surprised. He summoned the Marshal and asked why his order had not been carried out; and

154

then it came to light that he had won the same horse twice on the same day.

Other anecdotes reveal the sportive, almost schoolboy humour of Henry the Young. There was, for instance, the day at Bures in Normandy when he decided to invite to his table all those whose first name was William—the commonest Christian name at the time, after John; no fewer than a hundred and seventeen joined him at dinner that evening.

But Eleanor clearly thought more of her second son, Richard, whom she had made duke of Aquitaine. Though he might not possess quite as much charm as his elder brother, Richard was scarcely less prepossessing. He too was tall and handsome—for both were of more than average height, unlike their brothers Geoffrey and John. Richard was an exceptionally gifted man, a fine poet whose works (only two of them have come down to us) have not lost their power to stir the emotions, especially the one which he wrote during his imprisonment. He had inherited the grey eyes and flaming red hair of the Angevins, and likewise their proverbial fits of fury; but his poetic gifts, his sense of humour and his change-able disposition (his friend, the troubadour Bertrand de Born, calls him *Oc-e-No*, Yes-and-No) are more reminiscent of his Aquitaine forebears. Comparing the two princes, Giraldus Cambrensis declares that Henry was praised for his clemency, Richard for his justice; that one was the shield of the wrongdoer, the other the hammer.

Life flowed by joyously at the court of Poitiers, punctuated by tournaments and banquets and always to the strain of viol, lute and cithara. Eleanor looked on with pleasure as a host of young people gave themselves over to the delights of dancing and poetry. The gilded youth of Poitou and Aquitaine breathed an air that seemed to belong to some tale of chivalry. In addition to the princesses, and the princes with their wives or betrothed, there were the knights, ladies and damsels belonging to their retinues. From time to time there were even richer gatherings—at the time of the great religious festivals, or when some great lord or sovereign came on a visit. In June 1172, for example a most brilliant reception was held in Limoges in honour of the kings of Navarre and Aragon, Sancho and Alfonso II. The latter resembled the prince of Aquitaine

in being the friend of troubadours and a troubadour himself.
Indeed, he kept open house to poets: Peire Rogier, Peire Raimon de
Toulouse and Elie de Barjols all frequented his court.

Henry II was debarred from this festive scene. For two whole years
he was hardly ever to be found in Europe. The storm of censure
bearing down on him was in violent contrast to the idyllic picture
which has survived of existence at Eleanor's court.

When news of Becket's death reached him on New Year's Eve
1170, he was laid low for several days and remained shut away in
his room, refusing to eat, drink or be spoken to. In the end, the
people closest to him began to fear for his life; Arnulf, bishop of
Lisieux, and the archbishop of Rouen tried in vain to bring him a
measure of consolation. Yet when at last he showed his face, it
immediately became apparent that his chief aim was to reject or
minimize his guilt. He wrote a letter to the chapter of Canterbury
Cathedral, declaring that he had not wanted the killing and did
not feel responsible for it. Further, he twice sent envoys to the
pope: the first time, to cleanse his soul of this murder which the
whole world regarded as his doing; the second time, to entreat
absolution for the bishops who had supported him during the
quarrel with Becket—notably Roger of Pont-l'Evêque, archbishop
of York, and Gilbert Foliot, bishop of London. Then he set out for
Ireland. He felt that he needed to put a certain distance between
himself and events.

For these were relentlessly pursuing their course. Within days of
Becket's death, there were reports from Canterbury of miracles
attributable to the martyr: a blind man whose sight had been
restored, a crippled woman who could walk again . . . The pilgrims
flocked to the desecrated cathedral, where no service of any kind
was held for almost a year. Meanwhile, round about Easter, Pope
Alexander III formally excommunicated the murderers and their
accomplices. The whole of England was laid under an interdict.
Henry II was not allowed to set foot inside a church. The pope
claimed to have had a vision just as the archbishop was being

stabbed to death: he had seen Becket saying mass and seen his chasuble suddenly redden with blood.

Henry was not received back into the fold until he had publicly done penance in Avranches before his eldest son, the Norman clergy and a vast gathering of barons and commoners. On May 21st, 1172, after swearing on the Gospel that he had neither ordered nor desired the death of the archbishop, he knelt on the steps of the church and allowed the monks to scourge him. He solemnly undertook to restore Canterbury Cathedral to its full dignity, to renounce the Constitutions of Clarendon, which had brought the quarrel with Becket to a head, to fast, give alms and contribute to the defence of Jerusalem by paying for the upkeep of two hundred knights.

In 1172 Henry decided to hold his Christmas court at Chinon. Eleanor joined him there, just as she had joined him in Bures two years earlier, when the announcement of the killing had brought the festivities to such a tragic end. It was obvious to her that Henry wanted to test the strength of his authority in Aquitaine, and we may reasonably assume that she went out of her way to give a good impression of her reign. After the years of ceaseless conflict occasioned by his quarrel with Becket, Henry could flatter himself that he had re-established control over his kingdom, all the way from Ireland—now 'pacified'—to the Pyrenees. His dramatic act of penance in Avranches had put an end to his dispute with the church, and any remaining friction between himself and the king of France had been erased in September, when Henry and Marguerite had been solemnly crowned in Winchester Cathedral. Finally, again as a token of peace and repentance, the king set about building two religious foundations—the Carthusian monasteries at Le Liget, in Touraine, and Witham in England. All was calm: kingdom, family, prelates . . . His world lay securely in his grasp.

Two months later, in February 1173, Henry summoned his chief vassals to a meeting at Montferrand, in Auvergne. Here he received Count Humbert of Maurienne and opened negotiations with him; his object was to marry off the last of his sons, John. He had a special affection for this youngest boy, calling him John Lackland because the prince had not shared in the distribution at Montmirail, where Henry had divided his kingdom among his children. (In fact this distribution had been a sham: Henry the Young might be a crowned king, but he had not been given the smallest particle of power.)

Henry therefore decided to marry his son John, a child of seven at the time, to Alix, heiress to the county of Maurienne. By this action he was ensuring that John would one day be master of a huge province in the vicinity of the Lake of Geneva, stretching downwards through Savoy and providing outlets to Italy and Provence. To show that he was in earnest, Henry paid Humbert five thousand silver marks. In addition he promised that John, to whom he had already talked of giving conquered Ireland, would receive several strategically placed castles in central England and three key positions on the European mainland—Chinon, Loudun and Mirebeau, abutting on the domains of Poitou and Brittany. John was consequently very well endowed, for these castles were so many stepping-stones in a state which sliced the Plantagenets' inheritance in two, from east to west. And Henry's determination to secure outlets to Italy could only point to imperial aspirations.

A second conclave, more formal than the first, was held in Limoges. Henry Plantagenet intended to communicate his decisions to his principal barons. He proposed to appear before them in all his majesty and announce not one forthcoming marriage, but two; for apart from John and Alix, King William of Sicily had asked for the hand of Joanna, who alone among Henry's daughters was still unmarried or unbetrothed. Through his children, Henry Plantagenet now reigned over Europe; and his power was spreading still farther southwards, for—another reason for calling this meeting at Limoges—Count Raymond V of Toulouse had agreed to do homage to him for his lands. Thus Henry was gaining the sovereignty which Eleanor had always wanted to establish over Toulouse and which he had failed to obtain by force in 1159. (In fact, only a short time after the king of France had saved him from the siege, Raymond had treacherously cast off his wife, Constance of France, and married Richilda, widow of the count of Provence; and he had asked Henry, rather than Louis, to settle his disagreements with the king of Aragon.)

158

The conclave at Limoges was designed to call attention to the aggrandisement of empire achieved as a result of Henry's strong will; all the more disquieting, then, was the impression made on him by the manner of its conclusion. The homage ceremony had been enacted with due solemnity. Henry had apprised the assembled barons of his plans . . . And then suddenly, to the astonishment of everyone, Henry the Young rose up and protested hotly against the settlement which had been made on his brother John. Why should he, Richard and Geoffrey have to forfeit castles which were vital to the defence of their lands? Furthermore, it was time that he was granted effective powers of sovereignty; otherwise, said Henry the Young, the two coronation services had been a hollow farce.

It must have been a harsh blow to Henry II's pride. Since the death of Thomas Becket, no one had dared to oppose his will; only the church's interdicts had stood in his way—stemming, as they did, from an authority which simply had to be bowed to.

At the end of the meeting the count of Toulouse requested a private audience and asked how Henry could possibly be so deaf and blind to what was going on around him. Surely he could perceive the baleful influence which Eleanor had acquired over her children during the past few years? Did he not realize that a web of conspiracy had been painstakingly woven and that there was not a single vassal in the whole of Poitou and Aquitaine who was not ready to betray him?

Henry was only half-persuaded as to the truth of these accusations. No one knew the count of Toulouse better than he did, or was better able to assess the value of the charges which he had laid. When it came to treachery, Raymond was a past-master—and Henry was well aware of the count's grudge against Eleanor. Moreover, like many another autocrat, he was probably too obsessed with his own ambitions to stop and notice what was happening under his very nose. His contemporaries insist that he was acting like a despot by this time, 'a despot within his family and within his dominions'. A despot is seldom clear-sighted.

However, the unexpected outburst on the part of his eldest son at least served to open his eyes to the fact that Henry the Young was no longer completely tied to him. It might be Eleanor's

159

influence; it might also be that the young man had been strongly affected by his father's public act of penance in Avranches, which had obviously been a blow to his personal prestige; nor must it be forgotten that the prince had always felt a very strong affection for Becket, who had been in charge of his early education.

So when the meeting in Limoges broke up, Henry decided to take his son away with him. He must find out what motives—and if need be what ulterior motives—were guiding the young man's actions, and precisely what influences had impelled him to turn on his father; he must also scrutinize the men about him and put a brake on the extravagance which was the despair of the royal treasurers.

The two kings spent several days riding and hunting together in the Aveyron valley; then, as Henry Plantagenet was eager to return to Normandy, they headed northwards. On the evening of March 7th they broke their journey at Chinon castle. They slept in the same room, as they had been doing ever since their departure from Limoges. When Henry II woke next morning, his son was missing.

Nor was there any sign of him anywhere else in the castle. A swift investigation revealed that the drawbridge had been lowered before dawn. Who could have conspired to this end? Henry decided to seek the solution later; his first step was to dispatch messengers in every direction. By this means he learned that his son had forded the Loire and headed northwards. He sent strict orders to his castellans that the Young King was to be detained on sight, then went hurrying after him. But the escape had obviously been planned with considerable care, and fresh horses had been posted at intervals so that the fugitive should maintain a clear lead over his pursuers. He was reported in Alençon before his father had even got as far as Le Mans. There followed a hopeless chase through Maine and the confines of Normandy, until finally news reached Henry Plantagenet that his heir had arrived in Mortagne, within the domains of the count of Dreux, brother to the king of France. The Young King was safely out of reach, and could afford to proceed to Paris at a steadier pace.

Thus, at the very moment when Henry II imagined that his authority had reached its peak, his eldest son was in open rebellion against him: he must have sought protection from the king of France prior to making his escape. Like Becket before him, Henry the Young was turning to the king of France for shelter and protection. Surely Henry II was not going to have the same trouble all over again?

But so it turned out. He dispatched messengers to Paris, requesting the king of France to send his son and heir back to Normandy: if the Young King had any wrong to complain of, it would be put right. The scene provided Louis with a further opportunity to display his own quiet brand of humour.

'Who makes this request of me?' he asked the envoys courteously.

'The king of England.'

'The king of England?' Louis displayed the liveliest astonishment. 'He is here with me and he has made no request of me through you.'

The envoys looked somewhat baffled.

'Perhaps,' added Louis, 'you still apply the title to his father, who was formerly king of England. Mark my words: that king is dead. It would be better if he were to stop mistaking himself for a king, since in full view of the rest of the world he has made his kingdom over to his son.'

But by the time this gibe reached him, Henry Plantagenet had at last acknowledged the truth of the situation. His eldest son was not alone in deserting him. Both Richard and Geoffrey had set off for Paris, and the rebellion was spreading through Aquitaine like a forest fire. All castellans, treasurers and other dignitaries appointed by the king himself were being expelled; the Lusignans and Rancons and Larchevêques were repudiating his authority. Furthermore, in response to the examples set by the barons of Poitou and Aquitaine, the counts of Sainte-Maure—Hugh, William and Jocelyn, all three of them familiars at the court of Poitiers—came out in favour of the Young King. And even more catastrophic news was in store: the movement was gaining hold in the island domains. The English nobles were seizing the opportunity to protest against the crippling taxes imposed by their sovereign. The earls of Leicester and Norfolk and the bishop of Durham were all committed to the rebellion, while in the far north King William

161

of Scotland was also voicing open support for Henry the Young. There was even a strange scene in Canterbury. After being under an interdict for a year, the cathedral was awaiting its new archbishop. On June 3rd, 1173, he was duly and properly elected: the successful candidate was Richard of Dover; but on the very day of his induction envoys arrived from the Young King, protesting against the decision to hold an election without his consent. The ceremony had to be broken off. An appeal was made to the pope, who naturally confirmed the election, especially since it had come to light in the meantime that the Young King, acting at his mother's instigation, had simply gone through the motions of blocking the appointment as a means of displaying his determination to set himself up as king in place of his father.

For a while, Henry must have felt completely isolated. Only Normandy had remained loyal to him. Among the men closest to him there was fear for his life. The letter which he sent to the pope at this stage strikes a note of genuine pathos. He complains of 'the malice of his sons, so iniquitously turned against their own father that they regard it as a glory and a triumph to pursue him'. And he adds: 'my friends have drawn away from me, my familiars entertain designs on my life . . .'

Not surprisingly, Louis VII made the most of the situation. He did all he could to assist the cause of the rebel princes. As, for instance, in the matter of Henry the Young's seal. This seal, a personal marker, was of exceptional importance in an era when the signature was not in use. When a person of eminence died, his seal was either broken or buried with him: nobody else must ever use the seal, which was for certifying documents.

Louis VII therefore lost no time in having a new one made and assembled a brilliant gathering in Paris to introduce the seal to the barons of France and the Plantagenet kingdom. All the rebel vassals who had been able to reach the French court swore fealty to the Young King. Others declared that they would ally themselves with him and help him secure possession of his kingdom; among them were the powerful Philip of Flanders and his brother, the count of Boulogne. The Young King distributed deeds to reward these alliances, employing his new seal in the process. Philip received the county of Kent and Dover castle; King William of Scotland was granted borderland adjustments which would make his frontier bulge deeper into northern England; his brother David was allotted the county of Huntingdon; the count of Blois was credited with fiefs in Touraine ... The count of Champagne promised military assistance, and all—with one voice—declared that 'he who was previously king of England is king no longer'.

The first fighting occurred in Normandy. On June 29th, 1173, Philip of Flanders laid siege to Aumale while Louis, at the Young King's side, attacked Verneuil. In northern England castles fell one after another; and in Brittany itself, along the frontier with Normandy, rebel barons seized the fortress of Dol.

Henry was at first nonplussed by the scale of these events, but he was quick to realize that since he could count on the loyalty of only a very few of his vassals his immediate task must be to recruit mercenaries. Contemporary opinion was against their being used, and this feeling of disapproval carried more and more weight so that, by the thirteenth century, it had led to a ban on their employment—until Philip the Fair reintroduced them, a fatal day in the history of France. But this was not the only characteristic which made Henry closer in outlook to a monarch than to a feudal king. Moreover, this was the very measure which led to his salvation. He recruited twenty thousand Brabantines without quibbling over their pay; and since time was short, and circumstances were against the levying of a further tax in England, he had to pawn everything to raise the funds, even his diamond-encrusted state sword, the one used at his coronation. Thereafter he acted with the speed and strategic skill for which he was renowned. In the space of a week, August 12th–19th, he advanced his army of Brabantines all the way from Rouen to Saint-James de Beuvron, at a rate of twenty miles a day. At Drincourt and Verneuil and Dol he gave proof, yet again, of his military prowess.

As events unfurled, the truth of Count Raymond's allegations was borne in upon him. Only Eleanor could have fashioned a conspiracy on such a scale. There could be no doubt about it: in the brilliant setting of the court of Poitiers she had slowly but surely turned sons against their father, vassals against their overlord. Everything pointed to her guilt: not only the testimony of the prisoners who fell into his hands, but the mood of exultation displayed by his Poitevin vassals. 'Rejoice, O Aquitaine, be jubilant, O Poitou, for the sceptre of the king of the North Wind is drawing away from you . . .' writes a contemporary chronicler, Richard the Poitevin.

Henry induced one of the prelates who had remained loyal to him, Rotrou of Warwick, archbishop of Rouen, to send the queen a solemn reprimand: 'We all of us deplore, and are united in our sorrow, that you—a prudent wife, if ever there was one—should have parted from your husband . . . Once separated from the head, the limb no longer serves it. Still more terrible is the fact that you should have made the fruits of your union with our lord king rise up against their father . . . We know that unless you return to your husband you will be the cause of general ruin . . . Return then, O illustrious queen, to your husband and our lord . . . Before events carry us to a dire conclusion, return with your sons to the husband whom you must obey, and with whom it is your duty to live . . . Either you will return to your husband or else, by canon law, we shall be compelled and obliged to bring the censure of the Church to bear on you; we say this with great reluctance and shall do it, unless you repent, only with tears and sorrow . . .'

But at the time this missive was composed (the wording is attributed to the king's secretary, Peter of Blois, who a few years later was to be one of the queen's staunchest aides) Eleanor certainly had no thoughts of returning to the husband who had spurned and deserted her. From the military point of view, things were turning out badly for her and already there was talk of a truce. Now that he had nothing more to fear in Normandy, Henry unleashed his forces against Poitou and began to ravage the area between Tours and Poitiers. Realizing that the queen's mainstay in this troubled hour could be none other than the devoted Raoul of Faye, he laid siege to Faye-la-Vineuse. The stronghold was soon in his hands. But Eleanor was gone, if she had ever been there, and so was Raoul himself: he had sped along the road to Paris in the wake of the princes, doubtless intending to seek asylum for the queen herself. How pathetically she and her brood were turning for succour to this despised first husband, this 'crowned monk'!

It was to the north of Poitiers, well on the way to Chartres and not far from King Louis's royal domain, that one evening a body of men in the pay of the Plantagenet happened to stumble into a small party of knights. They took them prisoner, quite at random, simply because they were Poitevins. To their astonishment they found a lady among the party, attired in men's clothes: it was Queen Eleanor.

Queen Eleanor Captured by Plantagenets

XV

Piegz a de mort selh que viu cossiros,
E non a joy, mas dolor e temensa,
Pueys ve la ren que.l pogra far joyos,
On non troba socors ni mantenensa.

'Tis worse than death to lead a life of pain,
Joyless, and filled with suffering and grief,
When she who might turn all this loss to gain
Denies her suppliant succour and relief.

AIMERIC DE PEGULHAN

'TELL ME, Eagle with two heads, tell me: where were you when
your eaglets, flying from their nest, dared to raise their talons
against the king of the North Wind? It was you, we learn, who
urged them to rise against their father. That is why you have been
plucked from your own country and taken to a foreign land. Your
barons have cheated you by their conciliatory words. Your lyre has
assumed strains of sorrow, your flute the note of affliction. In the
old days, with your taste for luxury and refinement, you enjoyed a
royal freedom; you abounded in riches of every kind; your young
companions sang their sweet songs to the accompaniment of tambourine and cithara. You delighted in the melodies of the flute,
you rejoiced in the harmonies of your musicians. I beg of you,
Queen with two crowns, end your continual self-affliction! Why
consume yourself with sorrow, why ravage your heart with tears
each day? Return, O captive, return to your own lands, if you can.
If you cannot, may your plaint be that of the king of Jerusalem:
"Alas, my exile has been a long one! I have lived with a crude,
ignorant tribe." Return, return to your plaint and say: "Tears have
been my bread both day and night, while men have asked me ceaselessly: Where are the members of your family? Where are your
handmaidens, where are your counsellors?" Some have been
suddenly torn from their lands and condemned to a shameful

ELEANOR OF AQUITAINE

death, some have been deprived of their sight, some are wandering in various places and are counted fugitives. Eagle of the broken alliance, how much longer will you cry out unanswered? The king of the North Wind besieges you on every side. Shout with the prophet, do not weary, let your voice ring out like a bugle so that it may be heard by your children; for the day is truly coming when you will be set free by your sons and return to your own land.'

This moving exhortation was the work of the same Cluniac monk, Richard the Poitevin, who had previously issued threats to the 'king of the North Wind'. Its vehemence, so well suited to Eleanor's nature, captures the feeling that must have been harboured by the people of Poitou, who were deeply attached to their ruling family, and above all by regular guests at the court of Poitiers, one of thom had proclaimed that the queen was to poets what dawn was to birds. But that brilliant hearth of life had been extinguished, the ever-hospitable court was closed. The queen was a prisoner.

———◆———

After being captured and recognized, Eleanor was taken to the tower of Chinon. It was there, in all probability, that she spent the six months leading up to her transfer to England early in July, 1174.

The setting must have prompted strange memories of the day twenty years earlier when she and Henry had made their first stormy but triumphant crossing from this same port of Barfleur. And now she was a captive in the hands of her own husband, who had only himself to blame for the troubles which now beset him. It was he who had broken faith. There might be imputations of treachery on both sides, but the initial act of betrayal had come from him.

Once again the sea was rough and a storm was threatening—one of those summer storms which are all the more dangerous on account of their very suddenness. There were doubts as to the advisability of setting sail. Everything was uncertain, weather and events alike. For Henry could certainly not claim victory yet. He may have wrested Le Mans, Poitiers and Saintes from Richard,

167

but he had been driven back from the fortress of Taillebourg, where that staunch supporter of the dukes of Aquitaine, Geoffrey of Rancon, was entrenched. In England the fight appeared to be spreading, led by the king of Scotland, the bishop of Durham and various nobles, one of whom—Hugh Bigod—had hitherto shown himself to be a loyal servant of the Crown, but had now espoused the cause of Henry the Young. The great chamberlain of Normandy, William of Tancarville, had sought permission to sail back from England, where he had been residing; but instead of going to Rouen he had hastened to join the Young King. The latter was in Flanders, busily mustering the troops who were shortly to reinforce the rebel army in England. So the revolt was by no means over; but in capturing Eleanor Henry had gone to the very heart of the conspiracy. And the queen, who knew him better than anyone, must have realized that he would no more flinch from a storm than he had done twenty years earlier.

Sure enough he gave orders for the fleet to set sail. Then, standing on the deck of the leading ship, he bared his head and uttered a public prayer: 'Lord, if in my heart I nourish plans which will bring peace to the clergy and the people, if the King of Heaven has decreed in His infinite mercy that my arrival shall mark the return of peace, then may He grant that I come safely to harbour. If He is opposed to my purpose and has decided to punish my kingdom, may I never be allowed to reach its shores.'

On Henry's lips, it was not always easy to distinguish between prayer and imprecation.

That same evening the fleet reached Southampton after a rough crossing.

Everyone assumed that the king's first impulse would be to make for central England and attack Hugh Bigod, or else proceed directly to the far north and there do battle with the king of Scotland. He did neither. On arrival, he declined the meal that was set before him and rationed himself to a hunk of bread and a glass of water; he then announced his intention of setting out for Canterbury next morning.

Despite his despotic nature he was not devoid of sensitivity, and the truth is that he felt momentarily disheartened; after all, the whole of his immediate family was against him and it was still

168

possible that he might be about to lose control of his kingdom. And it would certainly seem to have been then, in this sudden hour of dejection, that a true repentance was born in him. At the time of the act of penance in Avranches his main concern had been to cleanse himself of sin in the eyes of his people and of the Church; that had been an official gesture, a necessary preliminary to returning to the fold. But when, on July 12th, 1174, Henry went to the cathedral city where his disagreements with the archbishop had begun ten years earlier, it must have been apparent that he was no longer satisfying outward requirements: this time he seemed to be answering the call of conscience. A few days before setting sail Henry had unbosomed himself to the archbishop of Rouen who, touched by the man's loneliness, had suggested that he should visit Becket's tomb 'as a humble pilgrim'.

'If you are willing to come with me,' the king had replied, 'I will go.'

Which was how he came to be trudging along the road to Canterbury that day, barefooted and clad in the penitent's garb of simple homespun with a plain cord round the waist. He refused to take food or drink when he arrived in the town, but went straight to the archbishop's shrine and spent the night in prayer. It was a year since Thomas the martyr had been canonized. By this time the pilgrimages which had begun spontaneously in the immediate aftermath of the murder were becoming more and more frequent; they were even making their mark on the topography of London and the surrounding countryside, with the sudden appearance of Pilgrims' Roads and Thomas Streets (all this was some two hundred years before Chaucer wrote the *Canterbury Tales*).

It is not difficult to imagine the feelings that must have been aroused in the king by this vigil beside the tomb of the man who had been his dearest friend. This was the scene of the crime, and he had not dared to visit it until then. It was here one evening, as dusk was falling, that four knights had emerged from the shadows and come hammering at the cloister door. 'Where is Becket the traitor?' they had shouted. And the archbishop had given orders for the door to be opened, while the monks fled in panic—all save young Edward Grim. Then Becket had exposed his slender frame to the killers' thrusts until at last he fell, head northwards, in front

169

of the altar of St John the Baptist, laid low but unconquered. Almost four years had passed since then.

Henry attended mass next morning and then, as at Avranches, cast off his robe and exposed his naked back for a scourging. Afterwards he went to the leper-house at Harbledown and there, as an additional act of atonement, undertook to pay an annual contribution of twenty marks—a contribution which is still paid to the local hospital by the Crown.

Then, after taking some refreshment, Henry set out for London. During the night a messenger arrived; he brought news of the defeat of the king of Scotland, who had fallen into the hands of Ranulph Glanville, the king's justiciar. The struggle was not quite over, but by the end of September Henry's sons had given in.

Eleanor looked on helplessly as all her handiwork crumbled about her. Everything was slipping from her grasp at once: power, honours, even her children—for from now on she was to be parted from them. She was about fifty-three; her active life as a woman was coming to an end, as well as her active life as a queen; she was alone with her disappointed hopes, and humiliated in her ambitions and affections alike.

When she reached England, she was taken—at Henry's orders—first to Winchester and then to Salisbury tower, which was her normal place of residence. This was not the Salisbury which we know today—the tall spire of the cathedral was not built until the thirteenth century—but Old Sarum. The site of the tower where she lived can still be located on the turfed crater which lies within the ruins of the circular wall of the castle. It was here that she was to spend the darkest hours of her life. Her pride was not spared in any way. Henry now paraded himself quite openly with Fair Rosamond; he attempted to obtain a divorce in 1175, and hopes of success in this direction were raised when Cardinal Uguccione of Sant' Angelo came on a visit to England. The king gave him a warm welcome, presented him with a magnificent team of horses and had a beautifully furnished suite in the palace of Westminster especially prepared for Uguccione and his aides. Yet all this munificence proved of no avail: the legate departed without even listening to the plea for an annulment.

How did the queen respond to these uneventful years? She was completely cut off from life, isolated from all that was happening on the continent. She was not a captive in the sense in which we understand the word today: several times she changed her place of residence, moving to a castle in Berkshire or Nottinghamshire; but always she was kept under surveillance by one of the king's staunchest men, Ranulph Glanville or Ralph Fitz-Stephen, and precautions were unquestionably taken to forestall any desire on her part to escape in response to Richard the Poitevin's entreaties. By keeping her in England, Henry was depriving her of any contact with her sons; it was his policy to reinforce this estrangement, and for a while he even succeeded in creating a rift, though a fleeting one, between her and Richard over the question of Aquitaine, which was still under the combined rule of mother and son.

We know almost nothing of Eleanor's life during this long period of detention. It is easy to picture her going through moments of despair and being laid low at times in the dark, fog-wrapped winter days when the cawing of the rooks as they circled the scrawny trees must have seemed a cruel substitute for that musical background of flute and cithara conjured up by the lament of Richard the Poitevin. But this is not the predominating impression if we consider this 'uneventful' period in the light of the events which went before, still less of those which came after. It was not in Eleanor's nature to remain downcast, nor to immure herself in regretful longing for the past. The future may have been an unknown quantity, but she certainly did not regard this as any reason for failing to turn the present to advantage. That she *did* turn it to advantage becomes abundantly clear as soon as we think of her manner and behaviour after release; for at that point she presents herself in a truly astonishing light—more resourceful and energetic, surer of touch, more of a woman, more of a queen, than ever before. Which prompts us to believe that the years of silent retreat were not wasted years for Eleanor. Her every deed testifies to the fact: the closing years of her life reveal that her passionate love of literature, intellectual curiosity and powers of observation were as keen as they had always been. Once this long spell of enforced inactivity was over, she would be ready for action again and determined to draw, in every sphere, on the lesson learned in the seemingly endless hours of solitude while the seasons unfurled under the English sky.

Various happenings must have disturbed the serenity which she learned to acquire in the course of this unwilling retreat. To begin with, Eleanor must certainly have been told of the death of Fair Rosamond. In 1176 Rosamond became ill and retired to the nunnery at Godstow—and there she died before the year was out. The date is sufficient to give the lie to the story of how Eleanor made her choose between dagger and poison, for the queen herself was a prisoner at the time. One would like to think that in her heart she had forgiven this rival who was the prime cause of her misfortunes. Afterwards, Henry sent an annual donation to the convent where Rosamond was buried. There are tales that the nuns venerated her grave and that when this came to the ear of Bishop Hugh of Lincoln he was indignant and ordered the removal of the mausoleum which had been erected upon it. But a similar legend has grown up around the burial of many other royal favourites, especially Agnes Sorel, and it cannot be viewed as anything more than pious sentimentality.

It would have taken more than this to induce Henry to mend his ways. By 1177 a serious allegation was going the rounds and eventually it was brought to the notice of Louis VII of France. Alarmed, King Louis addressed an appeal to Rome calling for the immediate celebration of the marriage, long since contracted, between his daughter Adelaide and Richard, heir to Poitou and Aquitaine. The question was left in abeyance and become a source of continual friction between the courts of France and England. It remained unsettled for almost twenty years. The truth was that the luckless Adelaide had been seduced by Henry and so could not marry Richard. Throughout this time she lived in a state of semi-captivity, a sort of hostage in the hands of the kings of England; when at last she was set free she married William of Ponthieu, a knight of no consequence.

In the year of Rosamond's death, Joanna—Eleanor's second youngest—left for Sicily to join her betrothed, William II, 'William

172

the Good' as he is known in history. The young princess was accompanied by a large and brilliant escort, made up of high-ranking prelates like the bishops of Winchester and Norwich and headed by her brothers Henry and Richard. Henry escorted her across his domain, from Rouen to Poitiers; then Richard took over and accompanied her as far as Saint-Gilles. Joanna was a girl of eleven when the marriage ceremony was performed in Palermo. In atmosphere, the court which she was entering was more akin than any other to that of Poitiers. Her husband, a gifted and cultured pupil of Peter of Blois (who had since become chancellor to Henry II) was a perfect knight; he was to prove as much a few years later by extending a courteous welcome to the daughter of the king of Morocco when her ship was wrecked on the Sicilian coast; ignoring those advisers who suggested that he should hold her as a hostage, William saw to it that she was nursed back to health in his own palace and then sent her home to her father, escorted by a fleet which had been fitted out at his expense; the king of Morocco was so impressed that he at once ceded two cities which the Saracens had captured from the Sicilians.

Another item of news which reached Eleanor during her captivity was the death of her first husband, Louis VII of France.

The last months of his life had been darkened by an event which might well have ended in tragedy: an accident had befallen his only son. Partly because of the state of his own health, and partly because the boy was fourteen and therefore of age, Louis decided that the time had come for Philip the God-given to be crowned. Arrangements were completed for the ceremony to be performed in Rheims on August 15th, 1179. On August 13th Philip took it into his head to break his journey and go hunting in the woods at Cuise-la-Motte, near Compiègne. Gradually, caught up in the excitement of the chase, he drew away from his companions until the moment came when he realized that he was alone in the dark, utterly lost in the depths of the forest. Panic-stricken, quite unable to find his bearings, he wandered about all night. Early next morning he was found by some charcoal-burners, pale and distraught, shaking in every limb. They took him to Compiègne, where his father came hurrying to his bedside. For several weeks the boy seemed beyond hope. The shock to his nervous system had been

173

so great that he appeared unlikely to recover. At this point Louis sought and obtained leave to visit the shrine of St Thomas of Canterbury. The king of England bade him welcome at Dover and insisted on escorting him to the cathedral city, where they spent two whole days together in deep meditation before the archbishop's tomb. The two old enemies came together at the last resting-place of the man who had been the living embodiment of the curbs which the Church imposed on the power of kings.

Before leaving the city, Louis presented the monastery with his own gold cup and promised the monks that they would receive a hundred hogsheads of wine from France each year.

This shared pilgrimage must surely have made a curious impression on Eleanor. She had sat enthroned beside both these men. One she had loved, the other had loved her. And now these two kings, whom she had set against each other, were reconciled in the sight of God. A slow reversal of feelings had induced her to break with Henry, that creature of passion and ambition, and seek protection and asylum from the man whom she had once scorned. But now that too was behind her. And no doubt Eleanor had by this time recovered sufficient self-possession to adjust to this state of non-attachment.

Louis did not long survive the pilgrimage. His son regained his health at last and was strong enough to go through the coronation service on the first day of November. The reconciliation between the kings of France and England was made whole when, this time with his father's consent, Henry the Young attended and took part in the crowning of the youth who was at once his overlord and his brother-in-law. He was characteristically generous in the provision of gold, silver, venison and princely gifts; the minstrels were unanimous in extolling his munificence. It was he who was accorded the honour of bearing the royal crown of France on a velvet cushion as the long procession filed through the cathedral; in recompense for this duty he was given the post—a purely honorary one—of seneschal of the realm.

A few months later, on September 18th, 1180, King Louis VII died peacefully at the Cistercian abbey of Saint-Port. One of the chroniclers who tell of his last moments (Geoffrey of Vigé) declares that the king's life had been beyond reproach except for the fact that he had been too well-disposed towards the Jews and conferred too many charters of freedom on towns within his jurisdiction. Every era has its reactionary historians, and this particular historian can hardly have suspected that a time would come when his strictures would be regarded as words of praise.

———————◆———————

It may have been through the verses of Bertrand de Born, warrior and troubadour, that Eleanor learned of the continued fighting between her sons and their father. Since her capture, Poitou was no longer the home of the courtly ideal. Bernard de Ventadour had retired to the Cistercian abbey of Dalon. As for his companions, the courts of Champagne and Flanders had reaped the benefit, attracting the troubadours and trouvères who no longer had any reason to linger in Aquitaine. But the southern muse was not easily silenced, and Bertrand de Born—castellan of Hautefort, and a member of the Young King's entourage—was distinguishing himself by the quality of his lyrics; in these *sirventès*, as they were called, war assumed the place which Bernard de Ventadour and others had given to courtly love. For armed disputes had broken out again, setting father against son and brother against brother.

Eleanor had been a prisoner for nine years when in June 1183 she was profoundly affected by a dream. She saw her son Henry, the Young King, lying on a couch with his hands pressed together, in the attitude of a recumbent figure on a tomb. On his finger he wore a ring set with a priceless sapphire, and on his head—above the smiling, handsome but colourless face—he seemed to wear two crowns. One was the crown which he had worn on the occasion of his coronation as king of England; the other appeared to be made of a substance unknown to mortal man; pure light it was, like the Holy Grail.

When, shortly afterwards, she was informed that the archdeacon of Wells wished to speak to her on behalf of her husband, she immediately sensed the purpose of his visit. She told him of the dream which had been haunting her for several days. The archdeacon—Thomas Agnell by name—has handed the story down to us.

It deserves telling for the light it sheds on the mentality of the age and the inner life of Eleanor herself. The archdeacon was clearly surprised to hear the queen interpret her dream in a manner which even the most pious of churchmen would have found unexceptionable. 'What other meaning than eternal bliss can be ascribed to a crown with no beginning and no end? And what can such brightness signify, so pure and so resplendent, if not the wonder of everlasting joy? This second crown was more beautiful than anything which can manifest itself to our senses here on earth. As the Gospel says: "Eye hath not seen, nor ear heard, neither have entered into the heart of man, the things which God hath prepared for them that love him."'

After returning to Wells, the archdeacon must often have thought of the vision which had been granted to the queen, especially as he climbed the famous steps of the north transept, which always gives the impression of being bathed in celestial light. He assures us that this noble lady, 'a woman of great discernment, fathomed the mystery of the dream and had in consequence borne the news of her son's death with strength and equanimity'.

The Young King had died within a few days from an illness which his physicians had been unable to halt. His last moments in Martel castle, on the banks of the Dordogne, had been marked by an admirable and memorable spirit of peace. Sensing early that he was not going to recover, Henry had dispatched the bishop of Agen to implore his father's forgiveness for his acts of rebellion, and for being at war with him even now. Filled with the mistrust which tightened its hold over him as the years went by, Henry Plantagenet was reluctant to believe the envoy's words. However, the bishop insisted on being given some token of forgiveness which he might deliver into the young man's hands, and eventually the king entrusted him with a magnificent sapphire ring; this, he said, should be the sign that he forgave the prince and was anxious for his recovery.

As soon as the bishop returned, Henry the Young took the ring, placed it on his finger and pressed his lips to it; then he asked those about him to take note of his dying wishes. First he turned to William the Marshal and asked him, as his most trusty companion, to make the pilgrimage to Jerusalem on his behalf, wearing the crusader's cloak which he himself had now donned. Then he asked everyone present to plead with his father for the release of Queen Eleanor. Finally he confessed his sins and received the Body and Blood of Christ and the holy oil. Afterwards he commanded that ashes be spread on the floor. His companions lifted him from his bed and laid him down with only the crusader's cloak about him. He entreated them to apply a halter to his neck, for he wished to die like a common thief as penance for the wrongs which he had committed in his lifetime. Lying on the ashes and the cold stone, he distributed all his worldly goods, even the articles of royal attire. He was already fighting for breath when a monk gently drew attention to the fact that he was still wearing the precious stone which his father had sent him.

'Do you not wish to divest yourself of it and thus achieve absolute poverty?' asked the monk.

'I am not keeping this ring out of any desire for possessions,' replied Henry, 'but because I wish my Judge to know that my father sent it to me as a token of forgiveness.'

However, he gave permission for it to be removed after death. But when, towards evening, the Young King closed his eyes, the ring could not be prised from his finger; and this was taken as a sign that the father's forgiveness of his son had met with favour in the sight of God. Henry the Young died on June 11th, 1183; he was twenty-eight years old.

6-11-1183
Henry the young dies

2 Requests:
1. Wm the Marshall go to Jerusalem
2. His mother be released

XVI

Bela m'es pressa de blezos,
Cobertz de teintz vermelhs e blaus,
D'entresenhs e de gonfanos
De diversas colors tretaus,
Tendas e traps e rics pavilhos tendre,
Lanzas frassar, escutz trancar e fendre
Elmes brunitz, e colps donar e prendre.
. . . No'm platz companha des basclos
Ni de las putanas venaus;
Sacs d'esterlis e de moutos
M'es laitz, quan son vengut de fraus;
E maisnadier eschars deuria hom pendre
E ric home, quand son donar vol vendre;
En domn' escharsa no's deuria hom entendre
Que per aver pot plegar et estendre.

I love the medley of blazons
Enamelled scarlet, gold and blue,
The standards and the gonfalons
Painted in every vivid hue;
I love the tents that decorate the field,
I love to break a lance, or pierce a shield,
Or cleave a helm and call on foes to yield.
. . . But rogues and robbers I eschew,
And rotten whores, and all the crew
Of cozeners, cheaters, liars, who
Disgust me by the deeds they do;
Death to the profit-maker of ill fame,
The rich man selling out should reap the same;
Turn a deaf ear to women of no shame
Who prostitute themselves in search of gain.

BERTRAND DE BORN

178

WHETHER OR NO it was in direct answer to the Young King's last wish, the strict controls imposed on his mother seemed to slacken somewhat after his death. The news of his passing had brought great sadness not only to the knights who had ridden with him and benefited from his liberality, but among the ordinary people, where the account of his death was widely circulated.

The troubadours mourned him—and none was more deeply affected than Bertrand de Born, who had been his companion at arms. Bertrand composed two beautiful *planhs* (laments) in his honour. He had participated in the Young King's rebellion with characteristic zeal and fury and was even accused of being the evil genius behind the revolt. His biographers relate how he afterwards came before the dead man's father, vanquished and repentant.

'Lord, I lack everything today.'

'Why should that be?' asked the king.

'Oh sire, the day your valiant son, the Young King, died I was deprived of consciousness, wits and direction.'

The story goes that when the king heard what Bertrand had to say about his son, tears came into his eyes and he was beside himself with grief. When he recovered he said to Bertrand: 'Nothing could be less wrong or unreasonable than that you should have lost your wits over my son: he thought more of you than of anyone else on earth. And I, for love of him, restore your freedom, your lands and your castle, and with them my love and favour.'

The tale is probably as inaccurate as most of the others set down about the troubadours by their biographers in the thirteenth century; yet it is true in so far as it conveys the genuine grief which the Young King's death inspired in everyone, even his father who had shamelessly used him as a pawn in his own political game and had only himself to blame for his son's constant acts of rebellion. Shortly afterwards, Peter of Blois wrote the king a letter implying that Henry sorrowed over this loss 'without any regard for royal majesty'. Peter did his best to console him: 'If it is godly to cry because of your son's death, it is also godly to rejoice—for he repented humbly ... May you derive full joy from the knowledge that such a son sprang from your loins, abounding in every natural gift ...'

A few months later Eleanor was allowed to receive a visit, in

Salisbury, from her daughter Matilda and the latter's husband, Henry the Lion, duke of Saxony. The duke had been exiled by the emperor for continually rebelling; his marriage to the eldest Plantagenet daughter, twenty-seven years his junior, had shifted the Angevin policy towards an alliance with the Guelphs, of which Henry the Lion was the leader. Henry and Matilda had been residing for a while at Argentan, in Normandy, where Bertrand of Born had lived as their guest until, following the familiar pattern of courtly love, he had offended the duke by the ardour of some of his verses addressed to Matilda. When Duke Henry sent him packing, he avenged himself by scoffing at the unspeakable boredom which prevailed, or so he said, at the court of Argentan.

In the following year, 1184, it was Eleanor's turn to visit her daughter, who was in Winchester, brought to bed of a son— William. And the queen spent Easter at Berkhamsted, one of the pleasantest of the royal residences, whose moats were supplied by a meandering river shaded with willows. Eleanor's name began to figure with renewed prominence in the royal accounts that year. Also, Henry gave her two presents—the first for a very long time; these were a splendid scarlet dress lined with miniver, and a saddle worked with gold and trimmed with fur. Finally he announced his intention of bringing the whole royal family together in the palace of Westminster on November 30th, the feast of St Andrew. At Christmas the family was united again, this time at Windsor. To mark this public reconciliation, Eleanor made a gift to the abbey of Fontevrault: an annuity of a hundred pounds to be derived from the provostry of Poitiers and the vineyard at Benon (Charente-Maritime); henceforth the nuns were to receive this sum at Martinmas, half at Poitiers and the other half at Marcilly, near Benon; the following year, Henry Plantagenet formally ratified this gift initiated by his wife.

Were these presents, social gatherings and displays of leniency an indication that the king of England had genuinely altered his attitude towards his wife? In fact, each of these acts seems to have been primarily political in motive; they were more or less isolated instances. The death of Henry the Young had upset the Plantagenet's plans for his sons' future. The logical step would have been for Richard, next in line of succession, to inherit the portion

180

previously set aside for his elder brother. But Richard was not so close to his father's heart as Henry the Young had been; it may well be that Eleanor's special regard for him was partly responsible for this lack of affection. It swiftly became apparent that the new favourite was to be John Lackland, Henry's last-born son, who had been reared in his mother's absence. The king's first step after the death of his heir was to invite Richard to cede Poitou and Aquitaine to John—not to Geoffrey, who was now second in line, but to John, the youngest.

This invitation was not at all to Richard's taste. He was a true Poitevin, even more so than his elder brother; added to which, he had been declared titular successor to William the Troubadour and had spent his youth hunting in Talmond woods, like Eleanor's forefathers; he looked upon Limoges and Poitiers as his home.

Consequently, the problems of succession arising from young Henry's death could not be properly settled without Eleanor's presence and assistance. Henry might be in the habit of behaving like a dictator, but in this matter he had to bow to the conventions of the day and become a feudal king again. A few years earlier, in 1179, he had forced Eleanor to cede her own rights to her son Richard, and according to some historians this had led to a momentary misunderstanding between mother and son. This in no way deterred them from allying in opposition to the Plantagenet's schemes; in vain—only a year later—did Henry dispatch Eleanor to Normandy and try to bring Richard to heel by threatening Poitou with an army led by its lawful duchess. Neither Richard nor Eleanor was taken in by this attempt at blackmail. A prophecy generally attributed to Merlin the magician was in circulation at the time: 'The Eagle of the broken alliance shall rejoice in its third brood.' The Eagle was Eleanor. She had been so termed from the very beginning of her era. Guernes of Pont-Sainte-Maxence, in his life of Thomas Becket, calls Eleanor the 'Eagless' and makes reference to the prophecy, while the tale of William the Marshal even goes so far as to suggest that Eleanor's name—Aliénor—derived, etymologically, from *alie* (eagle) and *or* (gold).

It is a pity there are no detailed accounts of the gatherings which Eleanor attended at her husband's side, royally arrayed—for however brief a time—in her robe of scarlet and miniver. In 1184 she was about sixty-two; she had been queen of England for exactly thirty years. But a third of that period had been spent in retirement, an unwilling retirement that had patently induced in Eleanor a kind of serenity which, with the help of age and experience, was now enabling her to look more deeply into people and affairs. It was excusable that she should feel a mother's pride as she gazed at the children gathered about her, especially Richard, so tall and handsome, with his typically Norman build, grey Angevin eyes and bright hair, to say nothing of his sprightly humour and gift for writing poetry, characteristics which he shared with his brother Geoffrey. They were very different from John, both in nature and appearance. John was below average height, dark and highly strung. At seventeen, he already showed signs of the instability peculiar to the Plantagenets, an instability which in his case would eventually lead to something worse.

It is intriguing to wonder which of the marriage partners showed to better advantage in this situation: Eleanor or Henry, who was only just turned fifty yet who, according to contemporaries, was prematurely aged as a result of excesses of every kind. It is impossible not to be struck by the unstinting praise which is lavished on Eleanor by those historians who knew her in old age. Among them was Richard of Devizes, a monk of Winchester, who extols the virtues of 'that beautiful and chaste woman, at once impressive and modest, humble and eloquent'. On the other hand, they are unanimous in painting a sorry picture of Henry in his declining years: he who had been a knight of such commanding presence had become a stout old man limping from a kick inflicted by a horse. Those who knew him best assert that he was a victim of that appalling affliction, the inability to achieve a state of calm: he could not keep still, but was for ever frenziedly gesticulating. He had always been casual in the way he dressed, and as he grew older this casualness turned into untidiness, reflecting the inner disorder of a man who had no control over himself. He might be a great administrator, but though he had successfully imposed his authority on the state, he had not made it orderly. In these last years, authority became despotism: mere hunting offences were punished with appalling ferocity—men were mutilated or imprisoned for the remainder of their days. He had always had an immoderate passion for hunting; and in England, where there were not many hunting-grounds and where the forests were thinly scattered, this passion roused him to barbarous acts against anyone who infringed the regulations: the death of a stag, it was said, meant the death of a man. But Henry's despotism had not brought peace to the land. His contempt for others' rights had involved him in the cruellest of wars: the war waged against him by his own children. Towards the end of his life, the image which he projected was as far removed as could be from the twelfth-century ideal of the urbane, cultivated prince, eschewing all excess and dispensing justice and liberality. The account which Peter of Blois gives us of the style of living adopted by Henry and his court comes within an ace of caricature: 'At mealtimes or out riding or during the long evenings, there is no order or restraint. The clerks and knights of the court feed on poor, ill-fermented, badly baked barley loaves, heavy as lead. To drink, they are given a tainted, murky, thick, rank, flavourless wine. I have seen wine set before persons of eminent rank which was so thick that to get it down a man had to close his eyes, clench his teeth and sift it rather than drink it, grimacing with horror. The beer tastes horrible and looks atrocious . . . Cattle is sold to the court whether it is healthy or diseased, and fish—four days old—is no cheaper for being putrid and foul-smelling . . .' And he goes on to describe the diabolical regime which the king, growing more and more restless, inflicted upon his familiars; sometimes, in the course of his protracted expeditions, they would quarrel among themselves as to who was to enjoy the luxury of spending the night in a hovel which even a pig would disdain; and indeed the king's retinue included persons of every description— mountebanks, prostitutes, dicers, buffons, mimes, jugglers, publicans, rogues, vagabonds . . .

Another contemporary, Walter Map, likens Henry's court to that of King Herla, as described in the old Celtic legends. According to these tales, King Herla attended the wedding of the king of the Pygmies, celebrated in the latter's underground palace. Afterwards, the king of the Pygmies showered presents upon Herla and his party and then conducted them to the surface. He handed his chief visitor a small hound and bade him hold it in his arms. 'Take good care,' he said, 'that neither you nor any of your courtiers dismount before this little hound jumps down.' Herla and his companions had a long ride ahead of them. After a while the king met a shepherd and asked him for news of the queen, his wife, from whose side he had departed only a few days ago. The shepherd was at a loss to understand him and replied that he did not know any queen of that name; he believed, however, that there had been such a queen some two hundred years ago, before the Saxons conquered the Britons. Immediately a number of courtiers leaped from the saddle, meaning to punish him for his insolence, but barely had their feet touched the ground than their whole bodies turned to dust. The king was greatly alarmed and reminded his familiars that they were not to dismount until the little hound jumped down. But the hound never did jump down, and Herla and his court have been roaming the forests ever since. The story goes that the men of Wales used often to see them riding in the Wye Valley, but no longer did so now that they were re-embodied in the court of Henry Plantagenet. It is easy to recognize the familiar theme of the wandering hunt, which other storytellers call the 'mesnie Hellequin' and which has spread from its Celtic origins to become part of international folklore.

This legend and others equally ominous are frequently met with in contemporary writings about Henry II. One of the most striking is recorded by Giraldus Cambrensis. He avers that in a room in the palace of Winchester there was a painting of an eagle and four eaglets; three of these eaglets were assailing the eagle's wings and back with their beaks and talons; the fourth—and smallest—was perching on the parent-bird's neck and trying to tear its eyes out. Apparently Henry remarked on the picture in the following terms: 'Those four eaglets are my sons, who will go on persecuting me until I am dead; the cruellest of all, the one who will hurt me worse than the other three, is the youngest—my favourite.'

These fateful words proved only too true in Henry's last years. Richard and Geoffrey were continually in conflict with their father, shrewdly abetted by King Philip Augustus of France. It was soon evident that, whatever other qualities he might lack, Philip Augustus would at least be a more gifted diplomat than his father. When Geoffrey died while at Philip's court he was given a splendid funeral in the newly-built chancel of Notre-Dame, which had been consecrated only three years earlier. Countess Marie of Champagne attended the ceremony, deeply upset by the loss of this half-brother whom she treasured and whose death, as the result of an accident in the lists, had come so tragically early.

As for Richard, the ins-and-outs of his long struggle with his father are related only indirectly to the story of Eleanor's life. But they resulted in his following the example set by his brothers and contracting an alliance with the king of France. It was his cousin, Count Philip of Flanders, who brought them together. Gervase of Canterbury, the monk who was the ever-vigilant chronicler of these dark years, relates how in 1197 Richard declared to the count of Flanders: 'I would gladly walk barefoot to Jerusalem if it would get me into his [Philip Augustus's] good graces.' To which the count of Flanders replied: 'It would be a waste of time walking there either barefoot or shod, but there is nothing to prevent you from seeking him out just as you are, on horseback, in your splendid armour.' Hence the first audience with Philip Augustus, and the establishment of an alliance which could only be to the cost of Henry Plantagenet. There were still a good many unsettled grievances between the latter and the king of France. High on the list was the question of the fortress of Gisors and of the Vexin borderland, abutting on Normandy; both had been the dowry of Marguerite of France and should have been returned to the French Crown on the death of Henry the Young. In 1186, the year of Geoffrey's death, Marguerite had married again—this time to King Bela of Hungary; nothing was left of the union upon which, thirty years earlier, Henry and Eleanor had built so many hopes. True, Gisors now formed part of Adelaide's dowry; but as there was no question of solemnizing her marriage to Richard, the king of France was free to demand the return of the princess herself or of the fortress. There were continual outbreaks of fighting over this, followed by peace talks which were usually held under the famous Gisors elm, several hundred years old and so massive that nine men linking hands could barely span its trunk.

One day in August 1188 Henry Plantagenet and his escort arrived early at the rendezvous and thoughtlessly took up all the room in the shade of the great elm, showing nothing but contempt and defiance for King Philip and his party. The negotiations dragged on for hours, and from beginning to end the king of England's men hogged the shade under the tree while the king of France and his courtiers were exposed to the full heat of the summer's day. Towards evening, after a continual exchange of messages between the two parties, an arrow issued from the ranks of the Welsh mercenaries escorting Henry Plantagenet. The French, already riled as a result of their long, irksome wait in the sun, were furious at this violation of the conventions; they hurled themselves upon the English, who, quite unprepared for such an attack, withdrew in disorder and took shelter behind the powerful walls of Gisors. Unable to get at them, Philip Augustus's men took their revenge on the elm, lopping off the branches and hacking at the trunk. This behaviour was not at all to the liking of the king of France, who observed that he had not journeyed out to play the part of wood-cutter.

But his anger could not restore the tree where the foes had so often parleyed, and the fortress of Gisors became more than ever a bone of contention between the houses of France and Normandy; it inspired war after war between Philip Augustus and his powerful vassal. But paradoxically Philip's position was to be strengthened, for a while at least, by the active support of his enemy's son— Richard, count of Poitou and heir to the English throne. An extraordinary scene was enacted at Bonmoulins a few months after the episode of Gisors. Henry and Philip had arranged to meet in yet another attempt to settle their differences. A painful surprise was in store for the king of England: when Philip arrived, he had Richard with him. Philip voiced his demand that the projected marriage between his sister Adelaide and the heir to the English throne be celebrated without further delay; he went on to insist that Richard be made master not only of Poitou, but of the whole group of provinces which had been set aside for him—Touraine, Anjou, Maine, Normandy; finally he urged that the time had come for the vassals to do homage to Richard as heir to the English throne.

Henry foresaw a renewal of the troubles which had rained down on him as a result of crowning the Young King; he was not in the least tempted to repeat the experience of a premature coronation. Or rather, he was firmly resolved not to surrender the smallest particle of power to his son Richard. 'You are asking something which I am not prepared to concede,' he replied.

At this, to the stupefaction of both escorts, Richard stepped forward: 'Something which seemed unbelievable before is now abundantly clear to me,' he declared. And with slow deliberation he unfastened his sword-belt, went down on his knees before the king of France and, placing his hands in Philip's, did immediate homage for his continental domains. He requested that Philip should, as his overlord, provide him with aid and protection; and these were promised there and then.

Doubtless the scene had been prearranged. For Richard, it was a declaration of war on his father; for Henry, a public affront, a challenge flung down by his own son, the heir to the throne. Not content with this, Richard followed the precedent established by his elder brother and set out for Paris as soon as the meeting was over, to spend Christmas with Philip Augustus. To all appearances, the two men were bound by the liveliest feelings of friendship: they ate from the same dish, slept in the same bed and appeared together in public at the various feasts and ceremonies traditionally associated with the time of year.

Meanwhile the old king was undermined by sickness and sorrow, and his vassals were deserting him one by one. His Christmas court, held in Saumur, was sombre and lonely, with no one to enliven it save John Lackland—on whom, so it was said, he thought of conferring Richard's inheritance.

The war began again with the coming of spring. Philip and Richard fought as partners, while only the loyallest of knights stayed with Henry: it needed a William the Marshal to stand firm at his sovereign's side in such circumstances, battling for a lost cause. One final meeting was held between the two kings—this time at Colombiers, near Azay-le-Rideau. Henry's state of exhaustion was so obvious that Philip took pity on him, folded his own cloak in four and offered it as a cushion. Henry declined the offer. A truce was arranged. The war was going in favour of the two allies: Tours had just fallen to them and so had the city of Le Mans, dearest of all to Henry's heart, for it was his birthplace and his father, Geoffrey, was buried there.

When he got back to Chinon, the king took to his bed and never

187

rose from it again. He had sent his chancellor, Master Roger, to ask Philip for a list of the nobles who had betrayed him; it was part of the agreement, in fact, that they should apprise one another of the names of all traitors. Henry asked William the Marshal to read the document out to him. William could not repress a cry of astonishment: at the head of the list was John Lackland, the cherished son for whose sake Henry had not hesitated to sow discord among the elder brothers. The Marshal made to go on with the reading, but the old king told him to desist: 'You have said enough.' And with that he turned his face to the wall and lay still. On the third day a small amount of blood issued from his mouth and nose: he was dead.

HENRY II
dies
7-6-1189

XVII

Ar vey qu'em vengut als jorns loncs,
Que.il flors s'arenguo sobr'els troncx,
Et aug d'auzelhs chans e refrims
Pe.ls playssatz qu'a tengutz embroncx
Le fregz, mas eras pe.ls soms sims,
Entre las flors e.ls brondelhs prims,
S'alegra quascus a son for.

I see the days are lengthening,
And winter trees are burgeoning;
I hear the trills and call-notes light
Of birds in thickets sheltering
Against the cold; but on the height,
Among young leaves and flowers bright,
Each one makes merry in his way.

GUILHEM DE CABESTANH

RICHARD had sent William the Marshal to England with instructions to secure the release of his mother, Queen Eleanor. He found her, he reported, 'at Winchester, already at liberty, and more the great lady than ever'.

After her few months of comparative freedom in 1184 and 1185, Eleanor had returned to the shadows; once again her husband had placed her in the care of Ralph Fitz-Stephen, Henry of Berneval and Ranulph Glanville, all three of whom were men of proven loyalty. It is easy to imagine the bitter feelings that must have been aroused in her. Henry had summoned her to Normandy simply to use her as a scarecrow: he had hoped to bring Richard to heel by threatening to re-establish her as ruler of her Poitevin domains. Afterwards she had reverted to her captive condition—a condition which was harder to bear after her brief taste of freedom.

But with Henry's death on July 6th, 1189, her hour of deliverance

189

had come. She promptly set herself free, and her concientious bodyguards were probably too worried about what was in store for them to voice any serious objection. At once she embarked on an extraordinary cavalcade. Only yesterday she had been a captive; now she rode from town to town, from castle to castle, releasing captives wherever she went, securing justice for all who had cause for complaint against the royal sheriffs, redressing the manifold abuses of power committed by her husband.

She brought a spirit of liberation with her; a new reign was beginning in which there need be no fear of being imprisoned, or even hanged, for a minor hunting offence. And some of the decisions now promulgated by the queen show the extent to which she had opened her mind to the problems of her time during those long years of confinement, instead of immuring herself in self-centred grief; for instance, she introduced a series of uniform weights and measures for corn, liquids and lengths of cloth, and she brought in a coinage which would be valid anywhere in England. This concern for the country's economic needs cannot but command admiration. In Poitiers, Eleanor had been the presiding spirit of those courts of love at which the intricacies of refined emotion had been debated so unflaggingly; she had succeeded in inspiring Bernard de Ventadour and may well have provided Chrétien of Troyes with themes for romances; she had been the living embodiment of that idealized Lady to whom knights and poets paid homage. Yet here she was, displaying a degree of practicality and a realization of the requirements of the day which had proved beyond her husband, for all his technical skill in matters of building and warfare. That the same length of cloth should be measured differently in York and London, that an identical quantity of wheat should be weighed by one standard in Cornwall and another in Surrey: this was extremely confusing to peasants and merchants alike. As for coinage, local variations profited nobody except the money-changers. In a country now at the height of economic prosperity, standardization was imperative; yet it would be a long, long time before a standard system was introduced in France.

Eleanor also founded a hospital. This was a popular gesture in those days: her husband had founded several, including the leper-house at Caen, the institution at Quevilly, near Rouen, and the hospital of Saint-Jean in Angers. Nor was this the only foundation for which Eleanor was personally responsible. But it is perhaps of more moment than the rest, for here was a hospital founded in England, the country where she had been a prisoner for so long. Also, the other foundations had been isolated acts—whereas references to this one in Surrey occur in the Pipe Rolls again and again; from this time forward, continual mention is made of the queen's hospital, the queen's poor, the sick and infirm in the queen's hospital, and so on, and this gives the impression of unstinting solicitude over a long period, comparable with her concern for Fontevrault./

Her considerateness towards the abbeys lying within her domains also deserves mention. Her husband had found it convenient to divide his reserve battlesteeds among them, making the monks responsible for the animals' upkeep; of this onerous burden she discharged them.

Finally Eleanor laid plans for the coronation of her son, the beloved son who was to inherit the Plantagenet empire. Until the day Henry died, she had probably lived in fear and trembling at the thought of his disinheriting Richard in favour of John, his favourite (for was this not the hidden reason for Henry's guardedness in his negotiations with Philip of France? and why else should he have suggested—at Gisors, on the famous occasion when the elm was hacked to pieces—that Philip's sister, betrothed to the heir to the English throne, should marry 'one or other' of his sons?). She was well aware that there were now two immediate obstacles, or at any rate two major problems, to be overcome on Richard's behalf. First, he would be exposed to his brother's jealousy. For John had always been jealous: his meanness, his disturbing underhandedness, everything about him was in marked contrast to this tall, great-hearted brother with his noble strength and terrible ire, a man to whom forgiveness came as readily as anger, but who never suspected guile. Secondly, Richard was more or less a foreigner in English eyes. Though born in Oxford, he had made only brief visits to the island; he could not speak the language; his tastes, habits and background all served to justify the name 'Richard the Poitevin', which he was generally accorded. What sort of reception would

191

he receive from the burghers of London and from the great nobles whom his father had found so hard to manage?

In 1189, the year Henry died, Eleanor was sixty-seven. She was still a formidable figure: the impression which she made on William the Marshal is indicative of the feelings inspired by her presence—that of a great lady who, far from being senile or broken, was fired by an inner flame that solitude had served to verify. Moreover, the style of dress which was then in favour flattered a woman of mature years, even though it emphasized the figure. It was in Eleanor's era that the wimple came into being: a light veil framing the face which certain orders of nuns still wear and which conveniently hid white hair and wrinkled necks. Finally, it would seem that she had accumulated a superb store of energy during her enforced retirement. Perhaps she told herself that she had a duty to expend it unreservedly in the course of her last few years on earth, for she could not know that she still had so long to live, and that the last phase was to be the fullest, the most intense, the most eventful of all.

To the task of serving Richard, and ensuring that it was he who wore the crown, she brought all her love as a mother and all her experience as a queen. And what other queen of her time could stand comparison with her? In succession she had reigned over these two western kingdoms of France and England which were then the third force in the European world, younger than the badly undermined eastern empire, sustained against the Turks only by western aid, which was both needed and resented; more effective than the western empire, which faced disaster precisely because its rulers' ambitions were so immoderate. In these two kingdoms, which she had at one time hoped to combine under the leadership of her eldest son, lay the mightiest and best administered fiefs, the most prosperous cities, the most thriving markets. Nowhere was there a greater profusion of abbeys, or a higher standard of scholarship and teaching; nowhere did new buildings show such boldness of conception. What other city could now rival the fame of Paris or London or Oxford? What cathedral could compare with Chartres (which had just acquired an Englishman, John of Salisbury, as its bishop)? What markets could hope to vie with the markets of Champagne, where the level of trade was still

of Champagne. Father of Henry, K of Jerusalem

rising, thanks to the continual efforts of Eleanor's son-in-law, Henry the Liberal? What poetic works reflected better than those of Chrétien of Troyes the courtly and chivalrous ideals, the flower of the age, ideals which were now being reflected even within the confines of the German Empire? And where else did spiritual communities exist that could match the fervour and vigour of Fontevrault, Rievaulx, Canterbury or, rising amid the waves, the two St Michael's Mounts—one in France, the other in Cornwall, at the farthermost western tip of the world?

Two kings were now to rule over this dual domain of France and England which Eleanor—eagle with two heads, *aquila bispertita*—seemed, by her very existence, to mould into one. France was now in the hands of King Philip whose birth, putting an end to her hopes that Henry the Young might eventually reign over both countries, had coincided with her husband's withdrawal of affection: it was as though the long-delayed rise in the Capets' fortunes had signalled the decline of the Plantagenets'. She had never met Philip. He appeared to be on the best of terms with her son Richard, but a mother's instinct bade her mistrust him. All reports told against him. He was an unkempt, rough-and-ready young man brought up in the backwoods; though his tutor, Philip of Flanders, had striven for a time to impart some less crude ways to him. What response could such a husband evoke in his wife, the fair, gentle, loving Isabella of Hainault? He had certainly been a thoroughly selfish son to his mother, never showing her the slightest consideration. Adela of Champagne had left court and now lived on her own estates. Finally, he did not like troubadours, which could not fail to damn him in Eleanor's eyes. Four years earlier he had proclaimed that he no longer intended to entertain poets and musicians at his court, as any prince of good birth did; instead of showering hospitality on them, he proposed to give to the poor.

There could be no escaping the fact that the alliance between Philip and Richard had been basically against King Henry. What was likely to happen between them now that they confronted one another independently? Philip was alleged to have made a significant observation while still a child: as he gazed from a distance at the fortress of Gisors, white in the sunshine, he had exclaimed: 'I wish those walls were made of gems, and I wish all the stonework

Two kings:
1) Philip augustus of France
2 Richard I of Engl.

was gold and silver—so long as no one knew, or had any means of telling, except me!' And when this admission was greeted with astonishment he added: 'No cause for amazement—the more valuable the fortress, the dearer it will be to me when it falls into my hands.'

Sooner or later the clash was bound to come. Who would Richard's allies be? From his brother John he could look for nothing but betrayal. His brother Geoffrey, heir to the duchy of Brittany, had died three years earlier, leaving only a daughter; but his wife Constance was with child at the time and had subsequently given birth to a son named Arthur in honour of the hero of the Round Table. But for some reason Constance of Brittany loathed the Plantagenets; perhaps she thought they were to blame for her husband's death. At all events, she had willingly handed her infant son over to King Philip; and he, asserting his sovereign rights, had ordered that the child be reared at the French court.

Then there were Eleanor's daughters, linking the Plantagenets by marriage to other European courts. Unfortunately the eldest—Matilda—had died in the same month as Henry; but at least her husband, the duke of Saxony, seemed a loyal ally. The second daughter, Eleanor, was married to the king of Castile, and through her it was possible to look for alliances beyond the Pyrenees which could be highly advantageous to a kingdom extending as far south as Bayonne. Finally Joanna, as wife of William of Sicily, was in a position to provide invaluable support for Richard's grand design.

For there was a grand design taking shape in western Christendom in that summer of 1189, one that stirred many a memory in Eleanor's heart. As in the days when she was the young queen of France, there was talk of a crusade of kings. It was exactly forty years since her uncle, Raymond of Poitiers, had met his death in battle with Nureddin; and throughout those forty years the annual mass arranged by Eleanor had been said for the repose of his soul. In the meantime the dreaded catastrophe had occurred: Jerusalem, the Holy City, was in Saracen hands again. It had fallen two years earlier, in 1187, when the army of Frankish barons had incautiously ventured into the Hattin deserts and been cut to pieces by Sultan Saladin's mamelukes. The future looked black for the frail Latin kingdom, now almost completely stripped of defenders. But from the shelter of their fortresses, the military religious orders—those Templars and Hospitallers who had survived the slaughter at Hattin—were still desperately holding their ground. And now, with the support of a few recent reinforcements, the ex-king of Jerusalem (Guy of Lusignan, from Poitou) had undertaken the re-conquest of the city of Acre. In fact, the barons in the Holy Land had for many years been addressing ever more urgent appeals to western Christendom. The prelates supported these pleas, urging all Christian princes to spurn rivalry and personal ambition and take the Cross together; it was in response to the Church's en-treaties that Henry Plantagenet had more than once met King Philip under the Gisors elm. In vain. The special tithe levied for the purpose had been sacrilegiously misused: Henry had spent it on mercenaries in the fight against his own sons.

It would seem, however, that Richard was now determined, come what may, to answer the call which his father had ignored. And Eleanor, for all her eagerness to safeguard his royal interests, had no intention of dissuading him from a project which carried her back to the time of her youth.

1186 Geoffrey d
1187 Jerusalem fell
1189 Henry II died

XVIII

D'ardimen vail Rollan et Olivier,
E de domnei Berart de Montdesdier,
Car soi tan pros, per aco n'ai bon lau
... En totas re semble ben cavalier
Si.m soi, e sai d'amor tot son mestier
E tot aisso c'a drudari' abau.

In courage Oliver and Roland's peer,
In courtesy Montdidier very near,
My knightly prowess flattering favour gains . . .
I seem, nay, am a perfect chevalier,
I know the ways of love and hold them dear,
And everything that unto love pertains.

PEIRE VIDAL

THE BRIGHT PEAL OF BELLS, the heralds' trumpets sounding through the London streets, an eager crowd surging forward and bringing the horses to a standstill so that they pawed the ground with impatience; the cheers and acclamations; the tapestries draped in front of the houses and stuck with nosegays and green garlands; the fresh rushes underfoot . . . how often in her life Eleanor had been at the heart of such festive scenes. Since the day when, as a girl of fifteen, she emerged from Bordeaux cathedral in her wedding-dress, she had been hailed on innumerable occasions by a joyous populace, and been escorted amid the rustle of silken standards and the jingle of golden spurs.

But never had she experienced a keener sense of joy than today. Previous coronations had been the handiwork of fate, but this one was her own handiwork and the service was about to set the seal on her efforts both as queen and mother. For the past two months her every thought and deed had been guided by a single unswerving purpose—that of securing the English throne, and command of the Plantagenet realm, for this cherished son Richard who was her pride and joy. It was as though the whole of her previous life, including the long years of humiliation and enforced loneliness, had been a preliminary to the present triumph. The prophecy made by Merlin—or rather by Geoffrey of Monmouth—was coming true on this third day of September, 1189; the Eagle was indeed rejoicing in her third brood.

Richard had not set sail from Barfleur until August 13th. He had landed at Portsmouth and joined Eleanor in Winchester the following day. They had travelled to Windsor together, and from there they had ridden in solemn procession to St Paul's Cathedral on September 1st. Finally, still escorted by the prelates and principal barons of the realm, they had come to Westminster, where all was ready for the coronation.

No extravagance had been spared in the effort to make the occasion memorably colourful and brilliant. It is clear from the Pipe Rolls that the Poitevins gave free rein to their traditional liking for pomp. Every horse ridden by a member of the royal party was freshly accoutred, and the prodigious sum of thirty-five pounds was expended on a quantity of 'miscellaneous cloths' in various brown and scarlet shades and textures, to say nothing of furs— squirrel, miniver, sable. The apparel worn by the queen and her attendants cost seven pounds and sixpence; Eleanor's cape alone, using five and a half ells of silk and trimmed with squirrel's fur and sable, came to four pounds one and seven. Other items, which she would need for the series of feasts and banquets after the service, called for ten ells of rich red cloth, two sables and a miniver; and in addition, of course, there was all the linen for the wimples and undergarments. And since Richard's largess extended to the whole entourage (as indeed was the general custom at such times) a pelisse of squirrel's fur was specially made for Adelaide, 'sister to the king of France', and two others were presented to the daughters of the earls of Chester and Gloucester; Havisa, the earl of Gloucester's child and heiress to one of the wealthiest counties in England, had been given in marriage to John Lackland, the king's brother. In addition there were pelisses for the nephews and nieces: one recipient was William, Matilda's four-year-old son; another was the earl of Striguil's daughter, who was going to marry William the Marshal.

Of the members of the solemn procession slowly moving forward beneath the vaults of Westminster Abbey, many had cause to be profoundly grateful to their new sovereign. Immediately after the clergy in their white surplices came Geoffrey of Lucé, bearing the royal skullcap; then came John the Marshal with the golden spurs, his son William with the sceptre with the cross, and William Patrick, earl of Salisbury, with the sceptre with the dove. All three had been loyal followers of Henry Plantagenet, up to and including the time of his open conflict with Richard. Their presence at Westminster today was proof of the new king's forgiveness, and it is worth pausing to give an account of the scene, so characteristic of the period, which had been enacted between Richard and William the Marshal when they came face to face at Fontevrault, within a few yards of the church where Henry II lay at rest. It was only a matter of days since their previous dramatic confrontation on the outskirts of the blazing city of Le Mans, at a time when William was still fighting in defence of Henry as the king retreated before his son. He had stood aiming his lance at the heir to the throne and Richard had cried: 'Marshal, do not kill me! That would be wrong, for I am defenceless!' It was true: he wore nothing that could protect him except a pourpoint and a light iron headpiece. 'May the Devil slay you,' exclaimed William, 'for I will not!' Whereupon he thrust at Richard's horse and killed it, so that Henry should have time to make good his escape. It was with the memory of this deed fresh in their minds that the two men eyed each other at Fontevrault. How would Richard react? Would he succumb to one of those legendary rages which sometimes convulsed him . . . ?

What followed was fully worthy of the age of chivalry. 'Marshal,' said Richard, looking straight into the eyes of his father's defender, 'you tried to kill me the other day and would have done so had I failed to knock your lance aside with my arm.'

'Sire,' returned William, 'I had no intention of killing you. I have sufficient skill to land my lance exactly where I aim at, and I could have struck you as easily as I struck your horse. But it was your horse I struck. I cannot believe I did wrong, and I do not rue the deed.'

'I forgive you,' said Richard, 'and I shall not hold it against you.'

So William the Marshal found himself escorting his sovereign to the throne, with the prospect of an early marriage to one of the richest heiresses in England, the young countess of Striguil.

And Richard had accorded similar treatment to most of the barons who had fought at his father's side. Only Ranulph Glanville and Stephen of Marzai had failed to win clemency. Ranulph, once known as the 'king's eye', had been faced with the choice of imprisonment or the fantastic fine of fifteen hundred pounds in silver. Stephen had served as seneschal of Anjou for Henry II and was renowned for his avarice—he had refused to make the traditional offerings to the poor after the king's death; now he was held captive in Winchester pending payment of an even larger ransom—three thousand pounds.

On the other hand, the three nobles walking in procession with the three swords of state in their gold scabbards all had special reason to rejoice at this great event. One was David of Huntingdon, who had always been a keen supporter of Richard. The second was Robert of Leicester: a few short months ago he had been a more or less penniless outcast, but as soon as Eleanor was free she had ordered the restitution of all the lands which had been taken from him as a punishment for abetting Richard's revolt. The third was none other than John Lackland—though Lackland was now a misnomer, for his brother had showered possessions upon him: he was lord of the county of Mortain, in Normandy, and of several castles in England, including Marlborough, Nottingham, Lancaster and Wallingford; and his marriage to Havisa of Gloucester made him master of one of the finest feudal estates in the land. Richard had been similarly generous to his father's bastard sons. Geoffrey, the elder of the two, had gone into the church, and Richard had promised him preferment as archbishop of York; the younger son, William, known as 'Longsword', who was subsequently, by marriage, to become earl of Salisbury, was also treated lavishly. Obviously a considerable measure of calculation lay behind Richard's generosity: it was important to secure the allegiance of men who might otherwise have been his rivals and hence his enemies. But there was also a great deal of instinctive generosity about it.

199

Meanwhile the procession moved on. A dozen dignitaries—six counts and six barons of England and Normandy—carried a sort of long table draped with velvet and spread with the traditional vestments and insignia of the coronation ceremony: the gold-embroidered sandals, the royal tunic, the linen veil, the dalmatic and the ermine-lined mantle of kingship. Then came William of Mandeville, count of Aumale, with a cushion bearing the crown of gold inlaid with precious stones. Last of all, advancing beneath a silk canopy which four barons held aloft on the tips of their lances, came Richard himself, flanked by two bishops—Reginald of Bath and Hugh of Durham.

Eleanor must have followed every step in the ancient ceremony with the watchful eye of a master of ceremonies. First there was the taking of the oath. The prelates were gathered before the altar, in the centre of the chancel. Among the English: Baldwin, archbishop of Canterbury, Gilbert of Rochester, Hugh of Lincoln (destined to be canonized), Hugh of Chester . . . Among the Normans: Walter of Coutances, archbishop of Rouen, Henry of Bayeux, John of Evreux. And in addition to these there were the abbots, the cathedral canons and clergy representing every order, all standing to listen to the royal oath. Richard knelt, laid his hands on the open Gospel and pledged himself as follows: each day of his life he would behave in a peaceable and honourable manner and show respect for God, His Holy Church and His ministers; he would dispense unimpeachable justice to the peoples entrusted to his care; should bad laws, written or unwritten, be practised within his kingdom, then he would destroy them; he would ratify and add to those laws which were good.

Then came the anointing, the most solemn part of the service. In those days it was looked upon as a kind of sacrament; some people did not hesitate to compare it to the consecration of a bishop. Richard was divested of his raiment until all he had on was his breeches and his shirt, unfastened to the waist. Gold-embroidered sandals were placed upon his feet, and Archbishop Baldwin of Canterbury (a loyal friend to the Plantagenets: his first act after enthronement had been to ask Henry II to ease the circumstances in which Eleanor was confined) applied the oil to his head, chest and arms, as a token of the pride, knowledge and strength which a king needed. Next a linen veil was laid upon his head, symbolizing the purity which must characterize his intentions, and then a kind of silken skullcap which would henceforth be his customary headwear. He donned the royal tunic, made of gold brocade, and a dalmatic shaped like a deacon's, as a sign of the close affinity between kingship and the priesthood. The archbishop handed him the sword with which he must ward off the enemies of the Church, and a pair of golden spurs—the insignia of knighthood—were fitted over the sandals. Finally, the heavy gold-embroidered cloak of rich red cloth was fastened to his shoulders.

Richard looked magnificent in this array. His light red hair caught the light as he stood head and shoulders above the men bustling about him. He advanced on the altar with a firm gait and halted on the steps to listen to the final solemn adjuration addressed to him by Archbishop Baldwin: 'I entreat you, in the name of the living God, to accept this honour only if you vow to keep your oath inviolable.'

'With God's help I shall observe it without deception!' thundered Richard. To him, no ceremony was so formal as to demand the rigid observance of convention. And it was with every sign of assurance that he took the heavy crown from the altar, handed it to the archbishop and knelt as it was set upon his head; two barons held it, partly on account of its weight and partly as an indication that a feudal king ruled with the aid of his Council. Then the archbishop placed in his right hand the royal sceptre surmounted by a cross, and in his left the lighter sceptre surmounted by a dove, which was a reminder that whenever called upon to act as judge the king should seek the help of the Holy Spirit. Now that he had received all the tokens of kingship Richard walked to the throne, preceded by a cleric holding a candle and by the three barons bearing the three swords. He sat down and high mass began.

———————◆———————

Yet the coronation day was to be marred by tragedy. After the serenity and grandeur of the service, Richard—acclaimed by the barons and the common people—laid the crown and the royal vestments upon the altar and donned a simple gold diadem and a lighter silk tunic before going to the great hall of Westminster for the banquet. Here the prelates and barons mingled before Eleanor's gaze and were waited on by citizens of London and the royal city of Winchester; the former had volunteered to serve drink, the latter to serve food. Outside the hall, ample provision had been made for lesser folk, and the beer was flowing freely. Suddenly cries of horror rang out amid the joyful tumult. To the Jews of the City, this festive hour had seemed an appropriate time to come and offer their gifts to the king. It was a misjudgment. They came upon an excitable mob containing men to whom more than one of them had lent money—for in London, as in most other trading centres, the Jews were generally usurers and pawnbrokers; in his account of the sorry scene the chronicler Richard of Devizes terms them *sanguisugas* (bloodsuckers). Brawling began, culminating in a veritable manhunt. None of the Jews survived, except those who managed to reach the shelter of the archbishop's palace, their traditional sanctuary when their lives were in danger.

The day after his coronation the king gave orders that the men responsible for the massacre should be tracked down and punished. And Richard of Devizes goes on to relate how the Jews were molested in other cities too—though not in Winchester, his own city; here, he claims, people always behaved in a civilized manner (*civiliter*).

It was not long before the citizens of London, who had extended such an enthusiastic welcome to King Richard the Poitevin, awoke to the fact that their prized new sovereign had but one thought in mind: namely, to depart from his island kingdom at the earliest possible moment. True, his purpose was an honourable one. He was obsessed with plans for a crusade. And soon, inspired by his example, the whole of England began to make ready for the expedition. In the first place, a tax was levied to help pay the expensed of the men at arms. Despite the unfortunate precedent of the 'Saladin Tithe', which instead of being used against Saladin has been misappropriated by Henry II to subsidize his personal quarrels, the new tax was raised without undue difficulty. Richard had a fertile imagination when it came to raising funds, and he saw no reason why he should not sell feudal rights. We learn from one of the chroniclers of his reign, Roger of Hoveden, that he put castles, towns and large estates up for sale. 'I would sell London itself,' the king declared shamelessly, 'if I could find a buyer for it.'

But raising financial support was only one aspect of the island's preparations for the crusade. In every English port, craftsmen were busily engaged in the task of building ships and *buzzes*—huge transport vessels capable of holding eighty horses and over three hundred passengers, excluding servants and crew. In the towns, ropes were being twined and sails woven. Whole armies of woodcutters were felling trees to make masts and keels, while in the clearings the smithies were so many hives of industry: in the Forest of Dean alone, fifty thousand horseshoes were specially forged, to say nothing of arms and armour and pliant, intricate coats of mail which called for skilled workmanship, as well as helmets and bucklers which could be hammered out on the anvil. Slender arrows needed fashioning, and stout bolts for crossbows. Hard wood had to be tempered for building engines of war, and there was a great demand for soft leather with which to make saddles and harnesses. Skilled men of every kind were hard at work. On their estates, the great barons—carried away by the same spirit of enthusiasm—were making their own preparations for the journey east; and the impulse spread even to the towns, where countless ordinary people came forward and offered to join in the crusade. A modern scholar, Dr William Urry, has written a history of his native Canterbury and successfully drawn up a list, house by house, of the families dwelling in the city in Eleanor's day; in one small area—at the intersection of Mercers' Street and High Street, between the Butter Market and St Mary's church—he has traced five humble men who took the cross. There was Hugh the Goldsmith and Philip of Mardres and, not far away, Vivien of Wiht; there was Adam of Tolwarth, who fought close to King Richard at the siege of Acre, and the house of Margaret Cauvel, whose husband—a Londoner—likewise took part in the expedition. All these people were working hard, hurrying to and fro, getting into debt and selling land in order to buy weapons and armour. The crusade was transforming people's lives and having repercussions in even

203

the humblest dwellings: in peasants' cottages, pigs were being slaughtered and sides of bacon cured; they could be sold at a good price to those about to depart on the long journey.

On both sides of the Channel, within the realms of the kings of France and England alike, there was the same mood of excitement as in the days when Louis VII and Eleanor had taken the Cross. Today the stakes were infinitely larger, and the circumstances infinitely graver, than they had been forty years earlier. At the time of the fall of Edessa, forty-five thousand Christians had been either slaughtered or enslaved and northern Syria had been in danger of attack by the Turks. But today Christendom was confronted by a crisis on a completely different scale: the Holy City itself was in Moslem hands again. For a hundred years the precarious Latin kingdom had been preserved on a day-by-day basis, frequently at the cost of heroic sacrifices—like that of the leprous little king who had died four years earlier and who, towards the end of his short life, had insisted on being carried out in a litter so that he could superintend the fighting. Now that kingdom seemed likely to vanish for ever.

The fall of Jerusalem had resulted in long lines of Christian slaves trudging towards the markets of Egypt and Syria under Moslem escort. For more than a month, between October 2nd and November 10th, 1187, a cruel sorting operation had been performed daily, emptying the Holy City of its Frankish population and breaking up individual families; Saladin's officers had ignored old people and children, but herded the young men and girls between the first and second walls of the city. As a result, even according to the most moderate estimates, between eleven and sixteen thousand had been reduced to slavery; of these, five thousand were sent to Egypt, where they provided the manpower needed for building fortifications. Yet the victor, Saladin, had displayed an exceptional generosity. True, his reasonably honourable surrender terms had been exacted only under threat of seeing the entire city destroyed including the mosque of Omar—a Moslem shrine. For the population of Jerusalem had been implacably determined to defend itself. The disaster at Hattin had more or less stripped the city of armed defenders; but one of the few nobles to escape the slaughter, Balian of Ibelin, had hastily organized resistance. He had conferred knighthoods on some threescore burghers, thereby transforming them into warriors, and however ill-prepared they may have been, they had succeeded in blocking Saladin's vanguard. Saladin was caught completely unawares, for he had supposed he was riding into an open city. Realizing that the Franks of Jerusalem were prepared to go to any lengths, he had eventually given the vanquished a chance to ransom themselves at the rate of ten besants per man, five per woman and one per child. But only two per cent of the Franks living in Jerusalem could raise such a sum (a besant was the equivalent of about twelve gold francs). Balian successfully negotiated the release of the poorer members of the community in exchange for a lump sum. Seven thousand men were to be set free at a cost of thirty thousand besants; the Templars and Hospitallers parted with the money, though only in response to threats. And Saladin, in a praiseworthy gesture, set another two thousand slaves at liberty, sharing the ransom price with his brother Malik-al-Adil. In addition, he was moved to pity by the advanced age of two of the city's inhabitants and he gave permission for them to go on living in Jerusalem: one of these men was over a hundred, a survivor of the First Crusade which had set out from western Europe in 1096 and recaptured the Holy Places after three years of heavy fighting.

It was the same story all over Syria and Palestine. Refugees flocked to the coast as Saladin crushed one Frankish stronghold after another—Châteauneuf, Saphet, Beauvoir, Beaufort—strongholds which for a century had miraculously safeguarded the narrow strip of territory that made up the kingdom of Jerusalem (although there was a border of some two hundred and twenty miles to defend, the kingdom measured only about fifty miles across at the broadest point). Meanwhile the new emperor of Byzantium, Isaac the Angel, was content to congratulate Saladin.

Everything seemed to point to the termination of any Christian presence in the vicinity of the Holy Places, with the possible exception of the Greeks. This would mean a return to the days when a pilgrimage to Jerusalem had been fraught with perils; once again pilgrims would have to reckon with marauding bands of Bedouins, recurrent Turkish threats and the extortionate demands of the

Byzantine custodians in charge of the Holy Sepulchre. Indeed, no other outcome had seemed likely since the time when Nureddin, and then Saladin, had succeeded in uniting the whole Moslem world from the falls of the Nile to the Euphrates, from Alexandria to Aleppo, so that Egypt and Syria were under the command of a single man.

And yet the Frankish kingdoms were to survive for another hundred years and more—though admittedly in a very different form from the one determined by the First Crusade. Some of the barons clung to the debris of their principalities as drowning men will cling to driftwood. The walls of Antioch were capable of withstanding even the fiercest onslaught, and so were the fortresses manned by the Hospitallers and Templars. The unexpected arrival of a squadron of Sicilian Normans under the count of Malta, Margarit of Brindisi, led to the rescue of Tripoli, on the coast. The city and port of Tyre were similarly saved by a half-German, half-Italian baron, Conrad of Montferrat; he lost no time in reinforcing the area lest Saladin should launch an early attack.

Conrad was one of those hard-headed people for whom ends are more important than means. He had arrived within sight of Tyre on July 14th, 1187, only ten days after the débâcle at Hattin. The Italian squadron with which he was sailing had a considerable number of traders aboard. In response to the inhabitants' entreaties he undertook to defend the city. He entrusted the military governorship to a Genoese, Ansaldo Bonvicini, and then proceeded to share it out, quarter by quarter, among the droves of merchants who were anxious to establish a firm foothold in this well-placed harbour town so as to increase their level of trade in the East. To the Pisans—no strangers to the city—he allotted part of the ancient domain to which the king of Jerusalem had clung, granting them all kinds of concessions. One commercial company from Pisa—the Vermiglioni—managed to secure an extraordinary range of privileges, not only in Tyre itself but in cities such as Jaffa and Acre which had still to be recaptured. The merchants from Barcelona were given a fort known as the Green Palace, complete with oven and trading facilities, and Conrad distributed similar establishments among natives of Saint-Gilles, Montpellier and Marseille.

This policy, placing the Frankish tenure of the Palestinian ports on a firmly economic footing, was to be imitated at several other points along the coast. As René Grousset has pointed out in our own day: 'Moralistically speaking, it was faith which had created the Latin East in the last years of the eleventh century; it was the quest for spices which kept it going in the thirteenth.' The chivalrous solution had been replaced by the commercial solution, and for several hundred years the latter was to stand in the way of the religious solution—the one which St Francis of Assisi was to lay before the sultan of Egypt.

But no one could have foreseen these long-term consequences as the kings of France and England and the Emperor Frederick Barbarossa made ready for departure. Nothing was certain except that the Poitevin knight, Guy of Lusignan, who still bore the absurdly inflated title of king of Jerusalem, had taken it into his head to besiege St John of Acre with a mere handful of supporters, and that the time had come for a rescue operation; for there was a grave risk that the siege, begun on August 28th, 1189, might end in tragedy. Saladin had moved up in defence of the fortress, and the luckless attackers were on the point of being trapped between the Moslem garrison in Acre and these powerful reinforcements. The small bands of pilgrims who still disembarked from time to time (Italians, Burgundians, Flemings, even Danes occasionally) might lend the king trifling support, but a full-scale operation demanded the presence of the royal crusades—or of Frederick Barbarossa's, which had set out in May 1189.

Richard eventually left England on December 11th. Eleanor did not join him on the continent until February 2nd, 1190. Between them, they had decided that it would be wise to pacify John by adding to the grants of land which Richard had made at the time of his coronation. John was now to receive the counties of Cornwall, Devon, Dorset and Somerset. Geoffrey the Bastard had been elected archbishop of York and was to be consecrated as soon as the pope had confirmed his appointment. Richard had made both swear that they would not return to England for at least three years: doubtless he was mindful of the fate which had befallen Robert Courthose, the son of William the Conqueror; while he was away fighting in the Holy Land, his authority had been usurped

207

by his younger brother, Henry Beauclerk. However, Eleanor herself interceded on John's behalf and he was released from his oath. Not that he was granted any share in the government of the island; the kingdom was left in the hands of Eleanor and the man who had been Richard's chancellor in the days when he was still only count of Poitiers—William Longchamp, now chancellor and grand justiciar of England. He was a strange, misshapen figure with a limp and a stammer; yet the penetrating eyes beneath his bushy brows testified to a brain so shrewd and able that he was generally credited with two right hands; he was in holy orders, and shortly after the coronation the bishopric of Ely came his way.

In view of the impending crusade, it was essential that the kings of France and England should be on good terms. Philip Augustus was still pressing for the early marriage of his sister Adelaide. Richard met him at Gisors (there was no elm, now, for them to shelter under) and cleverly talked him into setting this vexed issue aside until later.

It was probably then that Eleanor started to hatch her private scheme for Richard's marriage; but she kept her thoughts strictly to herself and the preparations for the crusade went on more energetically than ever. The documents reflect the activities of these months, listing the manifold gifts which were traditionally made on such an occasion to monasteries and other religious establishments. Not far from Talmond, Richard founded the monastery of Lieu-Dieu and presented it to some Augustinian monks. He made donations to the abbey of La Grâce-Dieu, in the Sèvres marshes, while Eleanor gave the Hospitallers the small port of Le Perrot, near La Rochelle on the Atlantic coast, to make it easier for them to reach their establishments in Poitou. Another foundation was created at Gourfaille, near Fontenay. Nor does it come as any surprise that the abbey of Fontevrault received renewed support from Eleanor, while Richard confirmed the gifts which his forefathers had accorded the same abbey, adding various contributions of his own, including one for thirty-five pounds drawable on the Exchequer in London.

This last gift is dated June 24th, 1190. On that very day Richard was saying goodbye to Eleanor in Chinon. It had been arranged that his fleet should sail to meet him in Marseille or one of the Italian ports. He himself had decided to journey straight to Vézelay, where the crusading armies were gathering.

When the moment of departure came, a staff and water-bottle—the traditional emblems of pilgrimage—were ceremoniously placed in his hands. The staff snapped. An inauspicious beginning.

6-24 -1190
Richard leaves Chinon

XIX

Altas ondas que venez suz la mar,
Que fai lo vent çay e lay demenar,
De mon amic savez novas contar,
Qui lay passet,—no lo vei retornar!
Et ay, Deu d'amor!
Ad hora.m dona joy et ad hora dolor

You towering waves that roll in from the sea,
Buffeted by the winds incessantly,
Bring some good tidings of my love to me,
For his returning sail I never see.
Ah, cruel fate,
How swiftly joy and sorrow alternate.

RAIMBAUT DE VAQUEYRAS

IT MIGHT HAVE BEEN EXPECTED that Eleanor would go straight back to England following Richard's departure—for surely her first duty was to keep his kingdom safe for him? Yet in fact she set out in precisely the opposite direction, making for the Pyrenees.

The historic voyage of the two kings had suffered several postponements. Philip Augustus had lost his wife, Isabella of Hainault, on March 15th, 1190. She had died giving birth to twins, and these did not survive her. She was not yet twenty and had already produced an heir to the French throne—the future Louis VIII, born three years earlier. King Philip accorded her a state funeral in the new chancel of Notre Dame cathedral; excavations in the nineteenth century uncovered her tomb, with the tiny coffins of her two babies resting beside it. His behaviour towards her had fallen considerably short of the courtly ideal. At the time of his dispute with Henry II he had threatened to cast her off as a means of intimidating his father-in-law, Baldwin of Hainault, who—together with the count of Flanders—had espoused the king of England's cause.

210

Richard and Philip finally met in the port of Messina, Sicily. Here they spent the winter of 1190, and it was six months before at last they left the island. The historians offer no explanation for this delay, which in all probability was simply due to adverse winds and to the dangers which their fleets would have run had they been exposed to the winter storms. As a rule, November was regarded as the latest possible time for embarking on the journey east; after this, no one dreamed of setting sail before the end of March. The sea must have been particularly rough that year, for on arriving in Marseille, where he expected to embark, Richard had learned that the vessels from England had been unable to negotiate the Straits of Gibraltar, on account of adverse winds. In the end, tired of waiting, he and his entourage had made the crossing on Pisan ships.

But whatever the reason for the delays, they did nothing to help the cause of Christendom in the Holy Land. The crusaders were scattering their strength at the very moment when they should have been mustering it in preparation for an immediate decisive blow. News had already reached the West of the death of Emperor Frederick Barbarossa, drowned in the waters of the Calycadnus on June 10th, 1190—an event which, in the phrase of the contemporary Austrian historian Ansbertus, 'decapitated' his crusade. Only a few handfuls of Germans had joined Guy of Lusignan below the walls of Acre. Guy had also been reinforced by Henry of Champagne, Eleanor's son-in-law, but these trickles of help were not sufficient to allow of a real reversal of the situation.

Still, these wasted months were to Eleanor's advantage, if to no one else's. Her *chevauchée* to the Pyrenees had a very specific purpose. 'With no thought for her age', she had braved the winter. According to some accounts, she proceeded as far as Bordeaux, according to others, as far as Navarre. Then she set out on a long intricate journey through the Alps and across Lombardy. After unsuccessful attempts to embark at Pisa, and afterwards at Naples, she had at last set sail from Brindisi, on her way to join Richard in Sicily.

She was not alone. There was a girl with her: Berengaria, daughter of King Sancho of Navarre. Eleanor had shrewdly recalled that, while attending a tournament in Pamplona organized

211

by Berengaria's brother, Richard had addressed some passionate lines of poetry to the princess. The historian Ambrose, who was a member of Richard's crusade, describes Berengaria as 'a prudent maid, a gentle lady, virtuous and fair . . . '

Adelaide, the king of France's sister, had been left securely guarded in Rouen. Eleanor was relentlessly opposed to the French marriage; indeed, it was out of the question, as even Philip had eventually agreed in the course of his somewhat turbulent discussions with Richard during their stay in Messina. But Berengaria's arrival finally slammed the door on the possibility of any further negotiation—and Philip saw the truth of this so clearly that he and his fleet departed on March 30th, 1191, the very day when Eleanor and the princess arrived in Messina in the ship which Richard had sent to Reggio to meet them.

As Labande points out, in undertaking this long and perilous journey at the age of nearly seventy Eleanor was acting both as mother and as queen. It was imperative that the king of England should father a legitimate heir. Richard had a bastard son named Philip, to whom he was later to marry Hélie of Cognac's daughter Amélie (her dowry took the form of a magnificent domain in the Gascon region). But he needed a son whose claim to the Plantagenet inheritance would be beyond dispute; at present that inheritance was exposed to the ambitions of his brother John and his nephew Arthur, neither of whom was a desirable successor in Eleanor's eyes. And he also needed a wife capable of keeping him in check, for his magnificent qualities were in danger of being stifled by the fierce ardour of a temperament prone to excesses of every kind. His legendary valour and noble nature fully entitled him to the name Lionheart, quite apart from the physical characteristic of his tawny mane. A delicate poet and refined musician, he would often rise from his seat in church and lead the monks in their singing. Everywhere, in whatever circumstances he found himself, he displayed a limitless curiosity and thirst for knowledge. His first real taste of seafaring (for until now he had merely journeyed back and forth across the Channel) had filled him with an immediate passion for working the sail and helm. Under the guidance of the Italian crew, he showed himself to be a natural sailor: no doubt it was his Norman blood stirring within him. In

212

Italy he had made a point of visiting the Roman remains around Naples, with all the enthusiasm of a dedicated archæologist. He had insisted on climbing Vesuvius and had proceeded to approach the crater and pick up fragments of lava with such disregard for his personal safety that his retinue had shuddered at the sight. In Calabria he had heard people talking about an old hermit, Joachim of Floris, who was said to extract amazing interpretations from the Apocalypse, and he had lost no time in paying him a visit: bystanders were treated to the extraordinary spectacle of the Calabrian monk expounding his prophetic theories to the king of England who, according to his companions, 'revelled in listening to him'. Joachim conjured up pictures of a new Church—the church of the contemplatives, founded on the principle of charity and perpetuating the spirit of St John—which, according to some rather baffling calculations, was destined to appear on earth in the year 1260.

In addition, Richard revealed himself as an unsurpassable warrior, a matchless horseman if the need arose but equally capable of marching for days at a time; during the siege of Acre he personally shouldered the wood required for the engines, after carefully selecting it and earmarking it for the benefit of the woodcutters. Ambrose, in his eyewitness account of the expedition, tells of a strange conversation between Sultan Saladin and Hubert Walter, bishop of Salisbury; between them, they agreed that if only it were possible to combine the complementary qualities of the opposing leaders (Richard's prowess and Saladin's sense of proportion), the result would have been a prince beyond compare.

Saladin had been given ample opportunity to assess alike the chivalrous foe and the headstrong ally capable of blind anger. One day, in his impatience at seeing the negotiations drag on in the usual oriental manner, Richard had gone back on his word and ordered the massacre of three thousand prisoners, after Saladin had spoken of paying ransom for them.

Eleanor was acting with a mother's wariness and forethought. She felt marriage might have a stabilizing effect on her prepossessing but outrageous son. Perhaps she had heard of the scene enacted in Messina a few weeks earlier. Richard had presented himself

213

at the door of one of the churches, and there—with bare head and bare shoulders, clad only in his breeches—he had knelt down and made a public confession, imploring forgiveness for the sins against nature in which he had indulged. This passionate man did not shrink from any kind of debauchery, but like many others of his time, he was capable of repenting as immoderately as he had sinned. Five years later he was to make a similar public act of penance, for precisely the same reason. A hermit had vainly admonished him several times: 'Remember the end which befell Sodom, refrain from what is forbidden, or the Lord shall exact just revenge.' Shortly afterwards, Richard was taken ill. This happened in Holy Week. Overcome with remorse, he promised to mend his ways, recalled his wife to his side and, on the Tuesday after Easter, made another public act of penance; this he extended by going to church every day and giving generous alms.

Eleanor's delight in being with Richard on the eve of the crusade was reinforced by the pleasure of meeting her daughter Joanna, whom she had not seen for fourteen years. Joanna was now a very beautiful young woman of twenty-five; of Eleanor's daughters, she was the most like her mother. She had been a widow for a year, and the arrival of her brother had provided her with unexpected assistance in coping with the difficulties which had beset her since the death of her husband, William the Good. Tancred of Lecce, a bastard son of Duke Roger (her husband's uncle), had seized power with the support of William's ex-chancellor, Matteo of Ajello, and the backing of a powerful Sicilian faction. The coup was not in fact aimed at Joanna herself, but at the woman who claimed succession to the Sicilian throne—Constance, wife of the German emperor, whose activities the Sicilians had good cause to fear. Anxious lest Richard should conspire against him, Tancred had deemed it wise to lay hold of Joanna and use her as a hostage, consigning her to the fortress of Palermo just as the English fleet sailed into Messina harbour to the wild cheering of the local populace. As soon as he heard that his sister was being held captive, Richard flew into one of his notorious rages. Tancred lost no time in setting the princess free, and she at once came looking for her brother in his camp outside the walls of Messina. But while he was spiritedly engaged in recovering her dowry for her, further com-

214

plications arose. At about this time, in fact, Richard was engaged in frequent talks with Philip Augustus. Joanna was invited to attend one of them, and she clearly made a powerful impression on Philip. A contemporary records that he quivered at the sight of her and that a sudden beam of joy illumined his normally impassive face. Richard was the first to notice this reaction. The very next day he conveyed Joanna to La Bagnara castle, in Calabria, where she would be safe from any advances on the part of Philip Augustus. From La Bagnara she proceeded to Reggio, scene of her rendez-vous with Eleanor.

The latter spent only four days in Sicily; by April 2nd she was saying goodbye to her children and setting sail in the company of the archbishop of Rouen and the knight who had been detailed to escort her, Gilbert Vascœuil. It had been decided that the crusaders should take advantage of the fine weather and favourable winds and set sail for the Holy Land, where Richard and Berengaria were to be married. And Eleanor, however reluctantly, insisted on re-turning to England as soon as possible, even though it meant being deprived of the spectacle of her son clad in the splendid garments which she had ordered for his wedding: a rose-coloured tunic worked with silver crescents, a scarlet cap with birds' feathers held in place by a gold clasp, a silken baldric supporting his sword in its gold and silver scabbard . . . The saddle on his charger was worked with gold, and its cantle was adorned with two lions affronté.

Berengaria was entrusted to Joanna's safekeeping, and a few days after Eleanor sailed the two young women went aboard a dromond commanded by one of Richard's knights, Robert of Thornham. No one suspected at the time that the wedding which was supposed to be celebrated in the Holy Land would in fact take place at Limassol, in Cyprus, after Richard had seized control of the island in a sudden fit of temper. The emperor of Byzantium, who was in residence there, had hoped to collect a rich ransom by impounding the vessel carrying the two royal ladies when it was driven ashore by rough weather. When Richard landed on the island, he was beside himself with fury to hear that his sister and his betrothed were being held captive and that their possessions had been con-fiscated by Isaac the Angel. Within three weeks the situation had been completely reversed: the emperor was a prisoner in one of his own fortresses and Cyprus was in the hands of the Franks. Whereupon Richard left the island in the safekeeping of a few reliable men and set off again, this time with Berengaria, who in the meantime had been declared his wife in Limassol Cathedral.

At long last, on June 8th, 1191, he came within sight of St John of Acre. This time the besieged city did not hold out for long: on July 17th, after an extraordinary display of valour, Richard made his triumphant entry. He rather put the king of France in the shade, for it has to be admitted that Philip Augustus could not claim credit for any of the feats which had earned the Lionheart renown throughout the Holy Land.

Eleanor's hasty departure from Messina was not entirely due to her anxiety about her son John and what he might get up to while his brother was away. Barely had she arrived in Sicily than she had learned of the death of Pope Clement III. Now, in the course of her journey south Eleanor had chanced to meet at Lodi the emperor of Germany, Henry VI, and his wife, Constance of Sicily (she was the daughter and sole remaining heir of Roger II, grandfather of William the Good); it might be as well if she were to keep a close eye on events . . .

Eleanor arrived in Rome on Easter Day, April 14th, 1191, the date of Hyacinthus Bobo's consecration as Celestine III. Henry and Constance were to receive their imperial crown from his hands. Eleanor had no particular wish to attend the ceremony, and after an audience of the new pope—who seemed well disposed towards the Plantagenets—she remained in Rome just long enough to obtain from the money-changers the eight hundred marks which she needed for the return journey. By June 24th she was back in Rouen, supervising the control of her son's kingdom.

Predictably enough, it was not long before problems arose. John Lackland was taking advantage of his position. He journeyed all over England, making himself known to everyone—barons, prelates, burghers—and deliberately creating the impression that Richard would never return from the Holy Land. In all his comings and goings, and in all his false claims, he met with hardly any opposition except for the distrust of his brother's supporters and the vigilance of William Longchamp, now bishop of Ely, who com-

216

bined the offices of chancellor and grand justiciar. Disagreements between the two men were inevitable, and over-zealousness on William's part was to turn these disagreements into an open quarrel. Geoffrey, the bastard son of Henry II, had been consecrated archbishop of York by the archbishop of Tours on August 18th, 1190 (Eleanor came back from Rome with the news that his election had the pope's blessing). Afterwards he attempted to journey to his archdiocese but was arrested—on the chancellor's orders—as soon as he stepped ashore at Dover, for breaking his oath not to return to England for at least three years.

Feeling ran high among the clergy and the ordinary people of the land—William Longchamp had a host of enemies. Archbishop Baldwin of Canterbury had recently died in the Holy Land, and there were churchmen who accused William of seeking to be made primate in his stead. Then again, his administration was notably harsh and he was loathed in London. Here was a splendid opportunity for John to step in and rid himself of the arrogant chancellor. He arranged that William, who had taken refuge in the Tower of London, should be called to account before several thousand Londoners, whose feelings had been skilfully whipped up. William confronted the storm courageously; he was even brave enough to denounce John's machinations and accuse him of seeking to supplant his brother at the very moment when Richard was risking his life in defence of the Holy Land. But this did not prevent him from being stripped of office by an assembly convened in St Paul's Cathedral; here, as a modern historian has pointed out, is an odd example of a ministerial downfall in the Middle Ages. Fearing for his life, William Longchamp left England, disguised as an old woman, and, as soon as he reached the continent, made for Paris like so many others before him with a grievance against the Plantagenets. There he met two cardinals, Jordan and Octavian, sent from Rome by Pope Celestine III, and managed to arouse their concern for his plight. The cardinals set out for Normandy without taking the precaution of asking the queen for right of passage and safe-conduct through her lands; in consequence, the drawbridge at Gisors was raised against them and the seneschal of Normandy refused to lower it. An extremely involved situation resulted, attended by a gale of excommunications—issued not only by the cardinals themselves, but by the bishop of Ely and other English prelates, headed by Geoffrey.

This was how matters stood in the days leading up to Christmas 1191. No one knew how the dispute would end. And then suddenly Eleanor, who was holding court at Bonneville-sur-Touques, got wind of an altogether surprising piece of news: the king of France had left the Holy Land; after requesting release from his crusader's vow, he had just arrived in Fontainebleau.

Eleanor immediately decided to fortify the castles along the entire border-length of the Plantagenet kingdom, and she dispatched messengers to her seneschals bearing instructions to this effect. It was as well she took this precaution, for by January 20th Philip Augustus was below the walls of Gisors, calling on the seneschal of Normandy to hand the stronghold over to him; he spoke of agreements concluded with King Richard during their stay in Sicily, but the seneschal had received categorical orders from the queen and it was a clear breach of convention to lay hands on a crusader's property while he was absent in the Holy Land. He refused and Philip Augustus had no choice but to withdraw. At this juncture the queen learned that her son John was assembling a fleet at Southampton and recruiting mercenaries; it was alleged that he was intending to do homage to Philip Augustus and claim the duchy of Normandy in exchange for the long-disputed fortress of Gisors.

By February 11th Eleanor was crossing the sea to England. On arrival, she at once called meetings of barons in Windsor, Oxford, London and Winchester: it was imperative to have them all swear oaths of fealty to Richard, and equally imperative to put an end to the false rumours which had been cunningly propagated, especially regarding his alleged intention of remaining in the Holy Land and setting himself up as king of Jerusalem; above all, it was imperative to cut off supplies from her youngest son and thus keep him from crossing the Channel.

Eleanor was successful, and John had to postpone his expedition. She sent message after message to Richard, begging him to come home; in reply, she was treated to accounts of his feats of valour. His renown grew and grew—not only within his own army, but among the citizens of France, who were resentful towards their

218

own king for giving up the crusade. Negotiations had been opened with Saladin, who had become more tractable since the fall of the city of Acre. For a while it was even considered possible that a romantic solution might be found for the age-old conflicts which set Christians and Turks at one another's throats. Richard put forward the suggestion that his sister Joanna should marry Saladin's brother, Malik-al-Adil. They would rule jointly in Jerusalem and the coastal cities would be ceded to them. Prisoners-of-war would be exchanged. The Templars and Hospitallers would take control of certain fortresses and villages, to ensure that the terms of the treaty were properly adhered to. An imposing prospect: a Plantagenet at the head of an eastern empire such as the world had never known; Moslems and Christians living side by side in perfect amity; pilgrims free to come and go as they wished, as they had been for hundreds of years until the Holy Land was conquered by the 'Saracens' . . . If she received word of the scheme, Eleanor must have been beguiled by this vision of Eastern domination, with her own daughter as the instrument of peaceful co-existence between two contrasting worlds. But any such dreams were dashed by the messages that followed. As soon as Joanna learned of the manner in which she figured in the negotiations, she flew into a rage which revealed her as a true Plantagenet. How dare they seek to betroth her without consulting her wishes! Never in a thousand years would she agree to marry a Moslem! Unless Saladin's brother undertook to become a Christian . . .

And so the war went on, with its characteristic alternation between battles and negotiations. Richard was nearly taken prisoner while defending the castle of Blanche-Garde; shortly afterwards he inflicted a severe defeat on Saladin's forces at Ascalon. Tales of his exploits sped across the country, and his fame increased among the Moslems as well as among the Christians; it was even said that Saracen mothers would quell their children's noise by threatening them with King Richard. He had succeeded in recapturing several coastal cities, including Jaffa, and when the whole of Saladin's army made a surprise attack on this latter city he put them to rout, though outnumbered ten to one; Richard himself wore hardly any armour during the attack, and victory was achieved as a result of his inspired alternation of pikemen and cross-bowmen.

Marie —
Eleanor's d. by Louis VII
m = Henry of Champagne

Son —
Henry of Champagne

Eleanor must have been moved when she heard that her daughter Marie's son, Henry of Champagne, who had been fighting in the Holy Land for the past two years, had been chosen by the barons to wear the crown as king of Jerusalem. A wholly symbolic crown, in fact, for Jerusalem was still in enemy hands: Richard had come within sight of the city walls, but been obliged to fall back. This was scarcely surprising: apart from the handful of barons fighting at his side, his resources derived mainly from the traders from Venice, Genoa and Pisa operating in the coastal towns. And they were concerned solely with the preservation of their trading-posts—Jerusalem itself was never, in fact, to be recaptured. The kingdom survived, but not its *raison d'être*. And the idea that the kingdom could be kept going by these clusters of traders in the ports already showed signs of being a myth; the crusaders themselves might not be fully alive to the fact, but their expeditions were turning into a trade war. The attempt to recapture the Holy Places was giving place to a general war against Islam, motivated by the urge to capture its markets. The day was coming when these crusaders, whose good faith can scarcely be impugned, were to find themselves taking part in the siege of Constantinople—a siege whose purpose was beyond the understanding of most of them, though perfectly clear to the wily Venetians.

Acknowledging that numerical inferiority rendered him more or less powerless against Saladin, Richard contented himself with inveighing against Philip Augustus's act of desertion: it was obvious that the bad blood between the two kings was largely to blame for the comparative failure of the expedition. In the end, after a further victory outside Jaffa, he decided to reach a compromise settlement with Saladin: the latter acknowledged the Europeans as rightful owners of the coastal strip between Tyre and Jaffa, and undertook that pilgrims should enjoy freedom of access to the Holy Places. The chronicler Ambrose touchingly conveys the disappointment felt by the humbler members of the crusade: 'You would have seen them in great distress, reviling the long wait to which they had been subjected . . . for they would not have asked to live another day after liberating Jerusalem!' When Richard learned that the sultan was prepared to grant him safe-conduct so that he might make a pilgrimage to the Holy City, he refused. A century later, Joinville recorded the story surrounding this refusal: Richard flung down his coat of mail and, weeping, said to Our Lord: 'Sweet Lord, I entreat Thee—do not suffer me to see Thy Holy City, since I am unable to deliver it from the hands of Thine enemies!'

On Michaelmas Day (September 29th) Eleanor heard at long last that the king had put his wife and sister aboard a ship bound for home, and that he himself was expecting to sail within a few days —he proposed to spend Christmas in England. The news brought her a tremendous sense of relief: her long wait was nearly over, her son was about to reclaim his threatened kingdom.

Little did either of them know that their difficulties were only just beginning.

Or sai je bien de voir certainement,
Que moi ne prisent né amin né parent.
Quand on me Jaist por or né por argent,
Moult est de moi; mais plus m'est de ma gent,
Qu'apres ma mort auront reprovier grant
Se longement sui pris.

I now perceive with bitter certainty,
Friend has he none who's in captivity,
Where I must lie for want of gold or fee;
I mourn myself, but more those close to me,
To whom my death a grave reproach will be—
I languish here so long.

RICHARD COEUR-DE-LION

WITH THE APPROACH OF AUTUMN the crusaders began to arrive
home in batches, bringing news of those who had yet to come.
Towards the end of November it was learned in England that
Joanna and Berengaria had disembarked at Brindisi and were bound
for Rome, where they expected to stay for a time. Not long afterwards reports arrived that the king had set sail on October 9th, but
his fleet had been obliged to put in at Corfu. It had been sighted off
Brindisi, seeking shelter from a storm. Since then, nothing had
been seen or heard of it.

The look-outs posted along the English coastline must often
have peered through the fog in the hope of identifying the royal
vessel. But the days went by and there was still no news of the king.
The fogs intensified, obscuring the towers and castles for a while
longer each morning, and in Winchester, Windsor and Oxford the
yeomen keeping watch for messengers saw nothing moving on the
waterlogged roads but an occasional peasant driving his cart. In the
churches and monasteries, clergy and people gathered to offer

222

prayers for King Richard's safety. The candles shed their light over the reliquaries, exposed night and day upon the altars. And everywhere the fear was growing that the hero of Christendom might have met with an unfitting end in some storm along the Adriatic coasts.

To Eleanor, this time of waiting must have been torture. For a whole long year she had managed to preserve law and order in the kingdom. She had secured the lifting of the Church's interdicts; she had put a brake on enmities and rivalries; and—for the time being, anyway—she had discouraged John from engaging in any treasonable acts against Richard. She had kept him from going to France—'fearing,' says Richard of Devizes, 'that in his fickle-mindedness the youth might lend an ear to the counsels of the French and plot his brother's downfall. For she was deeply agitated,' he goes on, 'and as a mother her heart was lacerated whenever she thought of the fate of her elder son . . . She was anxious that trust should exist between her children from now on, and that they should bring her greater happiness than they had brought their father.' Yet she, better than anyone, knew just how precarious was the balance which she had somehow contrived to maintain and that oaths and promises meant nothing to John. Richard of Devizes terms him a youth, though he was twenty-five years old at the time: undeniably he gave the impression of never acting other than impulsively, of being unable to achieve that complete self-control which is the mark of the true adult. And this impression was borne out by the whole of his subsequent history. He was an overgrown youth, an alarming, unstable adolescent. The more his actions revealed him, the more did his contemporaries come to look upon him as being laid under a spell. Not that he was devoid of intelligence—on the contrary, when the need arose he was capable of acting with shrewdness, even cunning; he could be tenacious, but the cold determination with which he carried out some of his plans was that of a man driven by an obsession, rather than of a man implementing a decision arrived at after mature reflection. At the very moment when his kingdom was going to rack and ruin, he refused to listen to the envoys of the city of Rouen (though he knew its plight was desperate), because listening to them would have meant interrupting his game of chess. His

223

acts of cruelty were gruesome, but in the second half of the twentieth century he would probably be thought of as a man of diminished responsibility. In his own day it was uneasily whispered that there was a devilish spirit at work in him: had he not refused to go to communion since the age of seven? He would be the only king of England not to receive communion on his coronation day. If ever living proof were given of the tales of ill-omen surrounding the Plantagenets, it lay in the person of John Lackland.

As anxiety tightened its grip on Richard's supporters, there were rumours that John was proposing to divorce his wife, Havisa of Gloucester, and marry Adelaide of France. And in clear anticipation of a more general attack on his brother's authority, he seized the royal castles at Windsor and Wallingford by suborning their constables. It was at this point that news arrived: King Richard was a prisoner.

———————◆———————

Eleanor's Christmas cannot have been happy. A few days later, the archbishop of Rouen sent her a copy of a letter which the king of France had received from the emperor of Germany on December 28th: '. . . We have deemed it proper to inform Your Nobleness, by means of these present letters, that while the enemy of our empire and the disturber of your kingdom, Richard, king of England, was sailing homeward to his dominions, it chanced that the winds caused him to be shipwrecked in the region of Istria . . . The roads being duly watched, and the entire area well-guarded, our dearly beloved cousin Leopold, duke of Austria, laid hold of the aforesaid king in a humble village household near Vienna . . .'

Already the news had been spread by word of mouth, sowing consternation in London and throughout England, as well as in the Plantagenets' continental fiefs. A detailed account of the king's voyage and of the circumstances in which he was taken prisoner has been set down by an eyewitness—Anselm, Richard's chaplain, who had been a member of the party but had been released almost at once and had made his way back to England. It is a true tale of high adventure, even containing the note of comedy which invariably steals into tribulations of this kind.

The king had set sail in his galley, the *Franche-Nef*, together with Anselm, Philip his clerk, two noblemen—Baldwin of Béthune and William of l'Etang—and a number of Templars. The stormy weather drove them hither and thither for six weeks, at the end of which time they came within sight of Marseille. There was talk of landing there, but the king was not in favour of passing through the lands of the count of Toulouse, since Raymond V was notorious for his treachery; he therefore decided to head back to Corfu. From there they hugged the shores of the Adriatic. By this time the galley was too badly battered to stand up to any more storms, so they came to terms with some pirates, who undertook to transport them back to Italy. Once again the weather turned rough; they were blown past Zara and Pola and finally washed up at a point between Aquila and Venice. Resigning himself to the fact that they could hope to journey no farther by sea, Richard learned that the area was ruled by a castellan, Count Mainard of Görtz, who was a vassal of Duke Leopold of Austria.

This was appalling luck, for Richard was on the worst possible terms with Leopold: one day, during the fighting at Acre, he had lost all patience with the duke of Austria's boastful ways and flung his banner into the filthy moat; the duke had sworn to have his revenge, and the threat was common knowledge. Richard decided to brave it out. He sent Baldwin of Béthune and two companions to the castle, with instructions to seek safe-conduct for themselves and for a certain merchant Hugo who was travelling with them. In the hope of winning the count's favour, he sent him a gold ring set with a magnificent ruby which he had bought from a Pisan jeweller. But it was as though the Devil had given Mainard the gift of second sight. Taking hold of the ring and turning it this way and that, he observed: 'It is not the merchant Hugo who sends me this gift, but King Richard. I swore that I would arrest any pilgrims who set foot on my shores, and that I would not think of accepting a present from them. However, in view of the value of this gift and the high estate of him who honours me with it, I shall send the ring back to him and give him leave to continue his journey.'

The envoys were amazed and deeply confused. This unwonted display of clemency might well conceal a trap. The king and his followers realized that they must act quickly; they bought the fastest horses they could find and set out for Carinthia that same night. Sure enough, Count Mainard's reluctance to act had stemmed solely from the unexpectedness of the encounter; when he had gathered his wits, he lost no time in alerting his brother, Frederick of Betesov, through whose territories the fugitives were compelled to pass. He bade Frederick send out armed men to apprehend the king of England.

After three days Richard and his followers came to the little town of Freisach, and there took shelter in a simple peasant's house. In an attempt to conceal his identity, Richard had donned the uniform of a squire and was pretending to be busy in the kitchen when, to their consternation, there was a knock at the door. It was one of the count of Betesov's henchmen, and he had been ordered to search every house in the district. The man strode in, leaving his escort outside. Richard pretended to stoke the fire, but he was wasting his time: he would have been instantly recognizable, even disguised as a beggar. Nothing could alter his height, his flaming hair, his regal bearing. His companions stood waiting in dread, but suddenly the count's henchman went down on his knees before the king and burst into tears. He begged him, in the purest Norman speech, to escape with all possible speed. He explained that he was Roger of Argenton, principal aide to the count of Betesov, having lived in the area for over twenty years and married the count's niece. He had instructions to arrest the king of England, but nothing would induce him to break the Truce of God and lay hands on the hero of all Christendom. Once again he entreated Richard to flee as fast as he could and promised to supply him with an excellent horse for the purpose.

Whereupon Roger of Argenton withdrew and took his escort with him, leaving the king and his companions speechless. Shortly afterwards, fresh horses were brought to them and Richard went on his way. He took only two men with him: William of l'Etang and a young clerk who spoke German. He reasoned that the smallness of the party would make it easier for him to pass unnoticed. The remainder left Freisach quite openly the following morning and were soon overtaken by the count of Betesov's men. Roger of Argenton had told the count that Richard was not among the foreign party, which seemed to consist solely of Count Baldwin of Béthune and his escort. Frederick had no choice but to yield to the evidence of his own eyes. Baldwin and the others were held for two days, then released and allowed to continue their journey.

Meanwhile, Richard had been riding hard, and almost without respite, for three days and three nights; but when they came to the little town of Ginana, on the banks of the Danube, he and his companions had no choice but to stop. He was tired out, and shaking badly from the fever which he had contracted in the Holy Land; also, the horses needed a rest. By a signal stroke of misfortune, Duke Leopold of Austria happened to be residing in that very village. Richard and William of l'Etang shut themselves away and sent the young clerk out to buy food and drink. He had no Austrian currency with him and when he reached the market-place he produced a gold besant. The villagers had never seen such wealth and started harassing him with questions; he pretended that he was travelling in the company of a wealthy Greek merchant, then slipped away, hurried back to the king and urged him to leave Ginana. But Richard was laid low by one of those attacks of quartan fever which were to torment him at intervals from now on, and it was quite plain that he could not stir from the inn. Returning to the village, the young man was incautious enough to wear his master's fur gloves because of the cold: they were embroidered with two handsome gold leopards and again attracted a crowd. He tried to dash away, but was grabbed by some of Duke Leopold's men. He was struck, threatened, until at last, more dead than alive, he was forced to indicate where his master was lodging. A baying pack hurried to the room where Richard and William were hiding, while a messenger ran off in search of Duke Leopold. This time there could be no question of escape or dissimulation. Richard drew himself up to his full height and confronted the intruders with characteristic courage and majesty. 'I am the king of England,' he declared. 'Summon your master—I shall surrender my sword to him, and him alone.' His noble presence restrained the mob until the duke arrived; then he gave himself up, without losing an ounce of dignity.

This had occurred on December 20th, 1192. Eleanor had probably heard an account of the scene from Anselm himself when he got back to England in March 1193. In the meantime, however sorely tried she may have been by the news of her son's imprisonment—and William the Marshal assures us that her sorrow was great—she had been quick to respond with her usual energy and resourcefulness. It took several months to find out where the duke of Austria had incarcerated his prisoner. She immediately dispatched two monks to Germany—the abbots of Boxley and Pontrobert—with instructions to roam Swabia and Bavaria and make inquiries as to what had become of her son. Savary, bishop of Bath, was sent straight to the imperial court of the Emperor Henry VI. Hubert Walter, bishop of Salisbury, was in Italy when he heard the news; instead of returning to England, as he had intended, he hastened to Germany in the hope of tracing his king. Even William Longchamp, still an exile, set out at once for the Holy Roman Empire: compared with the need to set Richard free, nothing else mattered. Indeed, feeling was running high in every corner of Christendom. There was great indignation at the impious deed perpetrated by the duke of Austria: the person and property of any crusader were inviolable, for they were insured under the Truce of God; and King Richard's exploits in the Holy Land had made him the most popular man alive.

The legend of Blondel de Nesles, the troubadour, was born at this time. He too, allegedly, set off in search of his master, wandering all over Germany with no luggage save his viol, singing the songs which he and Richard had composed between them, until the day came when from the castle wall above his head, he heard a familiar voice take up the refrain . . . Some people claim that Blondel was the cognomen of a knight of Artois renowned for his looks and the fairness of his hair, John II of Nesles—who was, true enough, highly thought of as a poet in his own day; so the legend may not be entirely unfounded.

At last it was learned that Richard had been imprisoned in the fortress of Dürrenstein, though in fact he was transferred to various other castles before Leopold finally handed him over to the emperor, who held him captive at Speyer on and after May 23rd. The emperor hated the king of England just as much as his vassal did; somewhat contemptibly, he was exacting revenge for the constant acts of rebellion directed against the empire by Richard's

228

brother-in-law, Henry the Lion, duke of Saxony; and he further accused Richard of having, while he was in Sicily, supported Tancred's claims in opposition to those of his wife Constance. Furthermore, Philip Augustus had engaged in a series of lengthy confabulations with the emperor on returning from the Holy Land and can hardly have failed to excite his wrath against the Plantagenet; it was even possible that an alliance had been concluded between them.

However that may be, Philip seemed to think that he was now free to do as he pleased. On April 12th, shortly after Easter, he once again rode up to the fortress of Gisors—and this time the seneschal, Gilbert Vascœuil, surrendered it without protest. This act of betrayal, laying the entire Vexin region open to the king of France, was an indication of what could be expected from now on. Richard's enemies plainly considered that he was no longer a force to be reckoned with: his kingdom had become a target for conquest.

Certainly John Lackland saw things in this light. He crossed over to Normandy and immediately called all the barons together, urging them to acknowledge him as rightful heir to the throne, but the meeting which he had tried to convene in Alençon was a failure. The Norman lords turned a deaf ear. And in Rouen, the seneschal—Robert of Leicester, whose lands had but lately been restored to him on Eleanor's instructions—was firm as a rock, as John well knew. John did not persevere with the issue; instead, he journeyed to Paris and eagerly did homage to Philip Augustus, confirming that the king of France was now the true owner of the Vexin. A few weeks later, Philip appeared outside the fortress of Rouen and demanded the immediate handing-over of the city and the release of his sister Adelaide. Robert replied that he had received no orders from the king to this effect; he added that he was quite prepared to admit Philip, alone and unescorted, and conduct him to the princess's quarters.

Philip had a lively imagination and was quick to realize how easily the tables might be turned on him, were he to accept the offer. He had only to step across that drawbridge, and the old queen would be in possession of an excellent hostage to barter against her beloved Richard! He withdrew, deeply chagrined.

Amid all this turmoil, Eleanor showed her true mettle. Constantly at her post, dispatching missive after missive, messenger after messenger, keeping in close touch with the seneschals on the continent and the chief barons in England, she contrived simultaneously to parry the threats which Philip and John levelled at the kingdom and to take every possible step to secure her son's release. She gave orders for defences to be established along the coasts of England, and for a close watch to be kept lest there should be any attempt at armed invasion. John had tried to recruit Welsh and Scottish mercenaries, but the king of Scotland had turned down his requests for assistance—for, like Robert of Leicester, William owed much to the queen. Three letters have survived, signed by Eleanor and addressed to Pope Celestine III. They were probably composed by her chancellor, Peter of Blois, but beneath the official prose there is an unmistakable note of indignation. How intolerable that the pope should not have lifted a finger to help Richard, when he had such powers at his disposal! The way these letters were signed was in itself a cry of pain: 'Eleanor, by the wrath of God queen of England'. And their contents amounted to a vehement protest which went so far as to threaten the Roman Curia:

'What afflicts the Church and sets the people murmuring and diminishes their respect for you is that, in spite of the tears and lamentations of entire provinces, you have not sent a single envoy. Often, over matters of little importance, your cardinals have been sent to the far ends of the earth with sovereign powers; yet given an issue as desperate and deplorable as this, you have not even dispatched the humblest subdeacon—not even an acolyte! The kings and princes of this earth have conspired against my son; remote from the Lord, he is kept in chains while others ravage his lands; he is held by the heels while others scourge him. And all this time, the sword of St Peter remains in its scabbard. Thrice you have promised to send legates, yet failed to do so . . . If my son were in prosperity, we should have seen them run in answer to his call, for well they know how generously he would have rewarded them. Is this what you promised me at Châteauroux, with such protestations of friendship and good faith? Alas, I know now that cardinals' promises are but empty words . . .'

And in her anger Eleanor went on to recall how her husband Henry, father of the present king, had put an end to schism by lending allegiance to Alexander while the emperor of Germany supported an antipope. She bluntly threatened Celestine III with a renewal of separatism: '. . . I declare to you that the day foretold by the Apostle is not far distant; the fateful moment is at hand when the seamless garment of Christ shall be diced for again, when the chains of St Peter shall be broken and Catholic unity dissolved.'

In fact, the pope had excommunicated Leopold as soon as he learned of Richard's arrest and imprisonment; he had threatened the king of France with an interdict if he dared to seize any of the lands belonging to his rival; and he was also holding the threat of interdict over the English churches and the English people, if they failed to raise the sum required for the ransom. But he hesitated to excommunicate the emperor. He was in no hurry to renew the endless series of quarrels and disagreements which for over a century had marred relations between the Holy See and the Holy Roman Empire.

Meanwhile Eleanor had received a direct communication from her son: a letter dated April 19th, 1193, had reached her through the good offices of William Longchamp. 'I would have you know,' wrote the king, 'that following the departure of Hubert, bishop of Salisbury, and William of Holy Mother Church, our cleric, we received a visit from our beloved chancellor, William, bishop of Ely; after an audience with the emperor, he secured our removal from the castle of Trifels, where we were formerly imprisoned, to Haguenau, where we were received with honour by the emperor and his court . . .' He went on to reveal that he could now entertain hopes of freedom, provided his ransom was paid. He asked that money and hostages should be collected, specifying that the sum so raised was to be entrusted 'to my mother, and by her to whomsoever she shall appoint.'

Eleanor lost no time in imposing a levy. Convention sanctioned such a step: any noble who was taken prisoner was entitled to expect that his vassals would contribute towards his ransom. The tax was a heavy one: every freeman was required to donate a quarter of his annual income. The churches were stripped of their treasures; the Cistercian monasteries, having no gold or silver to offer, gave a whole year's supply of wool from their sheep. For the ransom demanded was truly enormous. After prolonged negotiations it was set at a hundred and fifty thousand silver marks. Payment of a hundred thousand would secure the release of the royal prisoner; a further fifty thousand were to be sent later, but as a guarantee of this two hundred hostages must be delivered into the emperor's hands. Altogether a hundred and fifty thousand Cologne marks, the equivalent of some thirty-five tons of pure silver.

Such were the conditions laid down in the Golden Bull which William Longchamp had received from the emperor's hands and which was presented to the council convened at St Albans on June 1st–5th. Eleanor appointed a number of officers to ensure that the sum was gathered: Hubert Walter, who had just been nominated archbishop of Canterbury and whom, before the year was out, she was to make grand justiciar of England; Richard, bishop of London; two nobles—William, earl of Arundel, and Amelin, earl of Warenne; and finally a mere burgher, Henry Fitz-Aylwin, mayor of London since the day two years earlier when, taking advantage of the disturbances caused by the dismissal of William Longchamp, the city had set itself up as a commune. A significant choice: Eleanor was mindful of the growing influence of the bourgeoisie and determined that every power in the land should play a part in securing the release of her son.

Before long the bags of gold and silver, and other valuables, began to pile up in the crypt of St Paul's, under the watchful eye of Eleanor and her agents. But it was to be a long time yet before Richard was set free. Not until October did the emperor's envoys arrive in London to check the weight and quality of the sums collected for his ransom. Gifts and tokens of consideration were showered upon them, in accordance with tradition—silverware, furs, lavish garments of every kind. Richard, now confined at either Speyer or Worms on the banks of the Rhine, insisted that Eleanor should personally accompany the precious cargo. Vessels were accordingly assembled at Ipswich, Dunwich and Oxford and solidly fitted out so that they would be able to withstand not only the winter storms but any armed attacks that might be launched against them: such a convoy could not fail to stimulate the greed of pirates, or indeed of the king of France, whose shores would be dangerously close. *1193*

Eleanor set sail in December, with an imposing escort; she had left the administration of the realm in the hands of Hubert Walter, who had by this time been enthroned as archbishop. The archbishop of Rouen sailed with her, and so did a number of other staunch supporters, including Saldebreuil, whom Richard subsequently dispatched to the Holy Land as moral support for his nephew, Henry of Champagne. There were also a number of Poitevins in her party: Berlay of Montreuil, Aimery, viscount of Thouars, Hugh le Brun of Lusignan, and the ever-faithful Baldwin of Béthune, who had shared the discomforts and tensions of the king's journey from Acre and who, after thus risking his life, had reputedly been the readiest of all the barons to contribute to the ransom fund. Another of the queen's companions was William Longchamp, bishop of Ely.

Eleanor arrived in Cologne in time for the feast of the Epiphany, 1194. She was welcomed by the archbishop, Adolf of Altena, but a bitter disappointment awaited her; she was refused permission to see her son. He was to have been released on January 17th, but the date had been put back. The emperor was evidently in no hurry to meet Eleanor, and strange rumours were circulating: it was said that Philip and John Lackland had schemingly offered a larger sum than the one brought by the queen. It is not hard to imagine how these days of uncertainty, and their threat of shameful treachery, must have weighed on a woman of seventy-two who had lived such a taxing life and been exposed to the rigours of such a long winter journey. *Cologne 1-6-1194*

Finally, on February 2nd, 1194—Candlemas, when thousands of candles were lighted in the churches as a reminder of Simeon's canticle bidding welcome to the light to lighten the gentiles—a vast assembly was convened in Mainz, in the course of which, to quote Gervase of Canterbury, Richard was 'restored to his mother and to freedom'; this assembly was held under the auspices of the archbishop of the city, Conrad of Wittelsbach, to whom Peter of Blois—who knew him personally—had addressed two urgent missives. The emperor, Henry VI, had Duke Leopold of Austria beside him, and the formal release of their prisoner turned out to *2-2-1194 Richard released* be the culmination of an alliance between them—an alliance which was sealed, as always in those days, by the announcement of marriages between members of these previously hostile families. Henry VI, who was addicted to unrealizable daydreams and liked to see himself as a new Charlemagne lording it over a continent whose political development was actually slipping from his grasp, had insisted that Richard should do homage to him for his kingdom. The chroniclers state explicitly that it was on his mother's advice that Richard consented to do so. With her unfailing practicality, Eleanor realized that obtaining his freedom must be the prime consideration; once he was back in England, this subordination to an empire whose power was more abstract than real would not count for much. So, as a token of vassalage, Richard placed his leather cap in the hands of the emperor, who returned it forthwith in exchange for a promise that an annual duty of five thousand pounds sterling would be paid into his exchequer. The king of England was free at last, and on February 4th he left Mainz, fêted and congratulated by all the princes and prelates who had been involved in these events.

For Richard—this captive who for over a year had been transferred from fortress to fortress, from Dürrenstein to Ochsenfurt, from Speyer to Haguenau—had acquired enormous popularity among the German princes. His noble presence and indomitable good humour, however grim his surroundings, had won their admiration. A true heir of William the Troubadour, he had gone on composing poems and songs throughout his seemingly endless period of captivity, and his innate generosity had continued to find an outlet, if only in sharing the wine at his table with his gaolers. Finally, his natural eloquence had been put to good use: he had effected a reconciliation between the emperor and his brother-in-law, Henry the Lion, and broken up the coalition formed against Henry VI by some of his most powerful feudatories, including the duke of Louvain and the bishops of Mainz and Cologne. And it was by pleading his own cause, with an eloquence which reputedly brought tears to the eyes of those who heard him, that he had ultimately wrested a favourable decision from the emperor—who at that time had still been in two minds as to whether he should part with so valuable a hostage.

When the tension of all these official wranglings was over and they set off up the Rhine on their way to the sea, Eleanor and Richard were treated to the most effusive demonstrations of friendship on the part of the German princes. When they reached Cologne the archbishop gave them a wonderful welcome, and—an imaginative touch, this—the mass celebrated in the cathedral was that of St Peter ad Vincula, with the Introit: 'Now I can tell for certain that the Lord has sent His angel to deliver me out of Herod's hands . . .' In Antwerp, the duke of Louvain had likewise laid on a state reception for them. Far from diminishing his prestige, Richard's long imprisonment had surrounded him with an aura of martyrdom—and on the practical plane it had earned him alliances which might one day be useful to him. One of his nephews, the son of Henry the Lion, had married a cousin of the emperor (the daughter of the count palatine of the Rhine, Conrad of Hohenstaufen); and there were plans for a marriage between the duke of Austria's son and Richard's niece, the eldest daughter of Geoffrey and Constance of Brittany, a girl named Eleanor.

———————◆———————

3-12-1194
Richard
back in
England

When Richard's ship sailed into Sandwich on March 12th, 1194, the sun is said to have shone with a new brightness, while a strange red glow hung on the horizon, strong and clear as a rainbow. As soon as he was ashore, Richard went to Canterbury and meditated at the shrine of Thomas Becket: this was becoming a traditional gesture for kings of England. Next day, on the road to Rochester, he met Archbishop Hubert Walter and the two men threw their arms round each other and wept. His arrival in London on March 23rd *3-23-1194* *London* was a scene of great triumph. The whole town came out to meet him, led by its mayor. With Eleanor at his side, he rode from the Strand to St Paul's amid the cheers of a populace gone wild with joy: in the eyes of every man there he was the champion of the holy war, the Lord's anointed, the hero, the idol. And this popularity was to pass into history—for Richard, arguably the king of England who had spent least time in his own country, was destined to remain an outstandingly popular figure. One has only to think of the famous ballads in which he appears with Robin Hood and his merry men. One of these tells how, on his return from the Holy Land, Richard disguises himself as an abbot and is held up by the outlaws in Sherwood Forest. However, Robin strikes up a friendship with the 'abbot' and invites him to a feast. He gives a loud blast on his horn and his men appear from out of the forest, unkempt and in rags. They all settle down beside the stream, and the 'abbot' and Robin drink a toast to the king's return. Afterwards, the latter reveals his true identity, takes the outlaw to London and makes him a peer of the realm.

True enough, Richard *did* spend a few days in Sherwood Forest early in April; not long before, Eleanor had relaxed the previously stringent forest laws—and this may have given rise to the legend. But by this time Richard had been to Westminster, made a pilgrimage to Bury St Edmunds, and speedily regained control of the English castles. On hearing of his release, his brother John had tried to get word to all his castellans, bidding them stand by to defend their strongholds. In vain. The man to whom he had entrusted the message was arrested by the mayor as soon as he reached London. Furthermore, the English bishops, meeting at Westminster, had vowed to excommunicate anyone guilty of an act of hostility against Richard, their lawful sovereign. Nowhere was there any real resistance: Marlborough castle yielded at the behest of the archbishop of Canterbury, Lancaster castle made a similar act of surrender to Theobald Walter, the archbishop's brother. From Huntingdon, where William the Marshal had come to greet him, Richard journeyed to Nottingham, which opened its gates to him on March 28th—the very day when he heard from the bishop of Durham that Tickhill had submitted; and it was said that in distant Cornwall the castellan of St Michael's Mount had died of shock when he learned of the king's return. Thus a fortnight had proved sufficient to smother all the conspiracies and attempts to rebel which might have been engendered by his long absence; without a blow struck in anger, Richard was master of his kingdom again—even to the castles which belonged to his brother. Only one thing remained to be done: John must be punished for his acts of treason. He was summoned to appear before the king's court by May 10th, failing which he would be deemed a traitor and banished from the realm.

236

Meanwhile Eleanor, active as ever, was busy preparing a ceremony which would efface—if there were any need to do so—the bad impression which might have been created by Richard's act of allegiance to the German emperor. There was to be a second coronation, even more impressive than the first, in St Swithin's, Winchester, on April 17th, 1194. As on the first occasion, Richard, flanked by the leading prelates—bishops John of Dublin, Richard of London, Gilbert of Rochester, and William Longchamp of Ely—received the crown from the hands of Hubert Walter in the presence of the massed barons. And the chroniclers draw attention to the fact that Eleanor, surrounded by her attendants, sat facing him throughout the ceremony from a dais especially raised for her in the north transept. Eleanor was queen of England. Yet was there not another queen, the same Berengaria of Navarre whom she had collected from beyond the Pyrenees and delivered to her son in Sicily? But Berengaria was not present. She was still in Rome, with the king's sister Joanna. And perhaps Eleanor was in no great hurry to part with her crown or her place at Richard's side.

A time was coming when she was to turn her thoughts to relaxation and retirement, but the impression given is that before she did so she wanted to make every effort to bring about a reconciliation between her two surviving sons. No one could be sure where John was hiding—most likely at the court of Philip Augustus. By this time the twin conspirators were shaking with fear. 'Beware, the devil is loose,' wrote Philip, and it is said that he so dreaded an attempt by Richard to poison him that he never touched his food until the dogs had sampled it.

Unquestionably Richard's mind was set on revenge. By the end of April he was in Portsmouth, itching to set sail for France; but adverse winds held him up until May 12th. In the meantime he had received the surrender of his half-brother Geoffrey, his father's natural son, and had remarkably made him a present of two castles in Anjou: Langeais and Beaugé. But everybody was wondering what fate was in store for John Lackland, whose capture could not be far distant.

On May 12th Richard stepped ashore at Barfleur, in Normandy. Eleanor was with him, and so was William the Marshal. The Norman populace greeted him with the same enthusiasm as the people of England; the peasants hurried from their fields, and there was such a crowd all along the route that it would have been impossible to hurl an apple in any direction without hitting someone. Richard made for Lisieux, where he and the queen were bidden welcome by one of their loyalest supporters—John of Alençon, archdeacon of Lisieux. The scene which occurred that evening has been set down by William the Marshal's biographer. The king had moved into the archdeacon's residence and was enjoying a rest before dinner. Suddenly John of Alençon was called outside. When he returned he looked downcast.

'Why such a long face?' asked Richard. And when the archdeacon sought to evade the question he continued: 'There is no need to lie. I know what it is: you have seen my brother. It is wrong of him to be afraid: let him come without fear. He is my brother. It may be true that he has acted rashly, but I shall not hold it against him. As for those who led him on, either they have met with their deserts or they will meet with them later.' Whereupon John was shown in. He flung himself at Richard's feet, but the king raised him gently and said: 'Do not be afraid, John—you are a child and you have been in bad care. Those who have misadvised you shall pay for it. Now get up and have something to eat.' Just then, some of the local burghers happened to call at the house with a present—a magnificent salmon. Instantly recapturing his usual gaiety, the king gave orders that the fish was to be cooked for his brother. There was singing and dancing all over the city, and church bells rang out. Young and old, the inhabitants came by in long processions chanting:

> God is come in His full might,
> The king of France shall be put to flight!

Roger of Hoveden, one of the chroniclers closest to these events, states explicitly that the king's clemency towards his brother was due to Eleanor's intervention. And indeed, in these last years she became a continual and ubiquitous instrument of peace. She even went so far as to offer asylum, in an attempt to aid his escape, to one of Richard's most valued prisoners—Philip of Dreux, bishop of Beauvais and cousin to the king of France, who had taken up arms against Richard in Normandy.

For it was in Normandy and Berry that the rivalry between

238

Richard and Philip Augustus was now being thrashed out. The latter had precipitated the struggle by attacking the town of Verneuil. To this, the king of England made a lightning riposte. In rapid succession he subjugated Evreux, Beaumont-le-Roger, Pont de l'Arche and Elbeuf, and then—at Fréteval, near Vendôme—he inflicted a disastrous defeat on the French armies: Philip was forced to flee, abandoning his treasury, his silver plate, his tents and pavilions, his archives, even his personal seal. By July, the foe had no choice but to sue for peace.

However, the queen had begun to view these events with a new remoteness. The walls of Fontevrault now stood between her and the world's hubbub. She had probably gone straight there after crossing the Channel with Richard, thereby realizing an ambition which she must have harboured during all those years of anguish and intense activity. On several occasions she had recently directed her thoughts, if not her steps, towards her favourite abbey. She had settled a dispute at Saumur over corn in the nuns' favour, and during the stressful year of 1193 she had twice solicited their prayers and made new gifts to them—once at Winchester and once at Westminster. Now that England lay at peace in the safe, experienced hands of Hubert Walter, and now that Richard was in confident pursuit of the knave who had tried to purloin his kingdom, she could with a quiet conscience devote her last remaining years to prayer, reading and meditation. At the time of her previous excursions to Sicily and Germany, it was generally remarked among her entourage that the queen was 'forgetting her age'; the hour had come when she must remember it. From now on, her name figures but rarely in the Pipe Rolls and official deeds, and then only in connection with payments due to her by virtue of her private dower or of personal entitlements. For instance, she was credited with the 'queen's gold'—for she was entitled to one gold mark every time a fine of a hundred silver marks was paid to the king; this royalty had been withheld from her while she was a prisoner, but was renewed as soon as Richard came to the throne (and indeed, the king had been unfailingly generous in the allocation of funds to his mother). Eleanor was still prepared to throw in her weight with the archbishop of Rouen, on behalf of the monks of Reading; or to side with the abbot of Bourgueil, who was finding it hard to pay the local wine-tax. But in general the queen had become merely a silent presence beneath the high vaults of the abbey of Fontevrault.

And the news which was brought to her during this retreat must have seemed ample compensation for past tribulations. For Richard was emerging as undisputed victor from this trial of strength with the king of France: before the year of his release (1194) was over, he had the satisfaction of learning of the death of his enemy, Duke Leopold of Austria, as the result of a trivial accident. Leopold had fallen from his horse while storming a snow-castle built by his pages. The surgeons had amputated his broken leg, but gangrene had set in and he had died shortly afterwards. He was still under the ban which had been laid on him for seizing Richard, so he had been denied a Christian burial. To put an end to the Church's sanctions, his son was compelled to return the English hostages, held pending payment of the balance of the king's ransom.

Everything was turning out very much in Richard's favour, and the next few years were to open up prospects of which he had not dared to dream. For in September 1197 the Emperor Henry VI died in Messina, still preoccupied with his claims against Sicily. His brother, Philip of Swabia, lost no time in pressing his claim as successor to the title. But the German princes were somewhat weary of the ambitious Hohenstaufens and still had glowing memories of Richard and his superb qualities. A deputation was sent, offering him the imperial crown. Acceptance would mean the realization of the lofty ambitions of his father, Henry Plantagenet.

However, Richard was not greatly inclined to exchange his beloved Anjou and Poitou for dwelling-places which brought back grim memories of imprisonment. Moreover, he had no intention of exposing his kingdom to the equally covetous desires of the king of France and his brother John—for well he knew that it was only his presence which held them in check. He declined the offer, but suggested to the German envoys that the right man to approach was his nephew, Otto of Brunswick, son of Matilda and Henry the Lion (the latter having died two years earlier). Otto had been brought up at the Plantagenet court, and Richard—in common with his mother—had a great affection for him, even seeing him as a possible successor; he had already invested him with the county of Poitou and the duchy of Aquitaine. The young man agreed to the suggestion and, relinquishing these two titles, rode into Aachen on July 10th, 1198. On July 11th he was married to Marie, daughter of the count of Lorraine, and on July 13th he was crowned emperor. The kingdom of France was now hemmed in by Richard's dominions on the one hand and a Plantagenet-controlled Empire on the other.

In addition, Richard had established secure alliances with Baldwin IX, count of Flanders and Hainault, and Renaud of Dammartin, count of Boulogne. He had also married his sister Joanna to the new count of Toulouse, Raymond VI, whose father had died in 1194. Thus Philip Augustus found himself threatened on every side, completely surrounded by enemies—and this at a time when he had fallen foul of the Church's authority; for his kingdom had been laid under an interdict as a result of his behaviour towards his wife Ingeborg, the king of Denmark's daughter, whom he had cast off after the wedding-night.

Richard was emerging as clear winner. Philip had nearly fallen into his hands several times, and now seemed reduced to the last stages of collapse. So great was the craving for peace among the people of Normandy that the clergy intervened, insisting that a truce be agreed at last. The two kings met along the Seine, at a point between Vernon and Les Andelys. Philip rode his horse to the edge of the river, while Richard remained on a barge in mid-stream. Not far away rose the superb fortress known as the Château-Gaillard, which the king of England had erected on this bend of the Seine as a token of defiance. Its construction took into account all the latest developments in the art of warfare, and it was regarded as impregnable. The kings mutually vowed themselves to five years of peace.

XXI

Reisme son, mas reis no ges,
E comtat, mas no coms ni bar
Las marchas son, mas nolh marques
E.lh ric chastel e.lh bel estar
Mas li chastela non i so.

Kingdoms there are, but no more kings,
And counties, but no counts dwell there,
No marcher from the marches springs,
Castles, domains, lie void and bare;
Gone are the mighty castellans.

BERTRAND DE BORN

ONE DAY IN APRIL—that favourite month with troubadours,
when the nights are short and the air soft—a messenger arrived at
the gates of Fontevrault. There were hurried comings and goings,
and even in the choir, where lauds was being said, sorrow intruded.
King Richard was dying and had sent for his mother, Queen
Eleanor.

She made ready for the journey with that same promptness
which she had always displayed when action was called for. The
chronicles say she travelled 'faster than the wind' to the little town
of Châlus, where her son was clinging to life until she came. She
probably sailed up the Vionne, for in those days it was quicker to
go by river than by road. On the morning of April 6th she arrived
at Richard's bedside just in time to hear his last testament.

A chance incident had given rise to this tragic death. A few weeks
earlier, a peasant tilling his plot of land on the outskirts of Châlus
had unearthed an amazing find—an object resembling a large altar-
piece, made of solid gold and depicting, according to popular
description, an emperor seated beside his wife and family; these
figures were admirably wrought. The peasant had dutifully taken
his discovery straight to his lord, Count Aymar of Limoges. As

soon as he heard of it, the king demanded his share as overlord. The count turned a deaf ear. Richard further suspected him of being in the pay of the king of France and of aspiring to a degree of independence to which he was simply not entitled. In a fit of fury, the king laid siege to the castle of Châlus. Peace was inducing a mood of slothfulness among the mercenaries whom he had originally hired for use against Philip—Gascons led by a famous captain named Mercadier.

On the evening of March 25th, 1199, Richard went out after supper to inspect the work performed by his sappers who, on this first day of the siege, had already started undermining the fortifications. Suddenly an arrow whistled down from the battlements. The bowman was an excellent shot, and the arrow hit the king in the shoulder. But what was a single arrow to King Richard, who had acquired the reputation in the Holy Land of looking like a pincushion when he returned from the fray? However, the arrow resisted all attempts to pull it out: the barb had gone deep into his back, catching the spine. A 'surgeon' in Mercadier's employ was brought to the king's tent, and in the uncertain light of the lantern he hacked at the flesh while Richard groaned on his couch; but for all the man's efforts, a fragment of lead remained lodged in the wound. Richard, however, chose to disregard the seriousness of it. Unable to control his restless spirit, he continued to indulge himself as usual, eating spicy foods, drinking potent wines and spending his nights with the fine-looking girls of Poitou. The wound festered, fever set in, and within a few days his condition had to be acknowledged as hopeless.

It was at this point that he had sent for his mother. The abbot of Turpenay had offered to escort her; before setting out she had asked Matilda, abbess of Fontevrault, to go and break the news to Queen Berengaria and John Lackland.

Richard was attended by his chaplain, Milo, abbot of Le Pin, an abbey which had been restored at his expense; it was his habit to give generously to religious establishments of every kind and, for all his strayings and unbridled passions, he had never stopped going to church. And now, in the face of death, this impetuous creature whose lifetime had been marked by all manner of dissoluteness (and even vice) displayed extraordinary serenity. He had

unreservedly confessed his sins and asked to be given the Body and
Blood of Christ, which he had not dared to receive since returning
from the Holy Land on account of the fierce hatred which he felt
for King Philip. But all hatred was extinguished now. Richard had
forgiven the king of France and he had likewise forgiven his killer,
whose life he had spared after summoning him to his tent. He
condemned his own action in violating the Lenten truce by laying
siege to the castle, and declared that as a penance for his appalling
sins he was prepared to dwell in Purgatory until the Last Judgment.
He died towards evening, in his mother's arms, after requesting
that his heart should be preserved in Rouen Cathedral and his body
laid to rest in the abbey of Fontevrault.

At once messengers were dispatched in all directions to inform
the king's familiars. One was sent to William the Marshal, then
living in Vaudreuil, Normandy. It was Saturday in Passion Week,
the eve of Palm Sunday. William was on the point of going to bed;
he had already started to undress when the fateful tidings came.
He put his clothes on again and went at once to Notre-Dame-du-
Pré, where the archbishop of Canterbury, Hubert Walter, was then
staying. He had only just heard of the king's serious condition.

'Ah!' he cried, realizing that a visit at this late hour could have
only one meaning. 'I know what brings you here—the king is
dead. What hope have we now? None—for with him gone, I can
think of no one capable of defending the kingdom. If you ask me,
the French will overrun us without meeting with any resistance.'

'We must lose no time in choosing his successor,' said the Marshal.

'In my view,' returned the archbishop, 'Arthur of Brittany would
be our best choice.'

'Oh, that would never do, Your Grace. Arthur has had bad
counsellors—he is irascible and overproud. If we put him at our
head we shall rue it, for he dislikes the English. But let us consider
Count John. In all conscience, he is his father's and brother's
nearest heir.'

'Marshal,' said the archbishop, 'is that your wish?'

'Yes, it is his due. The son has a better claim to his father's heritage than the nephew.'

'Marshal, it shall be as you desire—but I promise you, you will
regret it more than anything you have ever done.'

'That may be,' said William, 'but I have given you my considered opinion.'

Palm Sunday (April 11th, 1199) found Eleanor back at Fontevrault, where her son was to be buried. Hugh, the saintly bishop of Lincoln, conducted the Mass for the Dead, assisted by the bishops of Poitiers and Angers; beside the queen were Lucas, abbot of Turpenay, who had attended her throughout the journey, and Milo, the chaplain who had administered the last sacrament to her son.

With the death of Richard, all her hopes came tumbling down. Her beloved son had been taken from her at the height of his powers (he was only forty-one), and had left no direct heir. Queen Berengaria had never meant much to him, but so long as he was alive it had been possible to hope that a child would one day guarantee the Plantagenet line. But a cruel fate seemed to dog the king; was there really a curse on the Angevins? Five sons, and of those five only the last remained, an unbalanced creature, weak and dishonest, capable of anything except wearing the crown in a worthy manner. Did it occur to Eleanor to leave him to tussle with his subjects and his own nature, while she herself retired ever further into the seclusion of Fontevrault? She was seventy-seven. Was she still capable of playing an active part in affairs? Would it not be better to cut herself off from a world which no longer held any purpose for her? If any such idea came to her, she must have rejected it as the worst of temptations. For all the agony it occasioned her, the shock of Richard's death aroused that regal instinct which had become second nature and which seemed more deeply ingrained than ever now that she was no longer motivated by ambition. It was imperative that what had been achieved should be preserved and passed on. This was a woman's task and if she was to perform it she must be ready to take action, she must anticipate tomorrow's problems even while she was solving today's. And neither age, nor weariness, nor her present inexpressible sorrow were going to keep her from that task.

On the very day of her son's funeral, Eleanor made a new bequest to Fontevrault 'for the soul of her very dear lord, King

Richard'; Richard always appears in her official deeds as *carissimum*, very dear; John is simply *dilectum*, the term generally in use, a conventionalized form. That he might earn God's forgiveness sooner as a result of the nuns' prayers, she was according them (stated the document) a grant of one hundred Angevin pounds per annum, to provide habits.

The days which followed were marked by many similar donations. To the abbey of Our Lady in Turpenay she conceded Langeais pond, specifying in the wording of the deed that she 'was present at the death of her very dear son, the king, who reposed all his trust in her, next to God, and she intends that his wishes shall be carried out. She will attend to these wishes with motherly concern and is especially counting on the help of the abbot (Lucas), who was present at the death-bed and funeral of her very dear son, the king, and played a larger part in these events than anyone else.' She heaped gifts upon her son's servants. Adam, his cook, and his wife Joan received various properties in England and were confirmed in their right to those previously bestowed on them by 'her very dear son Richard—may his soul be at peace for ever'. Similarly, his butler Ingeran, or Enguerrand, was granted an English village. And as time went by, other members of Richard's household staff were to benefit on several occasions under deeds signed by Eleanor. For instance, there was a certain Renaud of Marin to whom she gave a bakehouse in Poitiers 'in consideration of services loyally rendered to ourselves and to our son of blessed memory, King Richard'. Corresponding acts of generosity were made in favour of Roger (another cook), Henry of Berneval, and old Agatha, governess to the royal children, who was presented with a manor in Devonshire.

But these tokens of affection, gratitude and motherly love did not keep her from devoting all her energies to the security of the realm present and future. Indeed, the days ahead were to bring a host of important figures to Fontevrault, including the papal legate, Peter of Capua, who called to present his condolences to the queen. Members of the family arrived, too—among them, Queen Berengaria and Eleanor's granddaughter, Matilda of Saxony, who by marriage had become countess of Le Perche. Finally there was John Lackland. He had been in Brittany at the time of Richard's death and was accused of conspiring against his brother; but on learning the news he had put his dark schemes aside and hurried to Chinon, where the continental part of the English royal treasury was maintained; the seneschal of Anjou, Robert of Thornham, had handed it over to him without hesitation—but not all Richard's officers (least of all the great barons) were to respond with the same eagerness. John was on his way to Angers when he heard, at Beaufort-la-Vallée, that the city and castle had been delivered into the hands of Constance of Brittany and her son Arthur, who was claiming to be Richard's rightful heir. Here was a first breach in the unity of the realm, a first challenge to John Lackland. Immediate action was called for. Mercadier was still available; with his army of mercenaries, he was sent to Anjou with instructions to liberate the city, while John—pausing only to secure control of Le Mans—hastened to Normandy, where on April 25th he was invested with the ducal sword and crown of golden roses. Meanwhile Hubert Walter and William the Marshal were on their way to England to make the necessary preparations for the coronation, due to be held on Ascension Day, May 27th.

John crowned Ascension Thursday 5-27-1199

For her part, Eleanor had set out on a remarkably extensive tour of her own dominions, Poitou and Aquitaine. In swift succession she paid official visits to Loudon (April 29th), Poitiers (May 4th), Montreuil-Bonnin (May 5th) and then to Niort, Andilly, La Rochelle, Saint-Jean-d'Angély and Saintes, until at last she came to Bordeaux (July 1st) and Soulac (July 4th). As E.-R. Labande has pointed out, the speed of her progress is a tribute not only to her incredible willpower—triumphing over physical tiredness and mindful only of the need to keep the Plantagenet kingdom as intact as possible—but also to the 'excellence of the roads and communications in her domains'.

A world of memories must have assailed the queen as, after an interval of fifty years, she toured the beautiful duchy where she had so often roamed in the days of her youth. No doubt her shrewd eye was assessing the changes wrought during that half-century, for it had been a time of great transformation. Whereas war had several times ravaged the area round Le Mans and certain districts of Anjou and Normandy, western France—from Poitou to the Pyrenees—had enjoyed untroubled peace and was at the height of its prosperity. Along the waterways, the mills could previously be counted in ones and twos; now they were to be counted in hundreds. And hydraulic power was not only used for driving corn-mills and mustard mills: it powered the bellows and tilt-hammers in forges, it ground tanbark and dyestuffs such as woad, it brewed beer, threshed hemp, fulled cloth and even worked lathes and saws for carpenters. Thus a whole host of manual tasks had been mechanized, and the change had brought benefit to the entire population. As always, prosperity found expression in intense architectural activity. More and more rib vaults were being raised; they were the great invention of the age. The impetus derived from the boldness which Abbot Suger had shown in rebuilding the abbey church at Saint-Denis. Now the new churches were growing taller and brighter; walls were being hollowed out with complete unconcern, and never had stone seemed softer or so easy to work. In the Plantagenet domains, the princes had set a good example. They had been unfailingly generous in their gifts to abbeys. The construction of Poitiers Cathedral, the ducal palace and a number of powerful fortresses was only one side of the coin: they could also claim credit for the covered market at Saumur and the bridge over the Vionne, at Chinon; for such works of art as the dyke at Les Ponts-de-Cé, designed to regularize the course of the Mayenne; and for a great many hospitals and even whole towns, like the one built by Richard at Saint-Rémy-de-la-Haye, on the Creuse, or the rows of new buildings which were going up near Château-Gaillard. The builders of western France were displaying great technical skill, and it was a theology teacher from Saintes—a certain Master Isambert—who two years later was to set about constructing the great new London Bridge.

For here, undoubtedly, lay the most striking feature of the age: economic expansion, the rising importance of towns and, side by side with this, the development of the countryside. The population was growing at an ever-increasing pace, but at the same time there were unrelenting efforts to make better use of natural resources: fallow land was being reclaimed; the science of sheep-breeding was being studied and applied; forestry resources were being exploited. And viewed at this distance in time, the proliferation of new townships may well impress us as the most remarkable thing of all.

Instead of allowing the cities already in existence to swell to an immoderate size, new ones were created. And because these were well scattered, a harmonious relationship was established between town and country—a far cry from the unbalanced development which leads to overgrown cities and deserted rural areas.

The presence of the town, with its walls rising in competition with those of the castle, was the predominant characteristic of the age—and the fact had not escaped Eleanor's notice. As a rule, a certain interval of time is needed to arrive at a clear assessment of a given phase of history. One of the things which is so extraordinary about Eleanor is her degree of alertness to the true nature of her own era, and the keen critical eye with which she was able to distinguish its lines of force. We have only to consider what happened on that protracted tour of her duchy. Certainly the queen did not neglect her feudal duties; as she went along, she saw to it that justice was dispensed to those whose rights had been infringed; she restored to the nuns of Sainte-Croix de Montreuil the woods which had been misappropriated for hunting; she settled a number of legal disputes; she even had occasion to effect transfers of sovereignty, ceding the domain of Talmond to Raoul of Mauléon in exchange for his promise to waive all claims to La Rochelle; she confirmed, in accordance with custom, donations previously made to religious institutions in Montierneuf, Saintes and Bordeaux. But above and beyond all this she conferred charters of independence on town after town, releasing the burghers from their obligations towards their local lord. One by one, all the main centres of population were invested with the civic liberties by which the townsmen set such store, and Eleanor herself was present at the election of the first mayor of La Rochelle, William of Montmirail. What thoughts must have passed through her head as she gave Poitiers its freedom, she who—some sixty years earlier—had been moved to such wrath by the arrogant claims of its burghers and had sought to inflict such harsh penalties on the principal families (even wanting to take two hundred young men and girls as hostages). She had been so angry with Abbot Suger and her first husband, the king of France, when they had rescinded these measures—and here she was, voluntarily granting the very rights which she had so bitterly opposed! Yet what better proof could there be of the change which life had wrought in her? Between the fickle, frivolous young woman and the aged queen lay a long succession of experiences, some of them happy, most of them painful, but none of them wasted. She had reached an age when she might have been expected to give up and retreat into a private world of vain regrets. Far from it! Drawing on the wisdom which experience had taught her, she showed that she was capable of acting effectively at the very time when all her handiwork seemed to have collapsed about her.

'We grant, to all the men of La Rochelle and to their heirs, a corporation . . . which shall enable them to defend and preserve their own rights more effectively . . . and we desire that their free customs . . . shall be inviolably observed and that, in order that they may maintain them and defend their rights and ours and those of our heirs, they shall exert and employ the strength and power of their commune, whenever necessary, against any man . . .'

One can imagine the queen dictating the text word by word to her chaplain Roger (a loyal aide for whom she was later, at Fontevrault, to found the chaplaincy of Saint-Laurent) or to the other clerks travelling with her, Josselin and Renoul. All the towns which she visited, and the Ile d'Oléron too, were granted a similar charter, inspired by the famous document which, thirty years earlier, had given Rouen the privileges of which it was so proud. Clearly, these charters satisfied the aspirations of the burghers, but at the same time they constituted a really shrewd stratagem. By this conciliatory gesture, Eleanor was obtaining extensive military aid; for while releasing them from previous impositions, she was making it compulsory for them to contribute to their own defence. The kingdom's military resources were usually supplied by the feudal lords; Eleanor was now adding a militia which the burghers would be responsible for manning. The measure was so ingenious that Philip Augustus lost no time in introducing it in France; when he granted the citizens of Tournai their freedom, he specified that they were to maintain 'three hundred well-armed foot-soldiers', whose services he could call on at any time.

Eleanor had no illusions as to her son's capabilities, nor as to the barons' feelings towards him. The feudal bond was a personal bond, and there was nothing in John's personality to win him the loyalty which an overlord traditionally expected from his vassals. The only answer was to equip him with this military reserve acquired under the term of his alliance with the city burghers.

And this was not all. Immediately after her extraordinary political tour, which had allowed her to play the liberal, open-handed queen while re-establishing complete control over her duchy, she appeared before Philip Augustus in mid-July at Tours and did homage to him for her lands. Of course, this feudal act of homage to her overlord, the king of France, was no more than his due. But to renew it in the present circumstances showed exceptional shrewdness on Eleanor's part. Her gesture implied that she stood aloof from the struggle for precedence which had dragged on for so long between successive kings of France and England; she controlled nearly the whole of western France, from the Loire to the Pyrenees; by making the traditional obeisance, she was robbing Philip Augustus of any excuse to launch an offensive against this sizeable part of the Plantagenet realm.

The chroniclers are extremely terse in their accounts of the scene, and do not give any details. A pity, for it would be interesting to know how the ceremony passed off, exactly where it took place and which barons were in attendance as Eleanor, in token of submission, placed her frail old hand between the rough palms of this king who was young enough to be her son. However, it is not difficult to imagine the glance they must have exchanged when she rose and he planted the traditional kiss on that hand.

Neither of them was taken in. Each knew that the other was full of schemes and ambitions. The queen's gesture was an act of defiance; the king of France was merely biding his time until he had a chance to put his plans into effect. Still, when she met her son John in Rouen on July 30th Eleanor could rightfully claim she had done everything in her power to safeguard his kingdom—everything, even to the point of swallowing her pride before Philip Augustus.

And indeed, John appears to have been alive to the full measure of this motherly devotion. The covenant which he made with Eleanor at this time strikes a filial note which is surprising in view of his general nature. 'We desire,' he stated, 'that she shall have Poitou throughout all the days of her life . . . and desire that she shall be Lady not only of all those territories which are ours, but also of ourself and of all our lands and possessions.'

At this point, however, Eleanor was beset by a worry which had nothing to do with political events. In Niort, she had been joined by her daughter Joanna. For the past three years Joanna had been the wife of Count Raymond VI of Toulouse. Eleanor may well have seen this marriage as the crowning of one of her oldest ambitions: the Plantagenets would become overlords of the county at last. Be that as it may, the match could not possibly be a happy one. Raymond VI was as shabby a figure as his father: his public and private actions were equally alien to the courtly ideal. Joanna was his fourth wife. He had buried the first, shut the second away in a Cathar convent and discarded the third within a few months of marrying her, in order to get his hands on the valuable dowry which King Richard had set aside for his sister—the city of Agen and the surrounding area. Afterwards he had returned to his dissolute ways. He led a debauched life and was always in dispute with one or other of his vassals, for the failure to stand by promises was a family failing with the counts of Toulouse. Joanna had borne him a son, who would one day be Raymond VII. She was with child for a second time when, almost single-handed, she had to put down a revolt on the part of the lords of Saint-Félix, while her husband was up to some mischief in northern Languedoc. Things went badly for her: while besieging the castle of Cassès she was betrayed by her own people, who set fire to her encampment. Somehow she managed to escape. Knowing how little she could rely on support from her husband, she decided to come and seek help from her brother, King Richard. On the way, she learned of his death. She was almost prostrate with grief and exhaustion when at last she met up with Eleanor, who was still making her tour of Poitou. The queen sent her to Fontevrault to recover; from there she travelled to Rouen. Almost at once she had to take to her bed; she made her will and then, to the astonishment of those about her, announced her intention of taking the veil and entering Fontevrault. The archbishop of Canterbury, Hubert Walter, who had returned to Rouen with John Lackland, tried in vain to dissuade her; she displayed such unshakable determination that in the end they had no choice but to override canon law and send word to the abbess of Fontevrault. Her health was declining as her time drew near: she was unable to rise when she took her vows and received the veil. A few days later, Eleanor closed her eyelids. Just after she died, she was successfully delivered of the child she was carrying; it lived long enough to be baptized. Joanna was thirty-four; she had been taken from the world five months after Richard.

The previous year (1198) had brought the death of Marie of Champagne. Thus, in swift succession, Eleanor had lost the three children dearest to her heart. Alix of Blois had died a short while earlier, and the queen had honoured her memory by conferring a gift on Alix's daughter, who bore the same name and was a nun at Fontevrault. Of the ten children Eleanor had borne, only two remained—the highly disturbing figure who was still known as John Lackland, and that other Eleanor who lived at her husband's court in far Castile.

XXII

Dieus, donatz mi saber et sen ab qu'ieu aprenda
Vostres sanhs mandamens e.ls auja e.ls entenda,
E vostra pietatz que.m gueris que.m defenda
    D'aquest segle terre
    Que no.m trabuc ab se;
    Quar ie.us ador e.us cre,
    Senher, e.us fauc ufrenda
    De me e de ma fe;
    Qu'aissi.s tanh e.s cove;
    Per so vos crit merce
    E de mes tortz esmenda.

God give me knowledge and the grace wherewith to apprehend
Thy holy ordinances, and their meaning comprehend,
And may Thy mercy save me, and also me defend
    From perils here below
    Which lurk where'er I go;
    For, Lord, I love Thee so
    That faith and self I send
    As the just due I owe—
    Such grace from Thee doth flow;
    Dear Lord, Thy favour show
    And all my faults amend.

FOLQUET DE MARSEILLE

IT WOULD HARDLY HAVE BEEN SURPRISING if Eleanor had been laid low after so tragic and hectic a year as 1199, for life had dealt mercilessly with her, bringing intense personal grief and a sudden blackening of the whole political horizon, worse than anyone could have foreseen.

And yet the documents show her on her travels again in the depths of the following winter: at the age of eighty, give or take a year, she was crossing the Pyrenees on the way to see her sole surviving daughter. (*Eleanor of Castile*) `1200`

For within a few months of Joanna's being laid to rest beneath the vaults of Fontevrault, a plan had taken shape—and Eleanor was conspicuously anxious to implement it. There had been a meeting between John Lackland and Philip Augustus. On his own initiative, the latter had proposed a truce and undertaken to call off the hostilities in which his forces were engaged in Normandy. William of Les Roches, one of the Angevin vassals on whom he most relied, had defected and thrown in his lot with the Plantagenets, while the count of Flanders was threatening his fiefs in Artois. Most serious of all, the king of France was on the worst possible terms with the Vatican. The church insisted that he should reinstate his wife, Ingeborg of Denmark. So far he had refused—indeed, he had contracted a new marriage with Agnes of Meran, the daughter of one of the princes of the Empire. On January 13th, 1200, the long-threatened interdict had fallen on the kingdom of France. Realizing that he was in no position to continue the struggle, Philip Augustus had hurriedly made peace with his adversary.

1-13-1200 Interdict falls on Fr.

INNOCENT III 1198-1216

As soon as the truce was agreed, Eleanor set out with an imposing escort: Elie of Malemort, archbishop of Bordeaux, was with her and so was Mercadier, the mercenary who had fought at Richard's side in his last campaigns. For under the terms of the truce, Louis—heir to the French throne—was to be married to one of Eleanor of Castile's daughters. A similar scheme had been tried once before, at the time of the final negotiations between Richard and Philip, but no one had seemed in any hurry to put it into effect. This time, on the other hand, Eleanor had set out forthwith and journeyed with remarkable speed. She was in Castile before the end of January—and this despite being held up en route by one of the Lusignans, Hugh le Brun; taking advantage of these special circumstances, he refused to let her go on her way until she had ceded the county of La Marche to him.

Louis (later L VIII to mr Eleanor of Castile's d BLANCHE

Why was she in such a hurry? Of course, when one has been nursing a scheme for twenty-four years it is only wise to bring it to a successful conclusion as swiftly as possible. All the same, there is something striking about the personal sense of urgency which Eleanor brought to the realization of a project which does not seem to have fired her imagination until then. When Richard had suggested marrying one of his nieces to Philip's heir, she had not taken much notice. Yet John had only to breathe a word of such a project and she went hurrying off in person, filled with the determination to return with one of her granddaughters. Then again, betrothals were generally supervised by any prelate who happened to be at hand—whereas the present mission had been entrusted to no less a person than the archbishop of Bordeaux, a devoted supporter of the Plantagenets.

After the series of bereavements which she had suffered, Eleanor may have been glad of the opportunity to visit the last of her daughters. But it is reasonable to infer that her long and hazardous expedition was inspired by something quite other than the desire to steep herself in family life again. As on the occasion when she had collected Berengaria of Navarre and taken her to Sicily, Eleanor was acting as queen and mother alike. And her decision to make the journey clearly derived from her anxiety to contribute as much as she could to the peace of the realm. So long as Richard was alive, Philip had been held in check and there had been no real danger to the Plantagenet kingdom. With Richard gone, the situation was reversed. Anything might happen: a few short years might bring total destruction to the magnificent realm which had been established by the union of Eleanor and Henry. Her mission to Castile was thus in key with all she had sought to achieve since coming out of retirement almost a year earlier. In her efforts to safeguard the kingdom and keep it as intact as possible, she had created new allies for John by giving the burghers their independence; she had effected a reconciliation between him and William of Les Roches; finally, by formally acknowledging the king of France as her overlord, she had made Philip Augustus responsible for the defence of Poitou and Aquitaine. And now she was making a further contribution to peace by going in search of the best possible token of alliance—the girl who was to marry Louis of France.

The English historian F. M. Powicke, in a masterly analysis of the period, has with considerable discernment drawn attention to the important part played by the womenfolk at this crucial stage in the Plantagenet story. Parallel with the dispute between Philip and John there was the struggle being waged, with equal keenness on either side, by Eleanor and her daughter-in-law, Constance of Brittany. For as a cover for his designs upon Normandy, Philip had set himself up as the champion of her son, young Arthur of Brittany. We have seen how, at the time of Richard's death, the barons had to choose between Henry's youngest son and his grandson. William the Marshal had chosen in the light of the convention then prevailing. But Constance was free to argue that John was merely the younger brother of her late husband Geoffrey; she insisted that the entire inheritance should pass to the latter's son, Arthur. She was rather an odd figure: some time after the death of Geoffrey she had married an English lord, Ranulf of Chester, who (the whys and wherefores of this act are not clear) subsequently cast her off, after holding her captive for a time in the castle of Saint-James de Beuvron, in Normandy. Later, not long after Richard's death, she married a Poitevin noble, Guy of Thouars; her son Arthur had been brought up at the royal court of France, and, predictably, Philip Augustus was taking full advantage of the antipathy which she had always shown towards her first husband's family.

In the background, other female figures were influencing events. First and foremost there was Ingeborg, the poor forsaken wife whose protests against her unjust fate had won the support of the pope himself—the forceful Innocent III was now master in St Peter's. Then there was her rival, Agnes of Meran, by whom Philip was to have two children—another Philip, called Hurepel, probably because he had inherited his father's thick mane, and Marie, whom Philip Augustus intended to marry to Arthur of Brittany. Finally there was Berengaria of Navarre, Richard's wife, a somewhat dull creature who had proved incapable of keeping her incorrigible husband in check and who was now ceaselessly clamouring for her dowry; in the end John guaranteed her an annual income of a thousand silver marks, two castles in Anjou and one in Bayeux.

In addition to these, two other female personalities were about to appear on the scene: the Castilian bride-to-be whom Eleanor had gone in search of, and Isabella of Angoulême—whose presence was to spark off a series of events which eventually led to the break-up of the Plantagenet kingdom.

Isabella was betrothed to the same Hugh le Brun of Lusignan

[handwritten marginal notes:]
WOMEN INFLUENCING EVENTS
1. INGEBORG
2. Agnes of Meran
3. Berengaria of Navarre

2 to come
1. Blanche of Castile
2. Isabella of Angoulême.

who had waylaid Eleanor and successfully demanded the county of La Marche. Marriage to his little fourteen-year-old bride would make this early-middle-aged man heir to the county of Angoulême: in short, fortune seemed to smile on him. However, he had the ill-fated idea of inviting his overlord, the king of England, to the betrothal ceremony. John was busy with his own matrimonial problems: he had decided to terminate his marriage to Havisa of Gloucester, who had failed to bear him a child, and had just sent envoys to King Sancho of Portugal, asking for the hand of one of his daughters. During the celebrations at Lusignan, Isabella of Angoulême was presented to him. Two months later, on August 24th, 1200, came the astonishing news that John—having sent Hugh le Brun on a diplomatic mission to England, in order to get him out of the way—had married young Isabella with the full consent of her father, Count Aymar of Angoulême.

This rash deed scarcely endeared him to the Poitevin barons, who were so jealous of their independence and never slow to parade it. The after-effects were incalculable, for Isabella's was one of those strong female natures which so often influenced the course of events in feudal times. For the present, this marriage—which was in the nature of a kidnapping, even though aided and abetted by the girl's father—was a first step towards the disintegration of the kingdom: it loosened the personal bond on which the vassals' loyalty depended; as a result, the barons—hitherto undecided—became resolutely hostile to the king of England.

But in the meantime a quite different event took place, likewise fraught with consequences, and destined to place another strong-willed woman upon the throne of France . . . We left Eleanor journeying along the roads of Old Castile. It was very likely in Burgos, or some neighbouring stronghold, that she met her daughter and grandchildren. Eleanor of Castile had borne eleven children to her husband, Alfonso VIII; their court was gay and brilliant, with an atmosphere closely akin to that of Poitiers. Like Catalonia, Castile extended a ready welcome to troubadours. One of them, Raimon Vidal de Bezalu, has left us a verse description of a literary gathering at the court of Alfonso VIII. It was presided over by Eleanor the younger. She was beautiful and modest; clad in a dress of bright red silk hemmed with silver thread, she appeared before the court, which included 'many a knight and many a jongleur'; she curtseyed to the king and took her place quite close to him. Together, they listened as the troubadour told his tale; it was so beautiful that afterwards there was no member of the court who did not wish to know it by heart.

Among the permanent guests was Guilhem de Berguedan, an earlier Don Juan with a fine gift for poetry and seduction, who had vainly aspired to the queen's love. Also to be met there were Folquet de Marseille, who was later to take holy orders and become bishop of Toulouse, Perdigan, Peire Roger, Guiraut de Calanson and, last but by no means least, Peire Vidal, who is unstinting in his praise of this hospitable court and its generous king and queen.

It is good to think of this visit, which to Eleanor of England must have seemed an oasis, a haven of comfort amid the storm-tossed years of her old age. At the court of Castile she found an atmosphere of youth, freshness, poetry. And so we find her tarrying in her daughter's company for over two months; after all, weddings were not performed during Lent, and however eager she might be to get this one over and done with, she had no reason to return to her domains before Easter—which fell, that year, on April 9th. What *is* surprising is that, when she eventually turned her back on the delightful court of Castile, the girl she took away was not the girl she had come for.

Eleanor the younger had, in fact, three daughters of marriageable age (i.e. between eleven and fifteen)—Berengaria, Urraca and Blanca. Berengaria, the eldest, was already betrothed to the heir of the kingdom of Leon; so it was the second girl, Urraca, who had been set aside for Louis. Yet Eleanor had Blanca with her as she made her way back through the Pyrenees. And it is clear from contemporary chronicles that the substitution was made at her express wish. The excuse provided was patently *only* an excuse: the queen's party thought that the French people would never adjust to a princess bearing so Spanish a name as Urraca, whereas Princess Blanca could easily become Queen Blanche—a thoroughly specious argument at a time when the queen of France was called Ingeborg (or Isambour) and the queen of England bore so un-English a name as Eleanor (or Aliénor). However, the choice was made and there was no alternative but to accept it. Urraca was promptly betrothed to the heir to the Portuguese throne, while Blanche—contrary to all expectation—set out on the road to France. Eleanor's protracted stay had given her ample opportunity to assess the qualities of all three girls, and it seems plain that she had once more brought her splendid perspicacity to bear—a perspicacity rendered all the sharper by age and experience. Whether as the result of affection born of natural affinity (for afterwards it became clear that Blanche of Castile took after her grandmother in more ways than one) or of carefully considered judgment, it was she who was to be installed on the throne of France; and she emerged as a resourceful queen and admirable mother.

Spring was coming to southern Europe as Blanche journeyed towards her country of adoption. We have no means of telling what words passed between the aged queen and the young girl who, in this first year of the thirteenth century, had such a glorious future ahead of her; but it seems reasonable to infer that Blanche was very much in awe of Eleanor, who had been queen of two great countries and was mother of two kings, and whose children and grandchildren were strewn among the courts of Spain and the Empire.

The journey home was accomplished safely—despite the tragic death of Mercadier, killed in a street brawl in Bordeaux while Eleanor and her granddaughter were resting in the Ombrière Palace. True, Mercadier was in no true sense superior to any other mercenary: they were a ruffianly breed, given to looting and acts of gross brutality; the employment of mercenaries had been one of the blots on the reputation of the Plantagenet kingdom; it had contributed substantially to the brutal nature of the war between Richard and Philip Augustus; fortunately this evil was due to be stamped out in the thirteenth century. But to return to Mercadier's personal savagery: it was on his instructions that the man who slew King Richard was flayed alive and hanged, even though the dying king had stipulated that the bowman's life should be spared.

Blanche and Louis were married on May 23rd in the neighbourhood of Port-Mort, in Normandy, just across the border from France. No religious ceremonies could be performed in France itself, for the kingdom was still under the interdict imposed by

260

Innocent III. Eleanor did not attend the service. She had broken her journey at Fontevrault, leaving her granddaughter in the care of the archbishop of Bordeaux. Her own task was fulfilled.

———————◆———————

It would be tempting to end the story on this note of muted triumph, with the young princess marrying Louis of France and Eleanor fading quietly into the shadows of Fontevrault.

But no, the final episode had yet to come. Once more she was going to have to emerge from her haven, and once more the circumstances were to be tragic.

And yet everything seemed calm enough. John Lackland crowned his young bride at Westminster on October 8th, 1200, and the impression was even given that the king of France had condoned his hot-headed act; for in the summer of 1201 the king and queen of England journeyed to the Ile de la Cité and—as contemporary observers point out—were given a much warmer welcome than anyone would have dared to hope. Nor had Eleanor been idle. Still tirelessly expending herself in efforts to guarantee peace —for without it, as she well knew, the kingdom would not survive in the hands of John—she had successfully brought about a reconciliation with the viscounts of Thouars, or at any rate with Amaury, brother of Guy and hence Arthur of Brittany's uncle by marriage. In the spring of 1201 she wrote to John and told him how the latter had visited her in Fontevrault at her request. She was unwell at the time, but had nevertheless conversed with Amaury of Thouars: '. . . the pleasure which I derived from his visit did me good.' Before taking his leave of her, he promised that he would do his best to maintain harmony and obedience among the barons of Poitou. At the very moment when this reconciliation was being effected, the luckless Constance of Brittany contracted leprosy: she was destined to die a few months later, on September 4th, 1201. Her death was narrowly preceded by that of Agnes of Meran—perhaps France would be released from the interdict which had been imposed because of the king's misdeeds with this woman; perhaps a new era of peace and stability was at hand.

But in fact it was only the complications stemming from the punitive measures adopted by the Church which had kept Philip Augustus from giving free rein to his desire to lay hands on Normandy and the whole Plantagenet kingdom. He was sufficiently well acquainted with his adversary to realize that he could well afford to bide his time. He intended choosing the best possible moment to play his trump cards. Chief among these was young Arthur of Brittany, brought up at his court and carefully sustained in the belief that he would one day be king of England. The death of Constance deprived the youth of counsels which had almost certainly been more sagacious and less self-interested than those which were daily poured out to him in Paris.

The conflict came to a head in 1202. Philip Augustus had an excuse ready to hand—the calls for assistance issued by the Poitevin barons, headed by the Lusignans but including many others whose pride and lawful rights John had carelessly tramped on (he acted without any consideration for local customs, was pointlessly arrogant to his vassals and took castles out of people's hands whenever he felt like it). So the king of France, acting in his capacity as overlord, summoned the king of England to appear before his court and answer the barons' complaints. When he refused, on April 28th, John was condemned by default; a challenge was issued to him, and war declared. Shortly afterwards, Arthur of Brittany was publicly knighted by Philip Augustus and did homage to him not only for Brittany, but for Anjou, Maine, Touraine and Poitou. In other words, no store was set by the homage which Eleanor had sworn in respect of this province which was part of her private domain. Arthur was impudently annexing the fief which was hers both in law and in fact. The Plantagenet kingdom was in process of being dismantled, and it was widely noted that in his speech of homage Arthur had made no reference to Normandy: the king of France had already earmarked it as his own property.

Without more ado Philip went into action, capturing a series of Norman strongpoints—Eu, Aumale, Gournay ... At the same time he equipped Arthur, excited at the thought of embarking on his first campaign, with a force of two hundred hand-picked knights, bidding him seize control of Poitou and join hands with the Lusignans. When word of these developments reached Eleanor she

262

decided that she was in jeopardy at Fontevrault. With a small escort she hurriedly set out for Poitiers, whose stout walls had sheltered her several times in the past.

Swift as her decision had been, however, the queen was outpaced by events: Arthur, supported by Hugh of Châtellerault, had already left Tours and reached Loudun. The queen barely had time to take cover in the castle of Mirebeau. The little town was immediately taken by storm; but the keep stood firm, and Eleanor found herself trapped inside it with a handful of men. Surely she was not going to suffer the ignominy of being taken prisoner by her grandson?

Her answer was to position all available archers on the battlements and at the loopholes, reinforce the gates and bridges and post look-outs on the turrets. Not content with this, she beguiled her assailants by pretending to bargain with them while two messengers hurried off in search of help; she sent one of these messengers to William of Les Roches, who was in Chinon, and the other to John Lackland himself, who at that time was in the neighbourhood of Le Mans. John came to the rescue with surprising speed: the messenger reached him during the night of July 30th; by first light on August 1st he was within sight of Mirebeau. With a lack of foresight which shows how certain they were of their prey, Arthur and his companions had chosen to block up all the gates of the little township to ensure that no one slipped through their fingers; only one had been left free, so that they themselves could obtain supplies. The story goes that one of their knights, Geoffrey of Lusignan, had just sat down to table and was tucking into a brace of roast pigeons when word was brought to him that the king of England and his men were approaching, with banners unfurled. He swore jestingly that he had no intention of stirring for a little thing like that and would finish his meal first. But that was all he had time to say, for he and Arthur and the thousand or so men who were besieging the fortress were caught like rats in a trap before they even had a chance to defend themselves.

Eleanor was released unharmed. But no one could have foreseen the appalling treatment that was in store for this multitude of prisoners. John Lackland had just demonstrated that, when the situation demanded, he could act with the speed and skill of a real warrior; the sequel to this incident reveals the satanic ferocity of which he was no less capable. Every possible humiliation was inflicted on the captured barons: he had them chained to carts and paraded through their own domains until they came to the keeps which were to be their prisons.

As for young Arthur of Brittany, John first of all entrusted him to his chamberlain, Hubert de Burgh, stipulating that he was to be blinded and castrated. Hubert de Burgh refused to be party to such a crime. Arthur was held prisoner in the tower of Rouen until Maundy Thursday, April 3rd, 1203, when John and a solitary companion—his henchman, William of Briouse—went to the cell where the young man was confined, put him aboard a small boat, slit his throat and threw his body into the Seine. Not a word leaked out of what had been done until, some seven years later, this same William of Briouse, now John's mortal enemy, fled to the French court and told what he had seen.

Not long afterwards, a messenger—Brother John of Valerant—brought Eleanor a letter which John Lackland had sent from Falaise on April 16th, 1203: 'God be thanked,' he wrote, 'things are going better for us than this man is able to tell you...' A terrifying communication which shows just how wicked the man was, but also how little aware of the true nature of his deeds; and we may conclude, since the messenger himself knew nothing of the crime and the queen never saw her son again, that she died without learning the full horror that was concealed between the lines.

Eleanor was destined to live one more year—just long enough to witness the collapse of the kingdom through the loss of Normandy, which had been the chief and most splendid fief of the kings of England. By this time, John's barbarousness had turned most of his barons against him and Philip Augustus was in an impregnable position. It was William of Les Roches himself who surrendered Touraine and Anjou to him; it was Amaury of Thouars who, after Eleanor's death, yielded part of Poitou. After an active phase, John had sunk into that brand of insuperable apathy which is the mark of the cyclothyme. He had watched the principal townships of Normandy fall into Philip Augustus's hands one by one: Sées, Conches, Falaise, Domfront, Bayeux, Caen, Avranches . . . And when Rouen, the last to hold out, sent word to him asking for help, he refused to admit the envoys—on the grounds, cited earlier, that it would have meant interrupting his game of chess.

On March 6th, 1204, the king of France had seized Château-Gaillard, the magnificent fortress which, only a few years earlier, had been King Richard's pride.

It has been said that the loss of this fortress came as a death-blow to Eleanor—for she died at Fontevrault a few weeks later, on March 31st or April 1st, 1204. But did she really die in a mood of despair? If that were so, her death would have been completely out of harmony with her life, for when had she suffered bad news, or a set-back, or a bereavement without responding in a courageous and positive manner? True, it may be argued that by now she was simply too old and frail to withstand another shock. But equally it may be argued that the loss, however cruel, came as no surprise to her: it was inevitable. With Richard gone, and no true heir to succeed him, the demise of the great Plantagenet kingdom was bound to follow. Eleanor could sense that better than anyone. She may have done her duty as a queen and as a mother by cosseting as many alliances as possible (and even creating new ones, in the shape of the burghers), but she must surely have acted without any illusions: John was not cut out to be a king; in his hands, the realm was bound to crumble.

It is her mission to Castile that stands out as the one great positive measure of these last years and reveals that her judgment was as fine as ever. It may have been prompted by her determination to secure peace, at a time when peace was essential to the preservation of the kingdom; but this does not alter the fact that it was she who placed Blanche of Castile on the throne of France, and who picked her, rather than another, to fill the post which she herself had once filled.

She had once nourished ambitions of seeing her son Henry become ruler of France through his marriage to young Marguerite. Now it was the other way round: under the pressure of events the future king of France was marrying a Plantagenet. For a while it even seemed that the amalgamation of France and England would be effected under French mandate—that Louis of France, Blanche's husband, would land in England with the support of a number of barons who could no longer endure the domination of John

265

Lackland. But it was left to their son, St Louis, to rise above the interplay of ambitions and work out a just solution: while officially quashing all English claims to Normandy, the outstandingly generous and imaginative treaty of 1259 restored some of Eleanor's former provinces to the king of England, in order to 'engender love' between her heirs. The latter, in the event, acknowledged their consanguinity—and thus Eleanor's ghost presided over this reconciliation between the two kingdoms.

The fortress of Château-Gaillard might tumble, and the strongholds surrender one by one; but to the queen, dwelling once more in the seclusion of Fontevrault, all this was merely an outward sign of the renunciation inherent in death, the inevitable sloughing-off of worldly goods; nothing mattered to her any more, except this baring of the soul which would allow her to be born a second time and so come into the presence of her Maker.

But it was not with any sense of despair that she took her leave of the world. On the contrary, her spirits were borne up by the vision of a young girl, her own grandchild, who showed every sign of being equal to the task, as a queen and as a woman, which she herself had shouldered for so long, and which Blanche might bring to a more successful conclusion.

April was coming in; after the rigours of winter, the sap was stirring in the withered trees round Fontevrault, and the breeze from Anjou brought a promise of renewal to the nuns' garden.

———————◆———————

Many criticisms have been levelled at Eleanor, both as to what she was and what she did; she has been depicted as a common whore, a woman possessed of the devil, a termagant driven by hatred, and so on and so forth. In the light of historical evidence, all such verdicts founder automatically; what endures is the image of a 'woman beyond compare', as Richard of Devizes calls her—an image marvellously captured by the unknown sculptor who carved the stone effigy on her tomb. Through his efforts she is revealed to us under the vaults of Fontevrault, that beloved abbey where she eventually took the veil. With a truer inspiration than most of the historians, writers and litterateurs who have sought to convey Eleanor's features, the artist has succeeded in bringing her back to life, instantly and fully. Here she is, with her body draped in the folds of her robe and cloak, and her features framed by her wimple. And sure enough she is reading a book.

This is no death mask; she seems alive beneath the paint. True, they did not sink, in her day, to the vulgar realism of the Renaissance, when all sculpture was thought to demand colour, which is life, and retained nothing of death except the human remains hidden within. But this fashion of the time takes on a special significance here at Fontevrault, where Eleanor, having experienced every nuance of human love, at last achieved the Love that has the power to transfigure. Small wonder that she should present the features of a woman risen from the dead—for who, more than she, could lay claim to the forgiveness promised to those who have shown great love?

Bibliographical Note

Index

BIBLIOGRAPHICAL NOTE

There has been a wealth of fascinating literature about Eleanor of Aquitaine, though the fascination stems chiefly from the mental attitudes of the authors and the intellectual climate in which they wrote. Three typical biographies are those by Isaac de Larrey (London, 1788), Countess Palamède de Macheco (Paris, 1822) and Louis de Villepreux (Paris, 1862). A common feature of all such works is a willingness to rely on literary sources (e.g. the jocular Ménestrel of Rheims or the Anecdotes of Stephen of Bourbon); authors had only to embroider on these, with a tolerable degree of imagination, until they successfully refashioned the tired, familiar portrait of Queen Eleanor.

It must be stated in their defence that many professedly 'serious' historians writing in our own day are guilty of the same offence: they too are content to stop short at the literary texts (more approachable than the charters or Pipe Rolls), promoting them to the rank of historical sources and using them as a basis for brilliant and almost effortless deductive reasoning. Suppose a scholar in the year 3000 were to use Genet, Ionesco and a batch of popular weeklies as his sole material for a social survey of the twentieth century!

There is little to counterbalance all this. Among French scholars, only E.-R. Labande (*Pour une image véridique d'Aliénor d'Aquitaine*) has brought a lively critical intelligence to bear on the task of sifting the twelfth-century documents. Labande's portrait of Eleanor is superlatively fresh and thorough, unforgettably convincing. Yet the general reader has not had an opportunity to reap the benefit; as so often happens in the field of mediaeval history, his study appeared in a specialist review intended only for the initiated (*Bulletin de la Société des Antiquaires de l'Ouest*, 4th series, volume II, third quarter 1952, pp. 175–234). This almost secretive presentation of original work of high quality is regrettable at a time when laymen are showing an ever-increasing interest in their mediaeval past.

Outside France, Eleanor has attracted some excellent historians —including the American, Amy Kelly, whose *Eleanor of Aquitaine and the Four Kings* (Cassell, 1952) is quite outstanding in soundness and zest.

All I had to do was follow the progress of these two works step by step. The first is wholly given over to Eleanor herself, while the second deals also with the lives of those about her—Louis VII, Henry II, Richard, and so on; and for all Miss Kelly's mastery of her material, we do occasionally lose sight of the main character.

However, neither author has made full use of Eleanor's letters and charters—an omission noted by H. G. Richardson in his highly pertinent and enlightening article, *The Letters and Charters of Eleanor of Aquitaine*, published in the *English Historical Review*, no. CCXCI, vol. LXXIV (1959), pp. 193–213. Together with the Pipe Rolls, these letters and charters provide a host of factual details and often reveal exactly how the queen's mind worked.

The present work likewise owes a great deal to the attractive and penetrating articles of Rita Lejeune, especially to *The Literary Role of Eleanor of Aquitaine*, published in *Cultura neolatina*, XIV (1954), pp. 5–57. And also, of course, to the five volumes of Reto Bezzola's *Les origines et la formation de la littérature courtoise en occident (500–1200)*, Paris, 1958–63.

There are many others I ought to list, including authors of standard works on Normandy and the Angevins: J. Boussard, R. Foreville, F. M. Powicke, etc.

But I should never forgive myself if I did not also include the names of the chroniclers and annalists on whom I have drawn most fully: William of Newburgh, Gervase of Canterbury, Roger of Hoveden, Richard of Devizes, Ralph of Coggeshall and above all Robert of Thorigny, whose chronicle is worthy of that other monument which, as abbot, he raised at Mont-Saint-Michel. All these have been admirably assembled in *The Chronicles and Memorials of Great Britain and Ireland during the Middle Ages* (Rolls Series, London, 1858–99). Readers will find an exhaustive list of references under this heading in both Labande and Kelly, so there is no point in repeating them here.

I must own to one notable gap: my book contains none of those peremptory judgments which have become a hallowed tradition among authors writing about the Middle Ages. Scholars seem quite unperturbed by the imperial orgies and court scandals of Antiquity and the Grand Siècle; yet the mediaeval scene immediately prompts them to the weightily expressed view that, despite the magnificent cathedrals and the noble ideals of courtliness and chivalry, the people living at that time were abysmally brutish and ignorant: the barons cruel, the clergy dissolute, the people ill-used and undernourished. Anyone who declines to fall in with this view is dismissed as naïve. And perhaps it *is* naïve to prefer Mont-Saint-Michel to the church of Saint-Sulpice, or the Madeleine in Vézelay to the Madeleine in Paris; anyone perverse enough to do so can expect to be reminded, with an indulgent smile, that the Middle Ages were far from idyllic. At which point one may legitimately wonder who is being naïve—for was there ever an era which could in any circumstances be termed idyllic? The Middle Ages span ten centuries: refusal to believe that they were uniformly 'Dark' does not imply belief that they were free of the horrors and imperfections which have always been man's lot.

INDEX

INDEX

Hervé, Prior of St-Denis, 20
Hommet, Richard du, 147
Hugh (St), Bishop of Lincoln, 172, 200, 245
Huntingdon, David of Scotland, Earl of, 163, 199

Ibelin, Balian, Lord of, 204-5
Innocent II, Pope, 36, 42
Innocent III, Pope, 257, 261
Isaac II, Byzantine Emperor, 205, 215
Isambert, Master, 248

Jéberron, Gerard, 68
Jerusalem, Kings and Queens of,
Baldwin I (of Boulogne), 48, 49
Baldwin III, 48, 70, 89
Fulke of Anjou, 88
Guy of Lusignan, 121, 195, 207, 211
Henry I (II of Champagne), 220
Melisande, 48, 70-1, 89
Sybil, 121
Joachim of Floris, 213
John, King of England: birth, 103, 134, 155; Henry II's especial affection for, 157, 181, 184, 188, 191; matrimonial plans for, 157-8; promised Ireland and castles in Anjou, 158; protest of Young King at this settlement, 159; Henry II plans to give him Poitou and Aquitaine, 181, 187; character of, 182, 191, 194; joins final revolt against Henry II, 188; marries Havisa of Gloucester, 197, 199; Richard I makes provision for, 199, 207; Eleanor intercedes for, 208; plots against Richard and secures dismissal of Longchamp, 216-17; plans to invade Normandy but is thwarted by Eleanor, 218; goes to Normandy and appeals to barons to recognize his claims, 229; tries to recruit Welsh and Scottish mercenaries, 230; makes efforts to keep Richard I in captivity, 233; summoned before King's court, 236;

submits to Richard, 238; succeeds to throne, 243; invested as Duke of Normandy, 247; relations with Eleanor, 250-1; marries Isabella of Angoulême, 257-8; crowned at Westminster, 261; conflict with France, 262; rescues Eleanor from Mirebeau, 263; seizes Arthur of Brittany, 264; loses Château-Gaillard and most of Angevin empire, 264-6
John II, Byzantine Emperor, 53, 54
John of Salisbury, see Chartres, Bishop of
John of Valerant, 264
Joigny, Count (Rainaut) and Countess (Aelis) of, 154
Joinville, Jean de, 220-1
Jordan, Cardinal, 217
Jordan, clerk to E, 146

Kiev, Anna of (Queen of France), 20, 103

Labande, E.-R., quoted, 136, 212, 247
Lancaster Castle, 199, 236
Langres, Geoffrey, Bishop of, 49
Laon, Bishop of, 35
Larchevêque, family of, 161
La Rochelle, 16, 249-50
Leicester, Robert, 3rd Earl of, 161, 199
Leicester, Robert, 4th Earl of, 229, 230
Le Mans, 160, 167, 187, 247, 263
Le Puy, Adhémar, Bishop of, Papal Legate, 67
Lezay, William of, 34
Limoges, city of, 83, 128, 145-6, 155, 158-60, 181
Limoges, Aimery, Count of, 67, 242
Lisieux, meeting of Richard I and John at, 237-8
Lisieux, Arnulf, Bishop of, 156
Lisieux, John of Alençon, Archdeacon of, 238
London, Gilbert Foliot, Bishop of, 156

281

Wells, Thomas Agnell, Archdeacon
of, 175-6
Westminster Abbey, 101, 121, 197 *et
seq.*, 261
Westminster Palace, 107, 108, 180,
236, 239
White Ship, the, 93-4
Wibald of Stavelot, quoted, 45
William I (the Conqueror), King of
England, 80, 93, 98, 100, 207
William I, King of Scotland, 162, 178,
170
William Atheling (son of Henry I),
93
William of Newburgh, 87, 90, 123
William of Saint-Thierry, quoted,
45
William of Tyr, 72
Winchester, 100, 103, 105, 157, 184,
189, 197, 199, 218, 222, 236, 239

Winchester, Bishops of—Richard of
Ilchester, 173
William of Blois, 99, 127
Windsor, 180, 197, 218, 222, 224
Woodstock, 107, 130, 136
Worcester, Henry II, coronation at,
121
Worcester, Roger of Gloucester,
Bishop of, 147
Worms, Richard I at, 232

York, Archbishops of—Geoffrey
Plantagenet, 135, 199, 207, 217, 237
Roger of Pont-L'Evêque, 147, 156
Young King, *see* Henry
Yves de Saint-Laurent (Papal Legate),
36

Zengi, Governor of Aleppo and
Mosul, 46, 68, 70, 89